Ngātokimatawhaorua

JEFF EVANS

Ngātokimatawhaorua

THE BIOGRAPHY OF A WAKA

Photographer and film-maker Jim Manley was able to take some stunning footage of *Ngātokimatawhaorua* being built and, later, once it had been launched. Clearly visible in this image are a number of women, including one paddling (left, fifth from the front). COURTESY OF THE MANLEY FAMILY

Contents

Introduction		8
1	Puketi, a forest of giants	14
2	Ancestral links	37
3	Tradition and ceremony	44
4	Reviving lost skills	76
5	A nation prepares	100
6	Reflection and hope: Waitangi Day 1940	123
7	An icon is relaunched	144
8	Dissent and protest	165
9	The Year of the Waka 1990	188
10	Lessons given, lessons learnt	199
11	Tent City	213
Appendices		233
Glossary		240
Notes		244
Further reading		249
Acknowledgements		250
About the author		253
Index		254

Foreword

Ka mahi au, ka inoi au, ka moe au, ka mahi ano.

Kōia tēnei tētahi kōrero nā Te Puea Hērangi, i a ia e amo ana i te kaupapa e pā ana ki te waka o *Ngātokimatawhaorua*. E rapa mai ana ēnei kupu i te pātu o te whare tūpuna, o Manu Koroki ki Mōtatau, hei mahara āke i ōna mahi nui kia tutuki pai te kaupapa.

Ngātokimatawhaorua is the pre-eminent waka of Tai Tokerau iwi. It is the largest ceremonial waka in existence and of national significance. For such an important taonga and with its history, it is a mystery why there is so little written information about this storied waka.

It is also why it gives me pleasure to introduce Jeff Evans' new volume on *Ngātokimatawhaorua*. The book fills this gap admirably and provides us with a deeply researched and layered history of the waka and the people connected to it. In compiling this book, Jeff builds on his earlier foundational work over the past two decades, including volumes on waka and Tā Heke-nuku-mai-ngā-iwi Busby.

Ngātokimatawhaorua has dual lines of history and significance for Northern iwi/Māori. The original *Ngātokimatawhaorua* was an ancestral waka, the waka Kupe re-adzed to complete the return trip to Hawaiki, following his arrival in Aotearoa. Its re-incarnation draws from this whakapapa. The modern waka then also represents a tupuna and it is right, in writing and producing the first book on *Ngātokimatawhaorua*, that it is referred to as a biography, rather than a history.

The story of *Ngātokimatawhaorua* is inextricably tied to the Waitangi Treaty Grounds. As Jeff outlines, it was the vision of Princess Te Puea Hērangi that led to the construction of the majestic vessel in all its 35.7-metre length. It was carved for the centennial of the signing of Te Tiriti o Waitangi in 1940 and was completed just prior.

Many were debating the price of citizenship and whether to join the war effort in the Second World War, and so in this context *Ngātokimatawhaorua*, a waka taua, stood as a gift to the nation from an iwi that had declined to join the conflict. It was carved as a partner to the whare rūnanga at the Waitangi Treaty Grounds, by many of the same carvers.

Jeff Evans skilfully traces back the origins of the waka from the depths of Puketi Forest through its construction and, later, its renovation for the visit of Queen Elizabeth II to the Treaty Grounds in 1974. In his diligent craft and engaging story-telling he carefully binds together the different parts, people and time periods into a coherent whole. There is a notable similarity to the way in which the waka builders worked to shape, bind and lash together the three different sections of kauri tree to form a strong single hull: Whano, whano! Haramai te toki! Haumi ē! Hui ē! Tāiki ē!

Ngātokimatawhaorua today takes its place proudly near the foreshore at Te Ana o Maikuku. It stands as a symbol of the past and is an integral part of the future vision of the Waitangi National Trust as we look to the bicentennial of the signing of Te Tiriti in 2040.

Kia kōtahi te hoe!

Pita Tipene
Chair
Waitangi National Trust

Introduction

FOR MOST VISITORS a trip to the Treaty Grounds at Waitangi is an opportunity to learn something about Aotearoa New Zealand's founding document, Te Tiriti o Waitangi (the Treaty of Waitangi), to look through the world-class museums, and to bask in the glorious views over Pēwhairangi Bay of Islands. They invariably wander through the Treaty House and beneath the shadow of the towering flagstaff on the lawn before it and, if they have the time, take in a cultural show in the ornately carved meeting house, the Whare Rūnanga. They might even stop to gaze up at the giant Norfolk pine planted by Agnes Busby, wife of the first British Resident, James Busby, in 1836.

But there is another must-see attraction — one that many don't know about before seeing it in person. It is the giant war canoe *Ngātokimatawhaorua*. Built for the 1940 centennial commemoration of the signing of Te Tiriti o Waitangi, in a project championed by Te Kirihaehae Te Puea Hērangi (Princess Te Puea), the 35.7-metre-long waka taua remains a powerful symbol of Māori identity, strength and pride.

Such was the pulling power of the waka that the *Auckland Star* noted:

> All who were present at the Waitangi Centennial celebrations on February 6 [1940] agree that though the re-enactment of the signing of the treaty and the opening of the whare runanga were deeply impressive, the feature which made the occasion real from the historic sense and provided a tangible link between past and present was the presence of the mighty war canoe Nga-toki-matawhao-rua.

> Many who went to Waitangi, both Maori and pakeha, had
> heard they would see there a Maori canoe, but until they
> arrived they did not realise the beauty, grace and even
> majesty of this craft nearly 120ft long, in the building of
> which the best of Polynesian culture found expression.[1]

Now, two decades into the twenty-first century, there are no surviving kaihoe from that glorious summer morning on 6 February 1940 to tell us what it was like to paddle the waka taua under the gaze of thousands of spectators, but they must surely have relished the opportunity to follow their ancestors onto the waters of Pēwhairangi.

As compelling as *Ngātokimatawhaorua*'s participation was, its future after the event was anything but assured. Dismantled within days of the commemoration finishing, the waka was relocated to the upper Treaty Grounds, where it would sit, landlocked beside the Whare Rūnanga, for the next 34 years. And that may have been where it stayed, a curio for tourists to wonder at, were it not for the resolve of a group of kaumātua who argued successfully for it to be refurbished and relaunched for the 1974 visit of Queen Elizabeth II.

Today, waka taua are a potent window into the past. Durable, reliable and built to withstand the rough and unpredictable seas surrounding Aotearoa, these war canoes sit at the pinnacle of traditional Māori waka design. With a lineage stretching back to the Polynesian ancestors of today's Māori, the design of these single-hulled waka was only possible because of what those explorers found when they arrived in Aotearoa — an abundance of very large, very tall trees, particularly kauri and tōtara.

Access to such massive trees gave the canoe builders in Aotearoa a considerable advantage over their counterparts in large parts of central and eastern Polynesia. Island-based canoe builders were restricted to building

Helped by willing tourists, *Ngātokimatawhaorua* is pushed from its shelter, Te Korowai ō Maikuku, along railway tracks toward the shore. It's a far cry from the early days, when the waka was rolled across logs in the traditional manner and then pulled back up to the canoe house with the help of a winch. JEFF EVANS

up their larger waka by securing hand-hewn planks together, edge on edge, resulting in a canoe that usually required a second hull, or an outrigger, to help stabilise it.

Canoe builders in Aotearoa, however, were able to source trees so big in circumference that when the logs were hollowed out, a thick, heavy 'backbone' could be left at the bottom of the hull. This extra weight lowered the waka's centre of gravity and drastically reduced the degree of side-to-side roll that the craft might otherwise experience in anything but the calmest of seas. The benefit of that was twofold. Waka could be built without a second hull or outrigger, and, just as importantly, the inherent strength afforded by the backbone allowed craftsmen to build extremely long waka.

The place of *Ngātokimatawhaorua* as a cultural icon has been cemented over the years by the hundreds of thousands of visitors who have spent time with it at the Treaty Grounds or witnessed it being paddled on the water. But more so, its status is due to the mana of those who designed and built it, and those who have crewed it over the decades. Add to this list the names of the foreign princes and princesses, politicians and dignitaries who have been entranced while riding in the waka and you begin to understand its special place in the story of Aotearoa.

At 35.7 metres long, *Ngātokimatawhaorua* carries a crew of 88, and has room for another 40 passengers seated down the centre. Launched for the 1940 centennial of the signing of Te Tiriti o Waitangi, the cultural icon remains a drawcard for kaihoe and tourists alike. RAWHITIROA PHOTOGRAPHY

1

Puketi, a forest of giants

NGĀPUHI HEARTLAND, October 1937. Rānui Maupakanga, possibly the last master waka builder of his generation and by then in his seventies, enters Puketi Forest. Heir to the skills and knowledge required to build waka taua, he will prove to be a vital link to the tohunga tārai waka of years gone by. He will also be a key figure in the revival of the Māori war canoe.

Born in the small settlement of Hauturu near the eastern shores of the Kawhia Harbour, Maupakanga is solidly built, his face oval and his eyes deep set. A wide moustache covers his upper lip. He has a habit of wearing a short-sleeved bush shirt over his woollen jumper, and on sunny days a well-worn fedora and a pair of round-framed sunglasses complete the picture. He has made the long trip north into Ngāpuhi territory from Waikato, at the request of Te Puea Hērangi, to oversee the building of a massive waka taua.

At a planned 120 feet (35.7 metres) long and 6 feet (2 metres) wide, the waka will be the largest ever built, and will represent northern Māori during the 1940 centennial commemoration of the signing of Te Tiriti o Waitangi. Maupakanga is in the forest to locate a pair of kauri trees suitable for the task. Stands of the tree dot the forest, but his challenge is to find two large enough to meet Princess Te Puea's requirements. Even with the help of knowledgeable local guides, the search takes him a full two weeks.

The week before I travelled to Puketi Forest, a low-pressure system had settled over much of the country, bringing with it the late onset of winter. After weeks of good weather, the days had suddenly turned wet and cold and dreary. The one saving grace was that the day I had chosen to explore the forest looked likely to be the driest day of the week, perhaps of the coming fortnight. Even so, the growing intensity of the showers dancing in my headlights began to make me nervous the further I drove. By daybreak I had passed Whangārei and the low-hanging clouds that hid Mount Hikurangi; ahead, the sky seemed to be darkening.

That I was driving north, alone and before daybreak, was thanks in large part to a couple of innocuous words I had seen handwritten on an old topographical map of Puketi Forest. Spelt out in black ink next to a minor forest trail were the words 'Canoe Track'. I hadn't quite believed it when I first saw the notation, but over the course of several years I had come to suspect that the logs used to build *Ngātokimatawhaorua* may have been taken from somewhere near the end of that track under the supervision of Te Puea's experts.

Te Puea, a granddaughter of the second Māori king, Tāwhiao Te Wherowhero, was in her mid-fifties when she sent Maupakanga north. Renowned for being warm and generous and able to connect with people of all backgrounds, she had devoted much of her life to improving the welfare of her people.

In *Te Puea: A life*, historian Michael King contended she wanted 'to raise and sustain Waikato morale; she sought to give people confidence in the present and future by drawing from the assurance of a Maori past'.[1] Able to call on learned kaumātua from within her iwi, she engaged experts in language, in music and in the oral traditions to help uplift her people, before extending the programme to support what King described as 'more ambitious and more visible cultural projects'.[2] These included several carved meeting houses and plans for seven waka taua, each representing one of the canoes that had brought a major tribal group to Aotearoa.

Tasked with locating two suitable kauri for the construction of the massive waka, Rānui Maupakanga, seen here climbing over one of the felled trees, also oversaw the initial shaping of the three hull sections before they were extracted from Puketi State Forest.
COURTESY OF THE MANLEY FAMILY

Michael King suggested that Te Puea's desire to build a fleet of waka stemmed directly from watching the waka taua *Taheretikitiki* being paddled on the Waikato River as a child. 'Nothing,' he wrote, 'had moved Te Puea more in her youth than the sight of a team of paddlers ferrying guests from Huntly to Waahi in Mahuta's ornately decorated canoe *Taheretikitiki*, and then it going through its paces and manoeuvres afterwards to salute and entertain the visitors.'[3]

Te Puea wanted to share that sense of awe. She instinctively understood that anyone, Māori or Pākehā, who saw waka taua on the water were enthralled by them. And that is what she wanted to create: a symbol to make Māori feel proud, and for Pākehā to admire.

I too have been transfixed by the power and majesty of waka taua. In the mid-1990s I attended the annual Tūrangawaewae regatta at Ngāruawāhia for the first time. The spectacle of several fully crewed waka taua gliding along the river, white-tipped hoe flashing in perfect time, is one not easily forgotten. When I visited the Treaty Grounds at Waitangi a few years later, and had the opportunity to spend time with *Ngātokimatawhaorua*, I found myself entranced anew. Everything about the giant waka seemed to speak to me. Its graceful design, particularly evident while it was sitting in its open-sided canoe shed, was mesmerising, and its mystique was reinforced when I ran my fingers over the carved figures that adorn much of the canoe, and even more so when I took a close look at how it was put together.

The more I saw, the more it drew me in. How many other people, I wondered, had asked themselves what it must have been like to paddle such a waka into battle? Would the muscle-burning effort required to race the final 200 metres to shore, to where your enemy was waiting, have aided or hindered your fighting ability once you got there?

I was eager to read about the waka, to learn something of its construction and its history, but precious little was available. All I could find were a few clippings from old newspaper articles, mostly from the late 1930s and 1940, and some from the mid-1970s. Then, in early 1999, I met the canoe's long-time kaitiaki, Heke-nuku-mai-ngā-iwi (Hec) Busby.

On the day we met, Busby was overseeing the launch of *Ngātokimatawhaorua* at Waitangi. He was in his late sixties, with thinning grey hair and the thick-set physique of a man who was slowing down. He wore a T-shirt and black shorts, a cap and a pair of old sandshoes that were fine for walking into the tide. A tattoo of his voyaging canoe, *Te Aurere*, was visible from under his left sleeve, and a carved whale tooth hung from his neck. He was there to ensure that the waka was moved with care. When he spoke, he did so with the authority of a man in charge.

Once the waka had been launched, I walked over and introduced myself. I asked him a couple of questions about *Ngātokimatawhaorua*, and then I asked whether he was interested in having his biography written. I don't know what gave me the confidence to put the question to him, but I had already written about waka, Māori weapons and migration traditions, and it seemed that all those subjects converged in this one man. To my delight he said he was open to the idea, so we set a date for me to travel to his home at Aurere in the Far North to discuss the project further.

Over the course of several dozen interviews I gradually learnt that Busby was a remarkable man. Committed to the survival of his culture, he was an expert in many aspects of Māoritanga, including the use of the taiaha, and ancient karakia, and he'd become a sought-after authority on land matters within his rohe. He was also a giant within the contemporary waka world. After teaching himself to build waka in the late 1980s, he would ultimately oversee the construction of 23 canoes, including five waka taua and two double-hulled voyaging canoes — the type that still sail from island group to island group throughout the Pacific. Part-way through a traditional navigation apprenticeship when we first met, he would later be capped a master navigator by the legendary Satawalese navigator Mau Piailug.

On the occasions we discussed *Ngātokimatawhaorua*, Busby told me much about the canoe's story post-1974, but his knowledge of the waka's earliest days was limited to what he had learnt from one or two of his kaumātua, as well as the little he had been able to find in Māori Land Court records. Asked where the trees for the waka had been taken from, he readily admitted he didn't know for sure. All he could tell me was that they were from Puketi Forest.

Busby's reply reinforced what I thought I knew, but it didn't get me any closer to pinpointing exactly where the kauri had once stood. It also left me with an uneasy realisation: if Busby didn't know where the trees had been felled, it was likely no one knew. It seemed that my only choice was to pull together a small team and go looking for any evidence that might remain at the end of 'Canoe Track'.

Because we were all converging on the forest from different towns and cities, we had agreed to rendezvous at the Department of Conservation (DOC) headquarters in Kerikeri before making our way inland to the forest. I was familiar with the building, having visited it half a dozen years earlier when I had first learnt of the existence of the topographical map we would be following. I'd heard about the map in a roundabout way. I was visiting Ewen Cameron, curator of botany at Tāmaki Paenga Hira Auckland War Memorial Museum, to find out about the habitat of the kauri tree. Specifically, I wanted to know why kauri are only found north of the 38th parallel south. Cameron told me he suspected it had something to do with a past mini ice age limiting the trees' dispersal, and as we were finishing up, he suggested that if I wanted to learn more about kauri in the north, I should contact Stephen King of the Waipoua Forest Trust.

King, it turned out, was a fount of knowledge, and during our correspondence he put me in touch with John Beachman, a retired environmental management officer for the New Zealand Forest Service who had worked in Puketi Forest during the 1970s. When I got to speak to Beachman a few weeks later, I asked him if by any chance he knew where the logs for *Ngātokimatawhaorua* had been taken from. His reply stunned me — he said he knew almost to the exact spot. What's more, he was pretty sure the location had been marked on an official map, a copy of which was held in the DOC office in Kerikeri.

Things were starting to get interesting. If the map still existed, this was an incredible stroke of luck. The few published eyewitness accounts from the 1930s offered no clues, and there were no living survivors from among the bushmen who had felled the great kauri. Even the few photos I had seen of the felling were unhelpful, as the surrounding forest was too closed in to divulge any landmarks.

I made an appointment to visit DOC's Kerikeri office the following week, where I was met at reception by Adrian Walker, a friendly and helpful ranger with the rugged look of a man who spent plenty of time outdoors. After brief introductions he led me down a long corridor to his office, where he flicked on his dated computer and opened a folder containing several files. Double-clicking one of them, Walker turned the screen towards me and we both watched as a map slowly appeared. Scrolling to the bottom of it, he pointed out a small area coloured in yellow, just left of centre. Written in fine lettering within a finger-shaped sliver were the two unmistakable words 'Canoe Track'.

So there is was, lit up in so many pixels — a possible key to locating a small but significant part of the story I was now chasing. With a copy of the map saved to a memory stick, I raced home to study it. The first thing to catch my eye was the incredible amount of detail. Everything imaginable seemed to have been included. The rivers and streams were predictably depicted in blue ink, while the fine brown contour lines, as distinctive as fingerprints, detailed the relief of the land, allowing the viewer to build a three-dimensional world consisting of valleys, hills and ridgelines.

Even the tree species were delineated. The stands of kauri I was interested in were divided into three groups: mature kauri were coloured yellow, kauri between 10 and 30 feet tall (3–9 metres) were red, and immature kauri were green. Elsewhere, light-brown patches depicted stands of podocarps, mostly rimu, kahikatea, miro, mataī and tōtara. Various shadings marked the position of nearby roads and outlined the boundaries of the forest. A legend to help unlock the rest of the map's coded knowledge completed the picture.

Just a few minutes' drive northeast of Kerikeri's town centre, the DOC office looked much the same as when I had last been there. Hidden behind a wall of trees, the single-storey building housed a reception area and offices where the rangers did their paperwork. A fenced-in compound secured their work vehicles overnight.

This time I was greeted by Kipa Munro, DOC's cultural adviser for Northland and chair of Te Rūnanga o Ngāti Rēhia. He had agreed to accompany me into Puketi Forest. Of Ngāti Rēhia, Ngāti Kuri and Ngāpuhi ancestry, Munro and his forebears had been guardians of the forest for generations, so it was more than appropriate that he form part of the expedition. It was also important to me that we had iwi approval to enter the forest.

Munro was in his early fifties and fiercely proud of his heritage. Aside from representing his people through the rūnanga, he taught mau rākau to anyone interested — Māori or Pākehā — free of charge. He did it, he told me, because mau rākau is an effective vehicle to teach Māori language, culture and history. Munro was also, I found out soon enough, quick to correct the slightest mispronunciation of his native tongue, reinforcing his displeasure through none-too-subtle grimaces at the offending individual.

After signing in at reception, I followed Munro to the staff cafeteria for a cup of tea and to await the rest of our party. Master waka builder Heemi Eruera was travelling down from Kaitaia with two of his workers to join us for the day. I had first met him a decade earlier when I interviewed him for the biography of Hec Busby, his long-time mentor, and we had kept in sporadic contact since. Quiet and observant, Eruera was the type who only joined a conversation when he had something important to say, and his input was always concise and insightful. In his forties, he had been heavily involved in the 2009 refit of *Ngātokimatawhaorua* and now runs his own waka-building operation from an old dairy company building in Awanui, a 15-minute commute from his Kaitaia home. Accompanying him would be his nephew and new hire, Jacob Eruera, and his long-time right-hand man, Billy Harrison.

While we waited, Munro introduced me to one of his colleagues. Dan O'Halloran was a 20-year veteran of the department, and Munro had invited him to join us and to act as our guide. On the face of it, ours would be a fairly straightforward excursion into the forest, but O'Halloran would be the only one among us who had walked the ridge before, so it was reassuring to have him along. That he was bringing a GPS unit and first aid kit was also comforting. Clearly built for tramping, he was a compact, supremely fit-looking man who seemed to radiate energy. Perhaps because of his sun-weathered skin, I found it hard to estimate his age. That he wore three earrings in his left ear and a ponytail further confused things.

When Eruera and his crew arrived a quarter of an hour later, I learnt that he and Munro knew each other well. In fact, Munro had recently

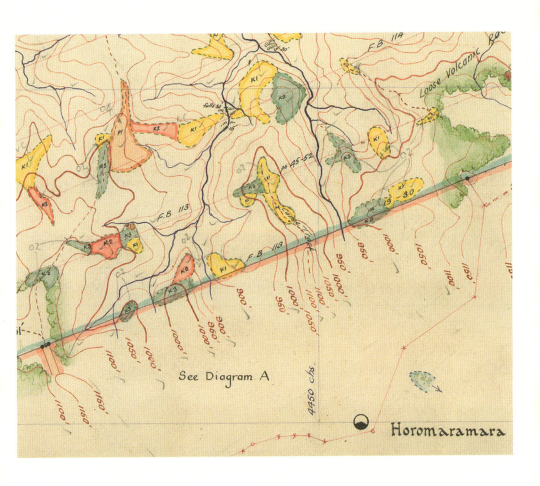

The section of the Department of Conservation map showing 'Canoe Track' (centre). Prepared by A. N. Sexton in the 1920s, the original map encompassed all of Puketi State Forest and was part of a New Zealand Forest Service survey to identify the remaining kauri stands. NEW ZEALAND FOREST SERVICE (SEXTON, C. 1920), COURTESY OF THE DEPARTMENT OF CONSERVATION

commissioned Eruera to build a waka for Ngāti Rēhia, and the pair of them had been in a forest bordering our destination the previous weekend.

After Munro had formally welcomed us all, we huddled around a laminated copy of the map as O'Halloran explained the colour coding for the kauri, then pointed to the dotted line marking the ridgeline we would be exploring.

My mind began to wander as he described what we could expect to see. I had obsessed over the map for months — years, really — but even with all the detail it held, it was still unclear exactly where our target trees had stood. There was no way to know how accurate these dotted lines were. Had the map-maker actually visited the site or was there guesswork involved? And how much had the forest changed over the years? Would the old photos we had be helpful or had decades of plant growth hidden what might once have been useful clues?

The morning cloud cover had disappeared by the time we made our way to our vehicles, pushed out over the Pacific by strong westerlies that unveiled a brilliant blue sky. Led by O'Halloran, our convoy of two 4 × 4s headed inland, past lifestyle blocks and orchards until we reached the intersection with State Highway 10 at Waipapa. From there, we travelled north for a few minutes before again turning inland to where paddocks of green flanked us.

At the top of a hill, O'Halloran brought our vehicle to a stop so we could take in the view. A hundred shades of green seemed to be floating before us, like a cloud hovering 10, 20, 30 metres off the ground. It was as if all 25,000 hectares of the forest were filling our view. Far to our right, a majestic kauri, standing alone like a sentinel, pierced the canopy.

In truth, what we were looking at was only a thin snapshot of the forest's southern border. I was beginning to reassess the challenge the canoe builders faced when they began their search for suitable kauri: the forest was immense. What, I wondered as O'Halloran gently accelerated, were the chances of us actually finding the site where the two kauri had once stood?

A little further along the road we stopped at a padlocked gate. Public access to the forest had been restricted after the recent discovery of kauri dieback. A microscopic, fungus-like pathogen that lives in the soil, kauri dieback infects the tree's roots, effectively damaging the tissues that feed the tree its nutrients and water. Stricken kauri, some of them hundreds of years old, were starving to death.

Munro jumped out and opened the gate, allowing both vehicles to pass through before he secured it behind us. Just inside the gate stood a recently introduced hygiene station, built to allow visitors to clean their footwear when entering and leaving the forest. DOC was doing everything it could — short of actually closing the forest — to restrict the transfer of the disease.

The station was of a utilitarian design, not totally dissimilar, I thought, to a cattle race for drenching. A hand-held spray-gun allowed me to moisten my boots with rainwater collected from the station's roof, before I ran each of them over a stiff upturned brush to dislodge any dirt. Then I stepped onto a foot pump that lowered under my weight and watched as an industrial-strength disinfectant was sprayed onto the soles of both boots. It was a simple, three-step process that gave kauri a fighting chance.

Back in the trucks, we set out again along the forestry road. Recent rain had washed away the shingle in several places, exposing its clay base, and the further we travelled, the more obvious it became that this would have been no place for a city car. As we crested one rise, Munro pointed out Mount Hikurangi, a sacred maunga, far to the south. I had passed it earlier in the day, but the significance of seeing it from here in Puketi

Forest only dawned on me later when I read a short piece written in 1940. It included one of the few descriptions I could find about the area the trees had come from.

> The said Kauri trees grew on Ngapuhi watershed midway between two coasts and their tops were in sight of all the mountains beloved by the Maoris of the North. Hence the choice of these trees for the canoe.[4]

The author, Frank Acheson, was an interesting character. Born in Riverton, Southland, he arrived in the Tai Tokerau district in 1924 with five years' experience as a Native Land Court judge and continued in that role until 1943. He was a serious-looking man with a long face and a closely cropped moustache, and he wore the sort of small, black-rimmed glasses you might imagine would be favoured by an intellectual of the period.

Over the course of his career, Acheson became friendly with many Māori leaders, including Princess Te Puea and Dame Whina Cooper, and he often lent an empathetic ear to their concerns. He is particularly remembered for several rulings related to lakebeds and the foreshore that were considered innovative at the time. He was also supportive of Māori land-development projects. And while his description wasn't specific enough to help us with our search, it did give a wonderful insight into the consideration given by kaumātua when choosing where the trees would come from.

Ten minutes after passing through the gate we pulled over into a layby of sorts and climbed out of our vehicles. O'Halloran, who would be leading us along the overgrown track, strapped on his protective gaiters, then grabbed his backpack and a pair of forestry loppers. Once the rest of us were ready, he led us the 100 metres or so back along the road to the start of the track. There Munro recited a karakia to the Māori deity Io, seeking guidance and protection for the period we would be here. Once he had finished, the group turned and entered the forest.

We started our expedition on the eastern side of a wide ridgeline. It seemed as though O'Halloran knew the territory like the back of his hand. Leading off at a cracking pace, he navigated the track with the assurance and speed with which I would walk a city footpath — despite the ground being slippery from the recent downpours that had drenched the country. Initially the only plant growth we had to deal with was kanono and karamu shrubs, with some kiokio fern and tātarāmoa vines encroaching on the path, but things got trickier the deeper into the forest we ventured. Before long we found ourselves regularly stepping over or skipping around the many juvenile mānuka that had taken root along the track.

Our sharp-eyed and knowledgeable guide provided occasional commentary along the way, and there was plenty to take in. A bowl-sized hole in the earth was the result of a pig rooting for food, and a peculiar miniature forest, spotted just off the track, turned out to be *Dawsonia superba*. Appropriately named giant moss, it is the tallest self-supporting moss in the world, growing to a height of 60 centimetres. From above, it looked remarkably like a plantation of tiny Christmas trees. Further down the track, O'Halloran pointed out the broken and empty shell of the giant carnivorous kauri snail known to the Māori as pūpūrangi. The shell was large — 6–7 centimetres across, and the unfortunate snail that had once inhabited it had probably been eaten by a wild pig, possibly the very one that had been foraging nearby.

Nature enveloped us. After 20 minutes or so of mostly downhill walking, I stepped off the track to let a couple of my companions pass by. I wanted to take a moment to absorb the forest's ambiance. It felt good to be here, away from civilisation. The air was fresh, clean and crisp after the rain, and the chilly westerly we had experienced when getting out of the trucks was absent, blocked by the close bush. A miromiro sang nearby, hidden from view among the trees, but there was precious little else to hear.

When I caught back up to the group, O'Halloran was using his loppers to clear a couple of overhanging branches. After he finished, I asked him to take a minute to describe what he could see around us. He began by pointing out the 4–5-metre-wide forestry road that our track overlaid. Now disused, the flattened road was covered in low-growing bush and young mānuka. I had missed it altogether, focused as I was on the twin challenges of keeping up and not falling down.

O'Halloran thought it probably marked the route loggers had used to drag trees out of the forest, but exactly how long ago he couldn't say. Did it date from the bullock train days we were interested in, back in 1937, or was it more recent? It was impossible to tell. But O'Halloran thought it was likely the logs for *Ngātokimatawhaorua* had come out along this road, if they had in fact been taken from this part of the forest. It would make more sense that later drivers would follow the same route rather than make a new one. He then pointed out a couple of 'young' kauri trees that were busy establishing themselves 20–30 metres off the track. They had probably been too small to harvest when the area was last picked over, and now had a chance to mature — at least if kauri dieback was held at bay.

The forebears of these young kauri were well known to northern iwi, who had quickly settled upon them as the tree of choice when it came to constructing their largest waka. Usually found in stands, and often in poor soil where other species struggle to establish themselves, kauri provided early Māori with a comparatively lightweight yet durable timber that was renowned for being straight-grained and free from knots. Importantly, it was relatively easy to work using stone adzes.

With mature kauri easily reaching 30–40 metres or more in height — the famous Tāne Mahuta, which is still standing in Northland's Waipoua Forest, tops out at an impressive 51.2 metres (half the length of a rugby field) — their circumference is large enough that waka builders could dispense with the second hull or the outrigger that was relied on for stability back in their ancestral homelands. The kauri canoe's width would deliver the balance they needed, and with a thick hull (keeping most of the weight below water level), they could maintain excellent stability on the water.

It is clear from the ships' logs and diaries of early European explorers that Māori waka builders were not the only admirers of the impressive tree. When Captain James Cook inspected them during his first visit to New Zealand in 1769, he judged them likely to provide fine masts and spars. Three years later Ambroise Bernard-Marie Le Jar du Clesmeur, sailing on the *Marquis de Castries*, made mention of the quality and size of the trees when the French sailed into the Bay of Islands to refit their ships:

> Now that our vessels were in a harbour sheltered from all winds, we thought only of refitting them. The *Mascarin*, having almost her whole port side unsheathed and the forepart unfastened, was making a lot of water. Mine was deficient only in the masts: in order to repair her, I searched up and down the coast, sometimes with Mr Marion and sometimes independently. Finally, after a lot of difficulty, some natives who had been made to understand what we wanted took us to a big cove about a league and a half from our vessels, where we found the finest timber. I do not exaggerate when I say that I saw trees more than 90 feet tall, without branches or knots.[5]

In fact, so enamoured were early explorers with the kauri that, once their reports reached the northern hemisphere, ships were sent specifically to obtain logs, in many cases for the Royal Navy shipyards. The first of these vessels arrived in 1794, and they kept coming. When naval demand eventually dropped away, the timber began to be exported for house, boat and furniture making. It was a financial bonanza for those involved in the industry, but the near-insatiable hunger for kauri devastated the native forests. Today, only around 7455 hectares of kauri forest remain from an estimated 1.2 million hectares.

As we got deeper into the forest, the bush immediately either side of the track began to thin out. Any mature trees that had once grown where the forestry road now lay had long been replaced by shrubs and spindly mānuka. So far, we had not seen any mature kauri close up, but it wasn't long before O'Halloran, some 30 metres ahead, slowed just long enough to call out over his shoulder that we should be seeing kauri any minute now. 'How can you tell?' I asked, but he was back in full flight by the time the words left my mouth. When I finally managed to catch up, he was pointing out clusters of cutty grass (*Carex geminate*) and kauri grass (*Astelia trinervia*). Both are known to grow near our target species, he explained, confirming that kauri are, or at least were, nearby.

The two grasses may have looked very much alike to my untrained eye (so much so that I still can't separate them with any confidence unless I have a guidebook with me), but they nevertheless turned out to be excellent indicators. Having made our way along the bush track for the best part of an hour, kauri came into view around the next corner. There, towering above us, were a half dozen majestic trees grouped at the base of a short rise, their spectacularly straight trunks reaching up to the heavens. More led up the slope and several were dotted about the summit.

We were only a short walk from the road, but we might as well have been a week's hard march from it. Civilisation was a distant memory now that these trees surrounded us. Somehow it felt as if we had stumbled on a prehistoric landscape, and I took a minute to take it all in. Then, as if to bring me back into the present, a pīwakawaka began fluttering among nearby branches, curious about who was invading its domain.

O'Halloran pulled out his GPS unit and confirmed that we were nearing the end of 'Canoe Track'. We agreed that this would be as good a place as any to begin our search, so we spread out and started looking for any sign of where the trees might have been felled, as there was a chance that either a stump or crown was still here. Eruera and his team started looking on the flat either side of the group of kauri we had first seen, while I followed O'Halloran up the incline in front of us to search among the other trees. Nothing up there caught our attention, but as we were returning, Munro called us over. He had found the remains of a huge kauri crown, partly sunk into the earth and covered with years of forest growth. The dank aroma of the decaying forest litter packed around it hung in the air.

I dug in my backpack for a photo I'd brought of the tree used to build the two end sections of the waka. Looking at the circumference of the crown in the photo, I thought the one before us certainly looked big enough, and the shape and angle of the branches raised our hopes further. Even after lying unprotected in the elements for over 80 years, Munro's find looked remarkably like the crown in the picture. One by one we pored over the photo, comparing it with what lay before us, trying to superimpose one image onto the other. There seemed to be little doubt that the shape and position of the branches matched, as did the terrain, sloping up to the right. It looked promising, but I needed more proof. I wanted to find the tree's stump.

Newspapers at the time reported that the trunk measured 67 feet (20.4 metres) from the ground to the first branch, so we had an idea of how far away the stump should be from the crown. Given the immense size of the crown, I could see that there was little chance it had been moved from

Puketi Forest and neighbouring Omahuta Forest comprise one of the largest tracts of native forest in Northland, at a combined 15,000 hectares (37,000 acres).

It was in this forest that the two massive kauri trees used to construct *Ngātokimatawhaorua* were felled. RAWHITIROA PHOTOGRAPHY

where it had first crashed to the ground. We should be able to locate the stump without too much trouble. The only real impediments were the tall grasses, and the decades of forest debris that had accumulated around the base of many of the stumps. Often piled as high as the stumps themselves, the debris effectively hid much of what remained.

Initially, I had trouble making out any stumps at all, but the much more experienced O'Halloran, Munro and Eruera could see through the camouflage to pick them out easily. We searched the whole area but nothing we found seemed a match for Maupakanga's kauri. This didn't make sense. There had to be a stump here to pair with the crown Munro found, even if it ended up not being the kauri we were looking for. So where was it?

I could think of only one possibility. There was a sizeable kauri stump on display at the Treaty Grounds in Waitangi that was supposedly associated with the construction of the waka. It was certainly large enough to be the one we were seeking, but the label stated that it originated in nearby Omahuta Forest. Could the provenance given to the Waitangi Trust when it was donated have been inaccurate? Could that stump have come from Puketi Forest instead? It was a long shot, and for the moment there was no way of telling.

Unsure how to proceed, I suggested that we take a break. The next closest stand of mature kauri was an hour's tramp to our north and we wouldn't be able to get there and back in the time we had left. There were also areas we wanted to avoid. Clearly marked on the map was a stream to our west. I had been told that warriors used its waters to cleanse themselves when they returned from battle, back when they fought to the death with taiaha and patu. The waters were still highly tapu and we wouldn't be venturing anywhere near them. For today, this section of forest would mark the limits of our expedition.

I looked for a place to rest, and, using my rolled-up jacket as a buffer from the damp forest floor, I sat and gazed at the bush that surrounded us. I wondered what it must have been like here before the first Polynesian explorers arrived in Aotearoa, when kauri dominated the northern landscape and birdsong rang out across the land. Then my thoughts drifted to those involved in building *Ngātokimatawhaorua*. Hardy and resourceful, these men had knowledge about how things were done when waka were still the main form of long-distance transport for Māori.

When Te Puea decided to build a fleet of waka taua, she found herself with a unique challenge. Before she could start, she first needed to find a tohunga tārai waka, an expert canoe builder, capable of building waka taua. The problem was that no waka taua had been built for the best part of 40 years. In Piri Poutapu — who would later play a major role in finishing *Ngātokimatawhaorua* — she had a skilled carver who learnt his craft at the School of Māori Arts at Ohinemutu in Rotorua, but he had no experience building war canoes. He was in his mid-thirties with the calloused hands of a man familiar with holding woodworking tools; but as gifted as Poutapu was, entrusting the project to him would have been risky at best. The construction of a massive war canoe was no job for a novice. So Te Puea went searching, raising the subject at every opportunity until, after either a tangi or a hui (accounts differ) at Rākaunui (near Kawhia) in 1936, Rānui Maupakanga presented himself. The elderly man rose to his feet and announced to those in the meeting house that he had built a waka taua for Te Puea's grandfather, Tāwhiao. Te Puea had found her man.

The first task Te Puea entrusted to him was to salvage and restore the old waka taua *Te Winika*. It had been dismantled by Gustavus von Tempsky's Forest Rangers during the Waikato War and, remarkably, the central section of the canoe was still intact, lying abandoned near Port Waikato. Work began almost immediately. Under Maupakanga's direction, the section of hull was recovered and transported to Ngāruawāhia, where it was received with an emotional pōwhiri. Poutapu then set to work shaping replacement haumi (the fore and aft sections, sometimes referred to as haumi kokomo) from freshly cut tōtara, under the old tohunga's supervision.

The refurbishment of *Te Winika* would turn into a masterclass for Poutapu. Not only did he learn the intricacies of adzing hulls directly from an expert, but he also acquired an encyclopaedia's worth of other knowledge about building waka; knowledge that would equip him well when he began work on *Ngātokimatawhaorua*. He learnt, for instance, the importance of submerging adzed timber in water (preferably salt water, but fresh would do) to draw out any sap. It was an old trick, Maupakanga explained, that greatly reduced the chances of the timber splitting. Poutapu also witnessed Maupakanga using an ember to draw the outline of the slot-end of a mortice-and-tenon join on the first of the new tōtara logs. So sure was the old man's hand that when the join was cut it fit perfectly with the existing central section. Later still, Maupakanga showed the younger man how to caulk and lash the joins. To complete the build, Poutapu, fellow carver Waka Kereama, and Poutapu's pupil and future opera singer Īnia Te Wīata, carved new rauawa, tauihu and taurapa (top boards, figurehead and sternpost) for the canoe.

Te Puea could only have been delighted when she inspected the restored waka. Encouraged, and confident now in the skills of Maupakanga and Poutapu, she dispatched a party to Oruanui Forest, near Mōkai in the central North Island, with instructions to search for suitable tōtara with which to construct the first of her new waka taua. Her dream was taking shape, but it had been a close-run thing. Had she delayed her search for a tohunga, or had Maupakanga not been at Rākaunui on the day of her visit, it's almost certain the direct line of knowledge of the ancient craft of waka building would have been lost forever.

2

Ancestral links

OF ALL THE QUESTIONS I wanted to find the answers to, one of the most fundamental was in regard to the naming of the great waka. Specifically, I wanted to know the origin story of the name *Ngātokimatawhaorua*. I knew that named waka hold a revered place within Māori society, so there must have been serious thought put in to choosing this particular name. I also knew that every iwi knows the name of the waka that brought the first of their people from Polynesia to Aotearoa, and that in many cases individual iwi members can trace their whakapapa back to the captain, the tohunga, or the crew who arrived on those early vessels. What I didn't know, however, was why the 1940 waka taua had been given the name *Ngātokimatawhaorua*.

The answer, when I found it, took me back to an era when Polynesian navigators confidently sailed into uncharted waters in search of adventure and new lands. And it was there, among the tales of those legendary explorers, that I was introduced to Kupe (the discoverer of Aotearoa), his double-hulled voyaging canoe *Matawhao* — or *Matahourua* as it is more commonly known — and the curious story of its renaming.

Keen to learn what I could of Kupe and to understand how his story relates to our modern-day waka taua, I arranged to meet with Heemi Eruera at Taipā, a sleepy coastal settlement 40 minutes northeast of

Kaitāia. As well as helping to keep alive the skills of his waka-building ancestors, Eruera is also extremely knowledgeable when it comes to the traditions of Te Tai Tokerau iwi. From previous talks with him I knew that there were narratives from the region that recounted the exploits of Kupe and some of the first voyagers to arrive in Aotearoa after him, so I was hopeful he could help me find the answers I was looking for.

Eruera started by explaining that there are a number of accounts of Kupe's voyage to Aotearoa and that each version has its place. 'And I suppose, just going back to my old man and how [his generation] viewed things, you can't actually say one is wrong and another is true. You just sort of take both versions and go "Oh, yeah. That's pretty good. We'll put that in our kete and we'll speak to that too."'

Eruera told me that according to his father Kupe's waka was named *Matawhao*.

> My understanding is that *Matawhao* was likely the original name of Kupe's waka. It comes from one of the names used for Tāne Mahuta, and that name was Tāne Matawhao. According to what I was taught, Matawhao is the face of the adze that was used to fell the tree, shape it, and then finish the waka.

It is probable that Kupe deduced the existence of the land he would discover after observing large flocks of migrating land-based birds flying to the southwest. Speculating that they were heading to rich feeding grounds, but unsure of how far away they might be, he set off from his homeland in the *Matawhao*, following the direction of their flight. Then, after perhaps three weeks at sea, Kupe's wife, Hine-i-te-apārangi, spotted the first sign of land. Still far from shore, she recognised the type of large, seemingly stationary cloud bank that often forms above a landmass. When she saw it, she famously exclaimed, 'He ao! He ao!' (A cloud! A cloud!) — and it is from this that the name Aotearoa evolved (ao — cloud; tea — white; roa — long).

After making landfall and exploring much of the coastline, Kupe settled for a time in what we now call Hokianga Harbour. Exactly how long he stayed there is unknown, but at some point, maybe after a few years, perhaps longer, he made the decision to return to his homeland. Before he departed, he was famously asked if he would ever return to Aotearoa, and it was from his reply that the Hokianga Harbour took its name: 'Hei konei rā e Te Puna o Te Ao Mārama. Ka hoki nei ahau? E kore ano ahau e hoki anga nui mai.' (Farewell, The Spring of Te Ao Mārama [the wellspring of life]. Will I return? I will not return.)

And that essentially concludes Kupe's time in Aotearoa. He came, he saw, he left. So why, you might ask, is the story of Kupe and *Matawhao* relevant to our twentieth-century war canoe? It's relevant because when Kupe returned to his homeland, his nephew Nukutawhiti (some say he was his grandson), asked him for his voyaging canoe. He wanted to travel to the newly discovered lands and explore them for himself. Kupe agreed.

According to Eruera, once the mana of the vessel had been transferred to Nukutawhiti, he quickly set about refurbishing the great waka.

> Part of the process of preparing the waka was to re-adze it: to clean it up and to lighten it. When that was completed, the waka received the name *Ngātokimatawhaorua* — the second adzing of *Matawhao*.

While the adze work was being completed, a second waka, named *Māmari* (which was built especially for this voyage and captained by Nukutawhiti's brother-in-law, Ruānui-o-Tāne), was also finished. Once the pair of waka were ready, the two men called on Kupe for the sailing instructions to reach the new land.

As Eruera mentioned earlier, there are a number of different versions of the tradition of Kupe's voyage to Aotearoa. In one well-known account we are told that the navigator used both Venus and a point on the horizon just to the left of the setting sun as guides, which is particularly interesting when taken in context with what Eruera shares about the sun a little later. For now, though, Eruera reveals the voyaging instructions that were passed down to him.

> So, you have Kupe's instructions, which are simple in nature: Hold the bow to Atutahi [Canopus] at night, and hold it to the Cloud Pillar during the day. Without applied knowledge, talk of a Cloud Pillar might sound a bit mythical, but it isn't.

The Cloud Pillar is, continued Eruera, what scientists call an orographic cloud. These clouds are created when moisture-heavy air meets a land mass, say, a mountain range, and is forced upwards. The rising air cools and, once it reaches a height where the water vapour in the air condenses, it forms a cloud. (The result of the phenomenon here in Aotearoa is famously long and white.)

> But the Cloud Pillar is more than an indication of land. I think it is also a mental construct that was used to describe the southwesterly direction when coming to Aotearoa from eastern Polynesia. Its name is 'Te Pou Kapua te Tonga-mā-uru' in the Hokianga kōrero, and it is actually an important directional marker.

If the sailing instructions handed down to Nukutawhiti seem uncomplicated, it's because they are. But why would Kupe's instructions be so minimal when other sailing instructions from the following era of migration list numerous stars and other heavenly bodies? In the *Tākitimu* legend, for example, there are at least nine stars and constellations named. One possible explanation is that when Kupe voyaged to Aotearoa he was heading down into unfamiliar latitudes, where the movement of the stars looked vastly different to what he was used to seeing. When viewed from his home in the tropics, the stars passing overhead rose near-perpendicularly from the eastern horizon, arched up to reach their apex, and then began to drop, again near-perpendicularly, before they disappeared below the western horizon. As the *Matawhao* left tropical waters, however, those same stars did something strange. They began to loop across the heavens.

This occurred because when the Earth tilts on its axis, say during the summer voyaging months, the view of the heavens from below the tropics becomes somewhat skewed, and the further south you travel, the more skewed it becomes. So during his voyage, not only did Kupe have to deal with the usual stresses involved in navigating a waka (including surviving on a couple of hours' sleep each night so that he could keep track of the waka's progress, watching for signs of changing weather and ensuring that his crew remained happy and healthy), but he also had to deal with a night sky that looked increasingly distorted.

And that begs the question, what would an experienced navigator do under those circumstances? He would reduce the possibility of getting lost by simplifying his processes wherever he could. One way to do that was to rely on two of the brightest objects in the sky: Venus and what is perhaps the key star available to a navigator, the sun.

Eruera explained to me that over the course of a year the rising and setting position of the sun slowly changes with the seasons, reaching its most southerly position in December. 'The sun actually starts to slow down in November, and by around the ninth of December there isn't a lot of change in its rising or setting positions at all.' It's about then, he continued, that for three short weeks the sun appears to rise each morning from the same spot on the eastern horizon and then set in one particular spot each evening in the west. That consistency made the alignment of a course based on the rising and setting positions of the sun relatively easy to follow, and helped reduce the risk of a navigator, his waka and his crew getting hopelessly lost.

As an aside, Eruera also told me during our conversation that there remains some interesting mātauranga regarding the voyages of that era within the traditions.

> Some of the written kōrero that is around is incredibly . . . I'll use the word 'thick', and by thick, I mean it's dense with kura huna — there's all these hidden little taonga in the kōrero. As we were talking before, unless you have some of that applied knowledge, some of that mātauranga will get lost in the realm of myth and legend — but if you have it, then you can kind of see things through a different lens.

> We know from other kōrero that they were leaving in the time of Ōrongonui me Matawhiti — which is the November– December period — and we know the best time of the month to leave was around Tamatea, the first quarter moon, because the moon was in the sky during the daytime and acted as a navigational aid.

And that is the beauty of studying traditions such as these. They can help us see into the minds of the navigators who sailed to Aotearoa; men like Kupe, Nukutawhiti and Ruānui-o-Tāne.

There's no doubt that *Ngātokimatawhaorua* and *Māmari* successfully completed the voyage to Aotearoa . Oral history confirms the fact and, as mentioned earlier, there are many individuals who can trace their whakapapa back to crew members from the two vessels.

Nukutawhiti and Ruānui-o-Tāne came, they saw and, unlike Kupe, they stayed — and over the generations their progeny spread throughout the north, taking the names of their ancestral waka with them. The result was that *Ngātokimatawhaorua* became synonymous with the region, particularly the Hokianga Harbour, and it remains to this day an important identifier for all iwi who whakapapa back to its crew.

So, what other name would suffice for a waka that was built to represent the five major iwi of Te Tai Tokerau? As one of the founding waka, with its mana magnified exponentially by its role in the discovery of Aotearoa under Kupe, the name *Ngātokimatawhaorua* — the second adzing of *Matawhao* — was a natural choice. It was perhaps the only option that was seriously considered for the great 1940 waka taua.

3

Tradition and ceremony

IT IS CLEAR FROM my research that Rānui Maupakanga, sent from Waikato by Te Puea, was almost certainly the last master canoe builder alive in 1937. What I didn't immediately appreciate was the discontent caused by his arrival in the north. According to court documents, a large gathering of northern rangatira descended on Kaikohe's modest courthouse in October 1937 to listen to Te Uri-o-Hau kaumātua Ripi Wihongi address the court in one of a series of meetings called to discuss Te Puea's waka plan.

Wihongi advised Judge Acheson that a 'very big and representative gathering of natives'[1] had themselves decided to build two waka taua. They would represent the five northern iwi — Ngāpuhi, Ngāti Whātua, Te Rarawa, Te Aupōuri and Ngāti Kahu — and were to be called *Ngātokimatawhaorua* and *Mātaatua*. The visit of Te Puea from Waikato, he continued, had stirred up the people from Tamaki to Te Rerenga-wairua:

> Te Puea passed through our territory like a shadow. We were
> hardly awake. Her visit awakened us. We have held meetings.
> We have linked up again with the spirits of our ancestors. We
> want to build our own canoes. First the two mentioned, and
> then others. But all the Northern tribes can go in these canoes.[2]

Acheson's reply to Wihongi suggests that he was surprised by what he heard. Perhaps he was formulating a response even as Wihongi's words echoed off the wooden courthouse walls. The judge pointed out that Ngāti Whātua, Te Rarawa, Te Aupōuri and Ngāti Kahu, along with the Ngāpuhi hapū of Pupuke, Matangirau and Matauri Bay, had all promised 'support for Te Puea's plan to build a great canoe to represent all the northern iwi — using Waikato experts and northern workmen'.[3] Not everyone in attendance agreed with the judge, however. Te Aupōuri representative Hemi Manuera immediately stood to deny Acheson's statement, insisting that his iwi had made no such promise. The judge then reminded those assembled of the promises he himself had witnessed, before noting that 'Te Puea has arranged for a suitable tree from the Puketi State Forest' and that her 'canoe experts are at the forest now to begin the work'.[4]

It was clear that a compromise was necessary, and ultimately Acheson could see no reason why another canoe, overseen and built entirely by local iwi, should not be built 'if the people wish it'.[5] The only concerns he expressed were that work on any waka would need to be completed, and that the vessels were to be properly housed and looked after, with 'proper conditions put in place to guard against damage by fire or otherwise'.[6]

In his closing summary the judge acknowledged the two waka-building projects and repeated 'the arrangements previously settled' to support Te Puea. 'People will be consulted from time to time,' he said, 'even though certain Hapus of Ngapuhi appear to wish to break away from the Northern Tribes.'[7]

The dispute between the northern hapū, some of whom claimed Te Puea had offended their mana by sending her craftsmen north without full consultation, would not be resolved until late January 1938, at another meeting of the Native Land Court. There to address the court was the charismatic Taurekareka (Tau) Hēnare, MP for Northern Māori since 1914 and at one time a bushman himself. Born in the northern settlement of Pipiwai, probably in 1877 or 1878, Hēnare was a direct descendant of Rāhiri, the founding ancestor of Ngāpuhi, and it seems likely that

Te Puea had personally asked him to step in to broker a way forward. They had developed a close friendship during their struggles to improve the welfare of Māori, and neither of them would have relished the prospect of this highly publicised project failing due to internal strife. A big man, renowned for his strong voice and refined sense of humour, Hēnare had become a skilled mediator by the late 1930s. He was certainly capable of swaying the opinion of the offended hapū during private discussions.

Hēnare reported to the court that the disagreements 'all had their origin in the failure of Te Puea and her advisors Mutu Kapa and others to consult Ngapuhi first'. However, he continued, it had been decided to 'heal the breach, and to reunite with all those who are supporting Te Puea's project. Two canoes will be supported, namely the one at Puketi State Forest to be under the control of Hohepa Heperi; the other the Ngaiotonga one to be under Rei [Rē] Kauere and others. When finished, both canoes are to be housed in the big Carved House to be erected on the Waitangi Reserve.'

Judge Acheson thanked Hēnare for his 'invaluable assistance' and said that the court was 'very pleased that harmony rules again'.[8]

As Acheson had pointed out, Te Puea's men were indeed already in Puketi State Forest (as it was officially known then). As soon as the logs for the waka that Waikato were building for themselves had arrived at Ngāruawāhia from Oruanui Forest, they were handed over to Poutapu and his students to shape, assemble and carve. This allowed Maupakanga and his right-hand man, Ropata Wirihana, to make the long trip north to begin their next assignment: to find suitable trees for the construction of a massive waka taua. Waiting for them was the well-respected local rangatira, Hohepa Heperi.

A bear of a man, standing over six foot (1.83 metres), Heperi, who owned a farm at Ōkaihau and had spent much of his life in the local forests logging trees for the government, would play a key role in the creation of *Ngātokimatawhaorua*. Not only did he manage the project on behalf of the northern iwi, but he also had the necessary knowledge to guide Maupakanga in his search for the trees needed to build the waka. Most important, though, his mana was sufficient to shield the Waikato contingent from any local discontent as they worked. There were elements in the north that resented their presence and, as we have seen, they were not afraid to speak their minds.

Armed with a permit from the State Forest Service authorising them to take two kauri, Heperi, Maupakanga, Wirihana and others entered Puketi State Forest on or about 11 October 1937. The expedition coincided with the arrival of spring and, as if overnight, the drab leaves of winter were overtaken by the new season's growth in myriad greens. Plants such as the carmine rātā were beginning to show off their new-season flowers, and perfume from the toropapa was starting to infuse the forest. The birdsong was growing more vociferous. Koekoeā (long-tailed cuckoo), famed for guiding early explorers to Aotearoa from their Pacific homelands, had begun to arrive back from their winter nesting grounds, while tūī, toutouwai (North Island robin) and hōrirerire (grey warbler) were busy nesting. Mature kōkako sang out to attract mates and to stake out their territory.

Knowing that he needed two trees in prime condition, Maupakanga refused to be rushed in his search. The kauri had to be large enough to make the substantial waka that Te Puea demanded, and he had to ensure they were free of rot, heart shakes (major cracks) and other faults. He also needed to consider the location of the trees. By the late 1930s, mature kauri were found in only a handful of stands through the forest, and there were few existing tracks capable of allowing access by truck or tractor. Maupakanga knew he would need a team of bullocks to extract the massive logs — though even bullock trains had their limitations.

Exactly where a tree stood in its environment also needed to be taken into account. Canoe builders of old understood that the western side of a ridge or hill produced a superior tree for their purposes. Master waka builder Hec Busby once told me that during the winter months, the south-western side of a tree is constantly assaulted by the wind and rain, slowing its growth and making that side heavier and stronger than the east-facing side. That strength, he said, helped keep the finished hull straight and true.

And that leads to the inevitable question: is the partially buried crown Munro had located at the end of 'Canoe Track' actually in Maupakanga's favourable location? I desperately wanted it to be. The lie of the land was right, and we were on the western side of the ridge. Although we couldn't locate the stump, the shape and size of the crown suggested this was indeed the place Maupakanga had selected at least one of the kauri used to build the giant waka. My mind began to race; but even as I tried to convince myself that we had uncovered part of the *Ngātokimatawhaorua* story, I knew deep down that we couldn't be certain.

Despite the doubt and the resulting frustration, it had been a worthwhile day exploring the forest. I had often wondered what it might have been like for Maupakanga and the others to live and work here, so it was useful to spend time under the Puketi canopy. We know from newspaper reports that it was six months from the time Maupakanga first entered the forest until he delivered the last of the canoe sections to Piri Poutapu at Kerikeri for finishing, and that Maupakanga and Wirihana lived in a simple nīkau hut while they were in the forest. We may never know exactly where their whare was built, but we can, however, assume that it was close to the worksite, yet sufficiently distant so that the storage and cooking of food would not interfere with the tapu nature of their purpose.

Another question I had not been able to answer was whether Heperi's bushmen also stayed at the campsite. Again, we don't know. If the kauri had indeed been taken from near this end of 'Canoe Track', it is conceivable that the locals returned to the comfort of their homes most evenings. It was less than an hour's walk back to the road, and there would certainly have been enough daylight available during the summer months.

Wherever the camp was situated, it would undoubtedly have been a rustic existence. The 'mattresses' in bush camps were regularly fashioned from mangemange vine that was coiled up and covered with sacking; upturned wooden boxes or timber offcuts functioned as seats. After-hours entertainment was often limited to playing cards or perhaps reading a copy of *The Weekly News*. After a long week working in the forest, Sundays were a welcome day off, and were devoted to odd jobs around camp such as washing laundry and sharpening axes.

With many hours of physical exertion ahead of the bushmen, work-days started with a basic but wholesome breakfast. It wasn't unusual for a cook to prepare a meal of beef stew and porridge accompanied by fresh bread baked in a camp oven. But that was for a well-provisioned camp. The cooks here probably needed to supplement store-bought supplies by foraging in the forest. Succulent kūkupa (and other birds) would have been a tempting addition to any menu, as would eel, pūhā and watercress. Even so, we know that food was still frequently in short supply.

The following caption accompanied a wonderful photograph (see page 51) taken of the bushmen, cooks and a welcome visitor at Maupakanga's campsite:

> It had been strenuous, appetite sharpening work and often
> food had been short at the bush camp, but typical Maori
> determination and single mindedness of purpose had

overcome all obstacles. Here all enjoy a specially appetising
lunch. Sea mullet, grilled around the open fire by their
cooks, who are at the rear left, supplied as a gift by coastal
fisherman Tommy Thoms, who is seated third from left
wearing a hat and holding a white enamel mug. Two sugar
bags full of these and other seafood so beloved of Maori
palate have been brought over that day from his coastal
village at Matauri Bay some 25 miles away. Every one of the
group who carried out this great work were Maori with sole
exception of the Yugoslav owner of the bullocks, second from
right. Front left is the white headed Hohepa Heperi, father of
Peta [sic] Heperi, supervising the undertaking.[9]

The photograph, taken by Reginald George Harwood (Jim) Manley,
was one of a number of glossy 8 × 12-inch (20 × 30-centimetre) prints I
had found buried in a manila folder in the archives of the Waitangi
Museum. Gazing at the photograph afresh after my trip to Puketi Forest,
I wondered about the unnamed bushmen before the camera's lens. Not
a great deal has been written about them or their daily lives. The
worksite had few visitors, given its tapu status, and those who came to
write about the build typically focused their precious column inches on
the waka itself.

There was one notable exception, and that was Frank Acheson.
Describing the bushmen's contribution in a letter to the Waitangi National
Trust Board he wrote:

The great majority of the Maori workers, many of whom
risked life and health in the forest, belonged to the North
and gave their services freely and without payment other
than their food. Their leader, Te Hoe Pita Heperi, worked on
the canoe for over two years without payment, supporting
himself and his family on his War Pension.[10]

ABOVE: Accompanied by forest ranger Jim Ogle (third from left), Te Hoe Pita Heperi (second from left) and four experienced bushmen contemplate the job ahead of them. Felled using axes, saws and wedges, the tree measured an impressive 67 feet from the ground to the first branch. COURTESY OF THE MANLEY FAMILY

BELOW: Esteemed rangatira Hohepa Heperi (front left, with white hair), who oversaw the construction of the waka, enjoys a well-deserved meal along with the rest of the work crew. Fish supplied by Tommy Thoms of Matauri Bay (seated third from left, wearing a hat and holding a white enamel mug) was a welcome change of diet for the bushmen. COURTESY OF THE MANLEY FAMILY

Te Hoe was, Acheson continued, 'a Returned Maori Soldier highly respected by Europeans and Maoris. He has a very pleasant and obliging manner and gets on well with everybody'.[11] He also mentioned that Te Hoe was an experienced carver, having trained at Ngāruawāhia.

As well as the authorised visitors, there was at least one unwelcome sightseer who caused much consternation. In December 1938 an article reviewing the progress of the build highlighted a serious breach of protocol:

> Tradition in symbol and ceremony is being observed in the building of the war-canoe. Regrettable though it was that a pakeha woman should have violated the tapu which always surrounds such work, a tohunga lifted that ban with an ancient ritual, conducted over the kauri trunks when they lay in the bush. At the time the tapu was broken — and one of the oldest Maori laws shattered by thoughtlessness — the incident aroused considerable feeling in the north.[12]

It is clear that the actions of the unnamed 'pakeha woman' could have had serious repercussions. The report concluded: 'So, in accordance with centuries of teaching, a priest chanted his most powerful karakia over the inert logs to atone the insult to Tāne, God of the Forest.'[13]

Any immediate crisis was averted, although we can never be sure whether this incident caused the difficulties encountered later in the project, when it came time to fell the second tree and move the hewn log from the forest, or during the launch of the waka itself. According to the tohunga of old, such breaches of protocol were often to blame.

Multiple accounts date the felling of the first kauri tree towards the end of October 1937. A handful of newspaper articles described the day, but the most valuable source of information was Jim Manley's black-and-white movie footage. Engaged by Te Puea to capture a lasting record of the project, Manley filmed extensively in both Oruanui and Puketi forests, creating a priceless visual record of the project.

Born in England, Manley was the grandson of Surgeon General William Manley, who had received the Victoria Cross for his actions at the Battle of Gate Pā during the New Zealand Wars. Jim seems to have been just as adventurous as his illustrious ancestor. His interest in film started after his family moved to America where, in 1915, as a 12-year-old, Manley bought a school friend's toy film projector. By the time he had left school he had also invested in a brand-new hand-cranked 35mm newsreel movie camera and sold a film to the London-based *Gaumont Graphic*. The sale would usher in a decades-long career that would eventually bring Manley to New Zealand, where he landed a job with a commercial film producer before incorporating his own company, Eppics Limited, in 1937.

That same year he was introduced to Te Puea and her husband, Rawiri Katipa, by Frank Acheson. Sitting at a table in Auckland's Old Majestic Theatre Coffee Lounge, Manley and the judge listened on as Te Puea described her dream of building several large waka taua for the centennial commemoration of the Treaty of Waitangi. Manley later recalled Acheson suggesting the construction be filmed, even though the judge appreciated that, 'according to Maori custom, the building of the carved canoes would be a strictly "tapu" undertaking during the progress of which photography, writing about the work in hand, or publishing such material, especially for personal gain, would be most unwelcome if not actually prohibited'.[14]

Acheson understood the issues, but recommended Manley for the job nonetheless. He told Te Puea that Manley was married to a woman from Te Arawa (Nimera Rikihana), and therefore understood 'the Maori heart' and 'would respect the Maori point of view, customs and beliefs'. Despite Manley being Pākehā, Te Puea could see the long-term value of such a recording, and found Acheson's recommendation compelling. She eventually agreed, on the proviso that the resulting footage would only be used to uphold the mana of the Māori people. Ultimately, 20,000 feet of 35mm negative motion picture film and several hundred feet of 16mm negative sound film were shot. In addition, Manley took hundreds of photographs, from which he put together a number of albums, each comprising nearly 200 enlarged prints.

Manley's enthusiasm for the project was never in doubt. He made countless trips to the forest, carrying his camera gear across rough and hilly terrain, and often slept in his car on overnight trips. His dedication to the project, and the related investment in time and resources would, however, ultimately cost him his business. As the Second World War began to rage on the far side of the world, commercial difficulties saw Manley's business put into voluntary liquidation in early 1940.

The following year Te Puea, worried what might happen to the footage as a consequence, approached the liquidator and negotiated to purchase the film. According to Manley she paid for it with her own money in order to ensure the film was 'preserved for her people for the future and not be allowed to fall into other hands'.[15] The acquisition, which included some 200 rolls of film, was eventually transported to Tūrangawaewae Marae in Ngāruawāhia, where it sat in negative form, unedited and slowly deteriorating. After being stored in several locations after Te Puea's death, it was eventually transferred to the New Zealand Film Archive (now Ngā Taonga Sound & Vision) in Te Whanganui-a-Tara Wellington for safekeeping.

'It was some of the finest film footage I had ever seen,' Sir Bob Harvey told me while reminiscing about the first time he watched Manley's film. As deputy chair of the Film Commission in the mid-1980s he had been one of a select group invited to the Film Archive to view some early silent films.

> Before we left, the director, Jonathan Dennis, asked if we might be interested in viewing some footage of the building of the canoes for the 1940 celebration, which of course we were. Well, I looked at about 10 minutes of the footage and I was absolutely in love with it. I was just stunned [at] how glorious it was.

Harvey, a former mayor of Waitakere City, is a tall man with eyes that dart playfully under cloud-white eyebrows, and he possesses an easy smile. He also has some pedigree when it comes to assessing film. He worked as an assistant projectionist in the 1950s and spent his time on the job studying some of the leading directors of the period, including John Ford, Billy Wilder, William Wyler, Alfred Hitchcock, and Aleksandr Ptushko. Movies, he told me, are in his blood, and have remained a passion throughout his life.

By the late 1980s Harvey had been appointed chair of the Commonwealth Games Arts Festival, which was being held in Tāmaki Makaurau Auckland alongside the 1990 Commonwealth Games. The cultural celebration was to feature artists from the competing countries. 'My mind leapt ahead while I was watching the footage, and I'm already thinking that this has to be part of the 1990 cultural festival,' recalled Harvey. 'We had to premier this film when they opened the games.'

With the backing of Judith McCann, CEO of the Film Commission, and the Commonwealth Games organising committee, Harvey went about securing financial support to start work on preparing the footage. The first step was for specialists at the Film Archive to transfer the footage from highly flammable and chemically unstable cellulose nitrate film to something safer and more durable.

Harvey recalls that everything seemed to be tracking well until he received a phone call from 'a woman who said she was Jim Manley's daughter. She had heard [about the project] and told me the family would not give permission for Jim Manley's work to be used. I replied that I was in terrible trouble then, and that I really needed the family's okay. She was steadfast: "Well, we're not giving it."'

Harvey turned for advice to Tainui elder and Film Commission kaumātua Rei Rakatau, who suggested that they visit the Māori queen, Dame Te Atairangikaahu, to seek her counsel. 'We drove down to Ngāruawāhia, where I told her that I thought it was the most wonderful, glorious piece of footage I'd ever seen. She replied, "I own the footage. Although Jim Manley shot it, he did so for Tainui, and he did it with the patronage of my mother. We will sort it out with the family."

'I can't tell you how bloody pleased I was. Rei and I left that meeting at 1 o'clock in the morning and we were absolutely delighted. But that's when the nightmare started. Manley's family weren't wearing this at all. They just weren't. They said we had no right to make the film; that [the footage] belonged to them. They were making all kinds of threats — you know, legal threats. They threatened to get Māori to oppose the making of this film. They threatened Jonathan [Dennis] that they would remove the footage from the [Film] Archive, take it back. Well, I knew I was getting involved in something over my head. I didn't have the clout, if you like, but I had the backing of Dame Te Ata.'

He also had the backing of the Film Commission. Judith McCann, determined to see the work completed in time to debut at the Arts Festival, contracted acclaimed Māori film director and producer Merata Mita, whose credits include *Patu!*, a documentary record of the protests against the 1981 Springbok tour, and *Mauri*. Experienced film editor Annie Collins was also signed up to work on the project.

'I was up to my neck fundraising,' Harvey recalled, 'while [Mita and Collins] were up to their necks editing the film, and I know they didn't know what parts went where. Manley didn't leave any sort of script and there was so much footage — Merata and Annie were looking at the footage thinking, "What the hell is that? Which bullocks are these, and where are they going?"'

Referring to the photo albums Jim Manley had put together helped, and fortunately they were also able to call upon the assistance of a number of Tainui kaumātua, some of whom had worked on the original 1940 canoe project. Nevertheless, progress was painstakingly slow, with Mita and Collins often reduced to working on a single frame at a time as they pieced the action together.

By the time the last of the frames were being spliced together, the first of two special viewings was organised. Shown at Ngāruawāhia, Dame Te Ata and invited elders watched on, engrossed as the 83-minute film brought their recent tribal history to life. Moved by what she had seen, Te Ata gave the film her seal of approval and the footage was subsequently carried up Tainui's sacred maunga, Taupiri, to be blessed.

Arrangements were then made for the film to be shown to sponsors and other stakeholders at a private theatre in Auckland.

On a warm mid-November evening in 1989, the invited guests began to filter into the small theatre and take their seats for what was supposed to be a celebration of the film.

Bob Harvey remembers feeling a growing apprehension as the evening progressed, initially triggered by the arrival of Jim Manley's daughter, Moana Whaanga, with three or four others. 'I don't know how she knew about it,' he said, recalling the night some 30 years later, 'and I was kind of pleased to see her, but I couldn't help but wonder why they had come.'

His unease increased when he noticed one of the Whaanga family take up a position outside the projection booth. Exactly what happened next is disputed. According to Harvey, about 30 minutes into the screening Moana Whaanga stood up and announced that no one was to leave the theatre. Her whānau then stood as one and headed out into the foyer. Harvey's version of events is largely echoed by Merata Mita in an interview published in the *New Zealand Herald*, though her account differed on some of the minutiae. According to Mita, for instance, Moana Whaanga waited until the end of the movie to make her demands, then stayed in the theatre to hand over a letter withdrawing 'all rights under the copyright' and order that 'any and all work is to cease',[16] while the rest of the group took possession of the film.

Not so, according to Moana Whaanga's son, Mel, who was also there on the night. When I asked him for the whānau version of events he told me he had been the one who had spoken, not his mother, that no one had been positioned outside the projection booth, and that he had not ordered anyone to remain in the theatre. Rather, he said, he explained that the whānau was unhappy with the film as it was presented by Mita, and that they were also unhappy with the way the New Zealand Film Archive had gone about securing the footage. The family, he said, believed that Jonathan Dennis had 'manipulated' Manley's widow into depositing her husband's work with the Archive. Mel Whaanga then declared to those assembled that, as the lawful owners of the film, they would be taking it with them when they left.

'Then there was shouting from the projection box,' remembered Harvey, 'and I thought, shit, something bad is happening.' Fearing the worst, he sprinted out into the foyer, arriving just in time to see a figure bolting from the projection box with a blur of yellow, which he later learnt was the basket in which Mita had carried the film to the screening. Inside the projection box he found a chaotic scene. Equipment was strewn everywhere and the rolls of film were gone. After checking the projectionist was okay, Harvey dashed down the stairs and out onto Hereford Street. But he was too late: by the time he reached the road the Whaanga whānau had been driven from the scene in a waiting car. The film was gone.

Well, sort of. What the Whaanga whānau had taken was the working print: a rough, unfinished copy of the film that lacked an audio track. Its loss was a setback but not an insurmountable one. It would take time and energy to replace it, but Mita and Collins had already spent so much time with the film they knew it backwards. Within days they were back working on a new copy.

That was not the end of the drama, however. During our conversation, Harvey claimed that as the film-makers were piecing together the replacement version in Ngāruawāhia, he continued to receive threats from the Whaanga whānau. When he went to a hui at Tūrangawaewae Marae, to which he had been summoned shortly after the uplift of the film, he felt as though he was the subject of a barrage of abuse. The hui had ostensibly been called to try to repair the relationship between the Commonwealth Games Arts Festival organisers and the Whaanga whānau, and to work out a way forward. Instead, Harvey claims, it devolved into a multi-hour personal attack that left him feeling isolated and vulnerable.

Even with Rei Rakatau at his side, Harvey said, he felt 'terribly alone'. 'I know some people considered me to be the villain in all of this, saying I forced their hand and stole the film off the Whaanga whānau, desecrated Jim Manley's mana and that of the whānau, but nothing could be further from the truth.'

The meeting continued deep into the night, until Dame Te Ata intervened. 'It was already midnight,' Harvey recalled, 'and she was suddenly standing at the door in her dressing gown. She said, "Kia ora, whānau. Why is this going on? Why are you saying such frightening things? The film was stolen, and now it's being finished here. This is a sacred, tapu moment with this film, and you are not to continue this

— I think she said *argy-bargy*. You are to give your honest and sincere acknowledgement to let this continue. I own this and I will take security of it, and I will guarantee its safety into the future. I will do this. It is my film. It is our film, and I want it to be shown for 1990, for all New Zealand."'

Dame Te Atairangikaahu had made it clear that the film was to be completed without further complications, and the resulting accord with the Whaanga whānau allowed Mita and Collins to complete their work uninterrupted. Harvey told me that although he was elated by Te Ata's support, he was 'an absolute bloody wreck' after the hui and was physically shaking for the entire drive back to Auckland.

Despite these difficulties, the film's premiere, at Auckland's Civic Theatre on 21 January 1990, was a triumph. Dame Te Ata, who arrived with a strong contingent from Tainui, had arranged for one of her iwi's waka taua to be transported north and displayed under floodlights in front of the theatre. Once inside, guests sat respectfully through speeches, waiata and karakia. Then the lights slowly dimmed and the opening credits flickered up on the screen. Five decades old, the images showed a way of life that few in the audience could imagine and even fewer had witnessed. What the film captured, so poignantly, was a way of life that had already faded from reality.

Away from the celebration, the agreement with the Whaanga whānau proved to be a temporary ceasefire rather than a lasting peace. Still troubled by the treatment they and the film had been subjected to, the whānau distanced themselves from the project as they contemplated their options. In the end they would take the dispute to the Waitangi Tribunal, an action that has seen restrictions placed on the availability of the film. At the time of writing it can be viewed only by appointment through the Ngā Taonga Sound & Vision offices in Wellington.

When I travelled to see the documentary, Ngā Taonga's building was temporarily closed, a victim of the 2016 Kaikōura earthquake. Instead of viewing it at their facility, I was directed to the Katherine Mansfield Reading Room of the nearby National Library. Modern and spacious, the room is cut off from the rest of the library by a glass wall, and contains a battery of large tables for the use of visiting researchers. I was greeted by a Ngā Taonga staff member, who had a digital copy of the film ready for me to watch. I put on a pair of headphones and settled in to watch Manley and Mita's creation.

The film commences with a medley of images from the 1940 centennial commemoration. A scene from the re-enactment of the signing of Te Tiriti o Waitangi is followed by footage of *Ngātokimatawhaorua* gliding across the bay, and then Captain William Hobson's pinnace is rowed towards the beach below the Treaty Grounds. The 28th (Māori) Battalion feature next, marching three abreast, before the camera's lens focuses on two waka taua, beached side by side, and then shots of the spectators who had travelled to witness the commemoration. Finally, the camera pans along the length of *Ngātokimatawhaorua* while it is being paddled out from Hobson Beach, before following it as it heads back to land. It is quite an appetiser.

With my focus primarily on the action shot in the north, I watched, enthralled, as footage showed Heperi and his fellow bushmen going about their work — saw, axe or adze in hand. Strong, well built, and possessing the stamina born of a lifetime of physical endeavour, each represented the quintessential Māori man of the 1930s. They wore the hard-wearing clothes needed for working in the forest: heavy woollen trousers held up by leather belts or braces, work shirts or bush singlets and leather work boots. Many of them wore hats to shade them from the summer sun.

The footage shot within Puketi State Forest began with the bushmen standing below a towering kauri, their faces turned towards the tree's crown high above them. The haunting call of a kōauau plays as they contemplate the enormity of their task. Then, as the voice of an elder began reciting a karakia, the men's sharp axes ripped into the tree to remove a wide, V-shaped wedge. Previously hidden by a thick layer of mottled grey bark, chips of kauri flesh formed a growing pile at the bushmen's feet.

Satisfied that enough wood had been removed, the foreman then called for the cross-cut saw. With a man at each end, the saw was soon slicing its way across the circumference of the trunk, the weight of the tree held up off the blade by a set of wedges. Once the saw had completed its work and been put aside, another of the bushmen reached for a heavy mallet. Swinging powerfully, he began to hammer in a new line of larger wedges, forcing them deep into the incision.

What happened next caught me somewhat off guard. Just as the final fibres holding the trunk to the stump were being severed, the movie unexpectedly went blank. Whether it was for effect, or whether the original footage had been damaged beyond repair, I couldn't tell. Either way, being left solely with the audio track was unsettling. Maupakanga, who would have been watching the scene unfold back in 1937 must have been anxious. Any miscalculation in his estimation of the balance of the weighty crown perched high above could see the tree fall in the wrong direction and collide with another, resulting in damage that could prematurely end the build.

When the footage resumed, the tree was lying on the forest floor. In some of Manley's photographs he captures a delighted Heperi and his team performing a spirited haka on top of the fallen giant. If any of that action was captured by Manley's movie camera it didn't make it into the film. Instead, the footage resumes with the bushmen cutting away the crown, then using their axes to remove a thick strip along the length of the log. This flat surface is where Maupakanga would mark out the shape of the

The bushmen cut a scarf into the trunk to ensure it falls in the intended direction, as well as to reduce the diameter so that the 8-foot-long cross-cut saw can be employed to finish the cut. COURTESY OF THE MANLEY FAMILY

canoe. Once their work was completed, the old master pulled a builder's string from his pocket, stretched it taut along the freshly exposed timber, and began to mark the tapering lines of a magnificent waka.

The principles of waka design — specifically the ratios required to build a strong, fast waka — would have been front of mind as he did so. The position of every line needed to be well considered, every dimension perfect. If the canoe was built too narrow, the strain on the hull would almost certainly lead to a catastrophic failure. Should the underside of the hull be too rounded, the waka would roll uncontrollably from side to side when on the water, leaving the crew with a disconcerting experience. Every decision Maupakanga made needed to be faultless.

Guide marks in place, the axemen began their relentless work, slowly transforming the kauri log into a semblance of the waka it would become. Footage from the site shows the forest floor covered with a thick carpet of kauri chips as the canoe began to take shape. Relying on tools that mirrored many of those used by tohunga tārai waka of old, the men worked quickly and efficiently. Aside from the cross-cut saw, waka builders looking on from centuries past would have been familiar with what they saw.

For an understanding of those tools we can turn to the journal of Jean Roux, a lieutenant aboard du Fresne's ship *Mascarin*, who took careful note of the implements and techniques employed by waka builders during his 1772 visit to the Bay of Islands:

> They make their tools of a stone resembling marble, very
> black and very hard. They make axes and adzes of it. They
> use the first for cutting down trees but they manage this
> only after a great deal of difficulty. To lessen the work it gives
> them, they dig away the earth right around the tree that they
> want to fell and set fire to it. They take precautions to ensure
> that the flame burns only the foot. When they have thus

felled it, they rough it down with their axes and finish it with their adzes; these stone tools cut quite well. Their chisels are made of a green stone like the one they carve their god from. This stone is extremely hard. They make one end very sharp and fit the chisel to a handle made of a small piece of wood. They attach it in such a way that it does not move when it is struck; they use it for doing delicate work.[17]

With the task of moving the log out of the forest still ahead of them, the men must have been tempted to cut away as much excess wood as possible, but Maupakanga would have had none of it. Conscious that they still had to drag the hull sections behind a team of bullocks, he knew to factor in a significant safety margin to ensure the logs were thick enough to withstand the move. He also left bulkheads in place, sometimes 45–50 centimetres thick, to provide structural support at each end, with another near the centre.

One of the final tasks before the bullocks were called for was to smooth the hull's surfaces, inside and out, with adzes. The practice left neat rows of vertical lines along the entire length of the hull and was a visual clue as to the skill of the workmen, as well as the pride they took in their work, given they knew that the hull would be adzed thinner still once Piri Poutapu got hold of it at Kerikeri.

One important aspect of the process that Manley did not capture on film (or if he did, it didn't survive) was the tohunga reciting a karakia to appease the guardian of the forest, Tāne Mahuta. Traditionally, there were numerous instances during a build when a karakia would have been needed — even before the first adze struck a tree. Karakia were

Wood chips litter the forest floor as work progresses on the two end sections of the waka. Jim Manley (left) captures one of the men shaping the hull with an axe, while the men in the foreground use adzes to flatten the top of the second section.
COURTESY OF THE MANLEY FAMILY

used to seek ongoing protection for the workmen, and even their tools, while they toiled away in the forest. In his seminal book *The Maori Canoe*, Elsdon Best shared several such karakia. In this excerpt he begins by setting the scene:

> The adept now returns to his companion at the base of the tree. The chopping at the trunk continues until many chips are collected. Another fire is then kindled by friction near the tree. This is the *ahi purakau* [ahi = fire]. The chips are burned in this fire; food is cooked. This is for the purpose of taking the *tapu* off, that the proceedings may be free from *tapu*. This rite is to [placate] Tane; the other, the *tumutumu whenua*, was to the gods. Now the adept chants the ritual of the *ahi purakau*:
>
> Hika ra taku ahi, e Tane! [Generate my fire, o Tane!]
> Hika ra taku ahi, e Tane!
> He ahi purakau, e Tane! [A purakau fire, o Tane!]
> Ka hika i te ihi, o Tane
> Ka hika i te mana, o Tane
> Ka hika i te marutuna, o Tane
> Ka hika i te maruwehi, o Tane
> Ka hika i te pukapuka, o Tane
> Ka hika i te mahamaha, o Tane
> Ka kai koe, e Tane! [You will eat, o Tane!]
> Ka kai hoku au, e Tane! [I also will eat, o Tane!]
> Ka mama nga pukenga [Thus will the teachers be freed]
> Ka mamanga wananga [Thus will the wise ones be cleansed]
> Ka mama hoki ahau, tenei tauira. [As I also, this disciple,
> will be freed.]

The 'placation of Tane,' Best noted, 'frees man from many ills and averts disaster.'[18]

68 NGĀTOKIMATAWHAORUA

It wouldn't be particularly surprising if Manley didn't film a karakia; such utterings were seldom suitable for the public domain, so it's likely he was not permitted to do so.

One legitimate criticism of his footage, however, is that he worked like a stills photographer when he captured his movie footage: setting his tripod, framing his shot, and shooting from a static position. As Merata Mita told journalist Peter Calder, it made the job of editing *Mana Waka* incredibly difficult 'because there is no continuity from one image to the other'.[19]

Nevertheless, it is still remarkable to be able to watch the film that resulted. The footage is mostly crisp and clean, and even though it occasionally bounces unintentionally between Puketi and Oruanui forests, it remains a phenomenal record of the project. It not only allows us to view a significant amount of the construction process for a waka taua (as overseen by Maupakanga, who, let's not forget, learnt the skills at the feet of nineteenth-century masters), but also gives us a brief insight into bush life in the 1930s. We can see for ourselves how backbreaking the work was, and how skilled those bushmen were, not only at felling the massive trees but also when it came time to pick up their adzes and shave fine slivers from the prone kauri. All I could think as the film credits faded away was how incredibly lucky we are to have such a record.

Our visit to Puketi Forest had been a good day but not a perfect one. The forest, it seemed, was determined to hold on to its secrets. At one point I saw Eruera looking up into the trees, his eyes squinting as he inspected one kauri after the another. I followed his gaze, wondering what he was looking for, but remained oblivious. He told me later he had been searching for any surface scarring on the bark, specifically any horizontal marks that might reveal where the bushmen had once wrapped ropes or chains around the trunks in order to help them manoeuvre the logs. He did spot some congealed gum high up on one tree, possibly where it had been grazed by a falling neighbour long ago, but nothing to help our immediate cause. Once Eruera had finished inspecting the trees I conceded reluctantly that it was time to call it a day.

The walk back to the trucks was largely uphill and, although the grade was far from challenging, I quickly found that the day had taken more out of me than I had expected. Looking around at the faces of one or two of my companions, I suspected I was not alone in feeling the pinch.

Our trek out was, of course, nothing compared to the effort required to haul the logs to the trucks back in 1937. Before the arrival of Europeans, the herculean task of moving the logs would have been carried out by an army of physically hardened men. Maupakanga, however, had the comparative luxury of a team of bullocks. In early December he sent word and the teams were summoned. The first of the canoe sections began their trip out of the forest on Monday 15 December 1937. An article in the *Auckland Star* by the young and enthusiastic reporter Frank Colwyn Jones — who was given privileged access by Te Puea to the worksites in both forests — revealed what transpired on the day.

> The scene is a little clearing in the great Puketi State forest near Kerikeri, in the North of Auckland. Begrudging even that little space of dappled sunlight and shade, sharply contrasted against the eternal twilight of the surrounding bush, the tall, riotously festooned trees crowd jealously in. And the only sounds are the falling cadence of the tui's call and the over-loud whirr of the native pigeon in flight. Suddenly, distantly up the rough bush track, noises fall.
>
> Men's voices shout, unintelligibly, peremptorily, and there is the slow, even sound of beasts walking in unison. Then, through the trees men run back and forwards, guiding the

awkward advance of a bullock train. Right into the clearing the
animals come. They stumble, they turn, they back, and finally
stand, heads lowered, depicting the patience of the ages.[20]

Bullocks in place, Jones then turned his attention to the animals' driver
and his helpers, who had fixed a steel hawser to one of the kauri logs:

The 'bullocky' shouts again. The 14 animals lean forward,
grunt, take the strain. Commands in an extraordinary
compound of cursing in English and pleading in Maori
ripped through the air. Skids were thrown under the hull
by sweating, eager helpers clad in all the miscellany of the
waybacks. The leaders bowed their heads, locked their
horns, stood like granite statues while their muscles rippled
and suddenly bunched. Small trees crashed; supplejack
vines burst asunder. The animals' legs moved like relentless
pistons — and the thing was done.[21]

It must have been another anxious time for all involved: one
miscalculation, one broken cable, one serious slip by the bullocks
and a hull section could have been damaged, perhaps irreparably. As
it was, the day went well. The two hull sections arrived at the trucks
undamaged and ready to be transported to Kerikeri Inlet, where they
would begin a period of seasoning in the tidal waters.

By the end of January 1938, Te Hoe and his men were back in the forest
preparing to fell the second kauri. At 70 feet (21.3 metres) it was 3 feet
(0.9 metres) taller than the first kauri, and it had a circumference of 28 feet
(8.5 metres) at its base. It would be used for the central section of the waka.

Uncertainty, confusion and contradiction abound when trying to determine the precise location this tree was felled. It had long been thought that the two trees Maupakanga chose had come from the same site, but that almost certainly is not the case. Close scrutiny of the footage in *Mana Waka* shows the three partially hewn waka sections (the two end pieces together and then the large central section) being moved through two quite different landscapes. In one scene, where one of the two end sections was being hauled along a bush track, the terrain looked similar to the route we walked. In contrast, the landscape through which the central section of the waka was dragged — yard by yard, sometimes foot by foot — resembled a cross-country path, where their passage necessitated the felling of small trees and the dodging of larger ones. The bullock crew faced steep hills that made for painfully slow progress. Watching the terrain closely and knowing how long the operation took left me in little doubt that the second tree had been taken from a location appreciably deeper in the forest.

As far as we know, the sequence used to cut the second tree down and then shape it in preparation for moving was the same as for the first tree, but this time the bushmen faced an unusual challenge. The mighty kauri, already cut most of the way through and with wedges driven in, teetered on the edge of falling and then . . . didn't. The wedges, designed to lift the sawn side of the trunk until the tree was off balance, had failed to do their job. Maupakanga ordered more wedges driven in but still the tree refused to fall. At that point, according to Hec Busby, Maupakanga called for the bullock train. If he couldn't tip the tree over, he would pull it down.

When the beasts arrived, there was one final challenge. Maupakanga needed a volunteer to climb the tree and attach the heavy steel cable that would be used to pull it down. Busby, who spent time with some of the original bush crew in the 1970s, said Tom Munu was the man who eventually scrambled up the towering trunk carrying the light rope with which he pulled up the heavy cable. His reward for risking life and limb was said to have been four crates of beer.

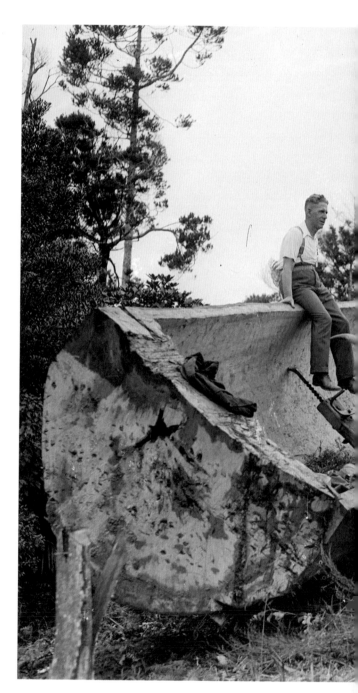

The massive central section of the waka took three weeks to extract from the forest using a team of 24 bullocks and a number of experienced bushmen armed with timber jacks (seen spanning the inside of the hull). W. B. BEATTIE, *NEW ZEALAND HERALD* GLASS PLATE COLLECTION, AUCKLAND LIBRARIES, 1370-M010-12

Once the tree had been brought down, the axes started to chip away at the massive log. Photographs taken after the initial shaping in the forest show that the top sides of the hull — where the rauawa would eventually be attached — were left 10–12 centimetres thick, and both the inside and outside surfaces were finished with the same tidy parallel adze markings used earlier on the front and back sections.

When it came time to drag the kauri out of the forest, the bullock train was assisted by additional workmen hired to operate the large timber jacks and winches needed to help manoeuvre the centre section over the hills. Even with 24 bullocks, it took three weeks to reach the waiting truck and trailer unit. Thankfully, rainfall records for nearby Kaikohe suggest that March was an unusually dry month. It is hard to imagine how they would have got on had a wet spell hit.

One thing I had puzzled over was how the logs had been lifted onto the trucks. I had come across several photos of the canoe sections on the back of a truck, but I couldn't work out how they got there. I imagined that the waka sections had been lifted by a crane, but it turns out that I was wrong. What I had seen as a formidable task was in fact quickly and efficiently accomplished. Manley's film had shown how Heperi had simply had the driver position his truck and trailer alongside a five-to-six-foot bank beside the road, and then, with the help of some skids and two teams of men pulling on ropes, they slid the hull section onto the truck, inch by inch.

Normally the transfer of the log to the truck would have signalled the end of the bullocks' work for the day, but not on this occasion. Struggling with the weight of the log, the truck was unable to climb the most modest of grassy rises until it was hitched to the back of the bullock team.

The details of the drive along the country roads to Kerikeri are interesting, if only for the preparation required to make it possible. Many of the corners along the chosen route could not accommodate the length of the truck and trailer and their radii needed to be increased. Some also needed to be reinforced in places. What in my mind's eye should have been a simple operation had turned into a mammoth one.

With the last of the three sections safely delivered to Kerikeri, it was time to celebrate. Hāngī stones were collected and then heated by fire, and once the meat and vegetables were added, the food was covered over by sacking and then soil, and watched over by experienced hāngī cooks. Any steam vents that broke through were covered over with additional sacking and then topped by a spade-full of soil. Fresh figs and watermelon followed. Experienced kaimahi ensured that there was enough food for workers and well-wishers alike.

The day is also remembered for the large numbers of Pākehā who turned up to see what the fuss was about, as well as the two busloads of children who attended the celebration, one from Ōkaihau East School and the other from Kerikeri. After sampling what was reported as the first hāngī for many of them, the children were invited to try out the waka for themselves: those brave enough were permitted to sit in the recently arrived central section of the hull as it bobbed about in the inlet. It must surely have been a once in a lifetime experience for them.

4
Reviving lost skills

THERE HAD BEEN TALK of towing the three hull sections to Waitangi once they had finished seasoning in the tidal waters at Kerikeri, but the move never eventuated. Instead, it was decided to complete the waka build near Waipapa Landing, where the Waipapa Stream enters Kerikeri Inlet. The site would be tapu, and this relatively secluded location would allow the construction crew a semblance of privacy. Waitangi was still within reach for the paddlers, at a distance reckoned to be eight miles.

When I visited Kerikeri to see if I could find exactly where the waka had been built and then launched from, it was a chilly, blustery day, and the large carpark at Waipapa Landing was empty.

Newspaper reports I had read named the launch site simply as 'Kerikeri', and the only clues I had were in a couple of screenshots I'd grabbed while watching Manley's movie, both of which included glimpses of the surrounding landscape. I hoped that these scenes, shot from nearly opposite angles, would help me pinpoint the site.

The first photo showed Piri Poutapu's men preparing to attach the feather puhi to the taurapa. To their left, partly hidden behind the hull, was a stream, and across the water in the distance was open farmland terminating in a small block of bush and what appeared to be a bluff dropping down to the tide. When I looked out from my car across the inlet, past some moored boats, I could see several low hills that had once been covered in grass. They now housed a well-established subdivision, but there was no doubt the underlying terrain was a match for the grass-covered hills in the photo.

The taurapa is checked for fitting at Waipapa Landing, on the banks of Kerikeri Inlet. The location of the worksite, beside Waipapa Stream (which is visible behind the waka), was still remote enough at the time to allow the work to be completed away from the gaze of the general public. COURTESY OF THE MANLEY FAMILY

The second photo was taken later, during the waka launch, probably from the bank on the far side of Waipapa Stream. Looking inland from that vantage point, the photographer could clearly see a pair of wooden buildings that had been constructed to house the men building the waka, and behind those structures a hill topped by a substantial wooden house. The hill, bare in 1940, was now covered with trees, and a newer house sat on the summit, but it was unmistakably the same location.

In October 1938 work began on the two accommodation units that would house around a dozen full-time workers who had been hired to finish the waka. A temporary nīkau structure was also built to shelter the waka during construction. But work on the waka itself did not begin until at least 10 months after the first sections had arrived in Kerikeri.

Heperi's workmen weren't the only ones who would suffer a frustrating wait, however. There had also been serious delays further south. Funds promised by the government to transport the logs to be used for Waikato's own waka from Oruanui Forest to Ngāruawāhia had failed to materialise, putting an already tight schedule further behind.

Cognisant of the government's record of efficiency in such matters, Te Puea had organised a fundraising tour by her concert party, Te Pou o Mangatāwhiri, as early as April 1937. It was scheduled to visit several North Auckland venues, but the outbreak of infantile paralysis in the region curtailed their programme. Instead, the troupe was restricted to playing at Auckland venues, including the State Theatre at Devonport and the Crystal Palace Theatre in Mount Eden. A second tour of the north was organised for late May through mid-July of the same year, and was, according to Te Puea, 'fairly successful financially', despite a run of inclement weather.[1]

The promotional poster for Te Puea's fundraising tour. A combination of bad luck and bad weather meant Te Puea's concert party, Te Pou o Mangatāwhiri, wasn't able to add substantially to the project's finances. FRANK O. V. ACHESON PAPERS, 1906-1948. MSS & ARCHIVES 96/1, FOLDER 2.4.2. SPECIAL COLLECTIONS, UNIVERSITY OF AUCKLAND LIBRARIES AND LEARNING SERVICES

The flow-on effect of the delays was that master carver Piri Poutapu, who was to oversee the finishing of *Ngātokimatawhaorua*, would not arrive in the north until early 1939.

Born Wiremu Te Ranga Poutapu in 1905 at Maungatautari in the Waikato, Poutapu had been enrolled by Te Puea in the first intake to the School of Māori Arts at Ohinemutu. Alongside fellow students Waka Kereama (Ngāti Korokī Kahukura), and brothers Hone Taiapa and Pine Taiapa (Ngāti Porou), he studied carving and the associated arts for three years under Eramiha Kapua and Tene Waitere, before returning home to the Waikato. His time at Ohinemutu was a period of intense study, and one in which Poutapu thrived. He learnt the properties of and uses for different species of tree, how to use an adze, and the finer points of surface carving.

Tohunga from the old school, Kapua and Waitere also taught their students the necessary chants and offerings to appease Tāne when they took his trees, the protocols to adhere to while working in the forest (no women, no food or cigarettes and no swearing), and how to dispose of any wooden chips left over after cutting a tree down or adzing one (the first chips were burned, and later ones buried). They were lessons Poutapu took to heart and that he would observe strictly throughout his career. He later insisted that his own students follow the same traditional practices when he established his carving school at Ngāruawāhia in 1932. Such was Poutapu's immersion in the art that he once told Michael King that he felt as if his ancestors were passing their mauri and tapu through him and into his work.[2]

The exact date of Poutapu's arrival in Kerikeri is unclear; he was still heavily involved with the finishing of Waikato's own waka throughout 1938 and into 1939. What we do know is that a mere 12 months before the Waitangi centennial celebrations were scheduled to take place, the hull of *Ngātokimatawhaorua* was still in the form of three logs lying on the banks of Kerikeri Inlet: each still in need of considerable adze work to trim them down. The sophisticated haumi joins that would hold the ihu, waenga, and te kei sections of the waka securely together also needed to be cut.

The *New Zealand Herald* reported in mid-February 1939:

> No work has been carried out for some time on the large Maori Centennial canoe that now lies at Kerikeri. It is stated that the carvers, who are to complete the building of the canoe, are still engaged on other canoes in the Waikato. The sections have lain in the waters of the Kerikeri inlet for some months to season the kauri wood, but these have now been hauled out and are lying on the bank, protected from the sun by shelters.[3]

Te Puea's fear that the fleet of waka would not be ready in time for the centennial commemoration was beginning to look a distinct possibility.

When work on the waka finally recommenced, the first task was to remove the excess timber Maupakanga had left in place to help protect the logs during the move through the forest. Taking up their adzes once more, Heperi and his crew got to work, methodically chipping away at the log under Poutapu's direction. It was exacting work that required a sharp eye and a steady hand, and the men excelled at their duty.

Poutapu had a choice of several finishes to consider for the outside of the hull, including a scalloped pattern (said to resemble fish scales) and the smooth finish that he eventually settled on. The reasoning for his choice was not recorded, but it is possible that it was a local preference, even though the scalloped option was also known in the north. Hare Hongi, a former student at the northern whare wānanga at Waitaha and a Native Land Court interpreter, once asked a master canoe builder why he had adopted the scalloped finish that left the outside of his canoe with wide vertical grooves separated by narrow intervening ridges. Hongi wrote:

> He explained to me that the toki umarua (double-shouldered adze) was specially made to pare-ngarungaru the exterior of the canoe (to prevent the water from clinging to the canoe, and so impeding its progress). The object, therefore, was to break up the water which the canoe was passing through, and so to give it greater speed, or to make the business of paddling easier.[4]

Once the hull sections had been thinned sufficiently, Poutapu took charge. It was time for the prow and stern sections — each measuring over 9 metres — to be joined to the central section. To do this, Poutapu would employ the highly effective haumi join. Elsdon Best described this as an elaborate mortice and tenon join, with each cut finished to ensure that when the two sections of the hull were brought together they interlocked.

Drawing on his experience rebuilding *Te Winika* with Maupakanga in 1936, and then his time helping to build Waikato's waka for the commemoration, Poutapu set to work marking the shape of the haumi joins on each section. Once drawn and checked, he reached for his saw. Footage of Poutapu working on the same sort of cut while building a waka at Ngāruawāhia shows him being particularly cautious, testing the fit between the two sections repeatedly as he got closer to the final form. When he was happy with the fit, holes were drilled along the edges of the join. The two sections were then lashed together through these holes, with hune (pappus of the seeds of the raupō), or a similar substance, sandwiched between the two surfaces. Finally, wooden battens or paewai were lashed over the join on the inside of the waka to form a near watertight seal.

While Poutapu was working on the hull, a team of men turned their attention to preparing the rest of the canoe's components. Timber for the rauawa, tauihu, taurapa and taumanu was purchased from a contractor and pit-sawn in Omahuta Forest, with additional timber coming from another source for the long battens that covered most of the joins, and for the 80 or more hoe.

Of the three largest components still incomplete, the tauihu or figurehead was perhaps the most impressive visually. There were two main designs of tauihu for tohunga tārai waka to choose from, depending on tribal preference. The first is the pitau style, which is most easily recognised — the forward-facing, human-like figure leaning out from the front of the waka, its tongue poking out in defiance and its arms stretched back.

The second design, and the one used for *Ngātokimatawhaorua*, is known in some regions as the tuere style. It has four separate components: the base, the central panel (quadrilateral-shaped and standing on one of its long edges), the rear splashguard, and a realistically carved human head affixed to the front underside of the hull just above the waterline. (The carving represents the god of war, Tūmatauenga.) Of all its parts, it is the central panel that makes the tuere so distinctive. Featuring carved manaia figures reaching out across its surface with their heads terminating on either the front or top edge, the panel looks alive, as if the stylised figures are leaning forward into their work, urging the waka onward.

As well as the tauihu, there was also the elaborately carved taurapa, or sternpost, to complete. Regularly standing 2–3 metres tall, the taurapa was a prized possession that, like the tauihu, was carefully stored away when the waka was not in use.

Intricately carved, a taurapa features a pair of curved 'ribs' that reach gracefully up from the base, terminating at a point approximately three-quarters of the way up its height. There are various narratives relating to these 'ribs'. Hec Busby once told me they represent the dual life principles: the taha wairua and the taha tangata, while another source suggested that they are a representation of the bill of the kōtuku or heron.

Finishing off the taurapa are several perforated spirals called pitau, and a human figure that sits solidly at the base of the taurapa, looking forward. It is interesting to note that most of the examples of taurapa that survive today, no matter where they originated, show a remarkable consistency of design, suggesting that there may be some long-held significance to the pattern that was recognised pan-tribally.

The final components of consequence to be fashioned were the rauawa. Long carved boards lashed edge on edge along the top of the hull, these were usually intricately carved with manaia and served two major purposes. The first was to increase the height of the hull, thus reducing the amount of water entering the vessel, and the second purpose was to increase the canoe's structural integrity. Lashed in place above the haumi joins, the rauawa lock down and help stop the joins from flexing.

To ensure the surface carving was appropriate for *Ngātokimatawhaorua*, Poutapu visited several museums to study taonga from the north and collected copies of pictures made by early visitors in the region. He also wrote to foreign museums asking for photographs of northern taonga in their collections. The tauihu that he used as a template was held in the British Museum collection.

According to Hec Busby, the photo of the tauihu arrived only a fortnight before the canoe's launch, and Tom Munu, who had climbed the second kauri to attach the cable that finally downed the tree, was given the task of carving it. He told Busby he had to work day and night to complete it in time: 'He remembered falling asleep sometimes while he was carving, and that old Piri Poutapu would let him sleep for an hour or so and then give him a nudge and up he would get.'[5] After the waka was launched, Munu and his wife lived at Ngāruawāhia for 12 months to repay Waikato for their assistance. 'He said he learnt a lot more down there with Piri Poutapu,' continued Busby.

It was Busby who explained to me the order in which Poutapu and his team likely put *Ngātokimatawhaorua* together. I joined him in his sunroom one March morning. The room was small — only big enough for Busby's recliner, two kitchen chairs and a small table — but it was the perfect spot for him to sit and read the tribal histories he enjoyed, or to look out over the sometimes moody Doubtless Bay, and it sheltered him from the worst of the elements in both winter and summer.

The first task, he said, was to join the three sections of the waka together, a skill that Tom Munu had shown him when they refurbished *Ngātokimatawhaorua* in 1974. Once these were in place, Busby said that they probably went about securing the tauihu and taurapa, first lashing them tightly in place, before filling any remaining gaps in the lashing holes with short plugs. Often shaped from kauri scrap, the circular plugs were pounded into the holes to keep the cord tightly in place, as well as to make the hole watertight. (From another source, I learnt that in the old days any remaining gaps were then filled with a tacky gum from the houhou tree called pia houhou or ware houhou).

Next, the two rauawa were lashed into position, before paewai were added both inside and out to cover the rauawa–hull join. Once that task was completed the taumanu were secured in place. Simple crossbeams with bevelled upper edges, the taumanu span the width of the waka every couple of metres along its length, helping to keep the rauawa spread and the hull rigid. They are habitually lashed in place directly above the hips of the carved figures on the rauawa, as if the figures themselves are taking the weight of the kaihoe from above.

The step before painting a waka, Busby said, would be to put the flooring in place. It was his understanding that the original floor for *Ngātokimatawhaorua* was a platform fashioned from mānuka sticks, suspended lengthways on crossbeams some 12–18 inches under the taumanu, with bundles of raupō placed on top of the mānuka stick floor.

Ngātokimatawhaorua then received its paint job. A dark shade of red (sometimes referred to as 'museum red') was used on the outside of the hull, and its tauihu and taurapa were finished in black. A puhoro design was also added to the underside of the hull, directly under the tauihu. Busby explained that this artwork, usually painted in a combination of red, black and white, is likened to the design on the top of a korowai. 'The tauihu is the head, and you've got the puhoro for the body.'

The final additions were items usually only attached for ceremonial purposes. First there was a row of feathers (often kūkupa or kākā) tied along the top and front edge of the tauihu. One source, collected from tohunga and historian Himiona Kāmira and translated by Bruce Biggs for the *Journal of the Polynesian Society*, named the upper row puhi-maroke (dry puhi, usually running along the top edge of the tauihu and over the splashboard), while the lower row was called puhi-mākū (wet puhi, affixed to the front and sometimes below the prow).[6]

At the other end of the waka two feather streamers were attached to the taurapa. Designed to trail the waka, the uppermost one is called puhi kai ariki, and the lower streamer puhi moana ariki. The name puhi rere is also sometimes used but seems to be a generic term to describe a pair of streamers trailing from the taurapa.

The final components were the ihiihi. Consisting of two hoops reaching out from the tauihu on slim rods, typically of mānuka or tanekaha, they were also decorated with feathers. Often referred to as karu atua, or the 'eyes of god', their original purpose seems to have been lost. We do know, however, that they were sometimes employed for sinister purposes, as George Forster witnessed at Queen Charlotte Sound in 1773: '[T]he war canoe in which a war party expedition had been made . . . had a carved head ornament with bunches of brown feathers, and a double pronged fork projected from it, on which the heart of their slain enemy was transfixed.'[7]

ABOVE: One of Piri Poutapu's team plugs the lashing holes below the tauihu with scrap kauri. The operation not only helped make the waka watertight, but it also kept the lashing cord securely in place.

BELOW: Beautifully carved, *Ngātokimatawhaorua*'s taurapa gets its final coat of paint.
COURTESY OF THE MANLEY FAMILY

In a nod to modern-day safety precautions, *Ngātokimatawhaorua* was also fitted with a pump, a convenience added to help empty the hull of any seawater that found its way in, either through its joins or from the splash of hoe.

As spring rolled into summer at the end of 1939, preparations for the centennial commemorations accelerated. While Poutapu, Te Hoe Heperi and their craftsmen raced to finish the waka, groups of women throughout the region were busy making the cloaks, belts and headbands that the waka crew and the hundreds of Māori participating in the commemorations would wear. Hohepa Heperi's wife, Erana, who had visited Ngāruawāhia to learn traditional weaving techniques and patterns, spent weeks travelling throughout the north to pass on her newly acquired knowledge. According to one report, 'The waistbands and headbands of the Ngāpuhi are being carried out in Taniko weaving in black and white, while black and white will also be the decorations on the cloaks, wool being used for these decorations as tufts of feathers are unobtainable.'[8]

Frank Acheson noted that Erana also oversaw the select group of women who helped paddle *Ngātokimatawhaorua* on the maiden voyage. With many of their young Māori men having already departed the north to join the armed forces, the women had been recruited to fill empty seats.

As the launch day neared, Poutapu and his crew saw to the final touches. The tauihu and taurapa, already checked for fitting, were removed from the waka and painted black. They then checked and rechecked the rest of the waka to ensure it was watertight. Hoe, now painted with red handles and white blades, were counted and stacked in piles.

The magnificent waka taua that had been a mere dream just a few years previously was ready. At 35.7 metres long, with a 1.8-metre beam and a 1.5-metre draft, *Ngātokimatawhaorua* could carry a crew of 88 and accommodate another 40 passengers seated down the centre.

That the waka had been completed in time was of course due to the efforts of the bushmen who had felled the kauri and the carvers who had completed the build, but also to the dutiful Hohepa Heperi. He was the quartermaster of the operation, working behind the scenes to ensure that things ran as smoothly as possible on the meagre budget available. Acheson, who took a keen interest in the venture from the beginning and who left a full record of the accounts, commented:

> Many people gave assistance without payment for their services. The Tokerau Judge thanks them all, and mentions particularly Mr and Mrs Hohepa Heperi and Mr Pita Heperi who gave continuous service for six years without payment or even refund for many expenses. Judge Acheson certifies that he has personally checked all expenditure in the fullest detail and found all accounts to be in perfect order. Mr Hohepa Heperi's accounts were models of accuracy, and a great help to the judge.[9]

Interest and then pride in the waka had grown over the months and years it had taken to build it. When *Ngātokimatawhaorua* was launched on Tuesday 30 January 1940, hundreds of well-wishers crowded the shoreline and tested the strength of the adjacent jetty. Others packed the decks of the pleasure craft that would escort the waka on its maiden voyage. The mood, initially buoyant, quickly muted, however, when it became obvious that the waka could not be moved when the time came. This great moment for northern Māori was threatening to dissolve into farce.

Among those who had gathered at Kerikeri to witness the launch was the respected rangatira Whina Cooper, of Panguru. Forty-five years old at the time, Cooper was, like Te Puea, a powerhouse for her people. She had been a leader of the northern Hokianga people since the early 1930s and had worked closely with Apirana Ngata to establish Māori land development schemes in her home district. In later years she would go on to be the founding president of the Māori Women's Welfare League and, at the age of 79, would become the face of the 1975 land march from Te Hāpua in the Far North to Parliament in Wellington.

She shared her recollections of the launch with Michael King:

> It was on rollers. In the creek that we were supposed to pull it to there was a barge with a winch on it. The idea was to pull the canoe along the rollers, using the winch and human labour. But when they tried to, it wouldn't budge. It just stuck fast, in spite of all the helpers and the wire ropes and everything. So they stopped trying and the old people had a conference about it. Te Puea was there, and said to them, 'Never mind the winch. That's all wrong. That's what's holding it back. We'll do it the Maori way.' So one of the tohungas, Pita Heperi, got up on top of the canoe and recited a karakia. Then he began a tauparapara and as he called out — jumping back and forth — all the Maoris pushed. Over the other side of the creek some old ladies began to call it to come forward. And do you know it did, it just slid beautifully down the slope and into the water like a swan. Old Heperi, dancing up and down it, waving his taiaha and calling out, didn't look like himself at all. He was taken over by his tupuna and became one of them.[10]

Film-maker Jim Manley was also in attendance. Perched on an elevated stage that was balanced on a large pontoon, he captured metres of film

ABOVE: Crew members place bundles of raupō on the suspended mānuka-stick floor. Added primarily for the comfort of the crew, the raupō also ensured the kaihoe would be high enough to reach over the rauawa when paddling. COURTESY OF THE MANLEY FAMILY

BELOW: The crew poses for the camera moments before departing Waipapa Landing for Waitangi. *Ngātokimatawhaorua*'s maiden voyage was a triumph for Piri Poutapu, the tohunga given the responsibility of overseeing the completion of the waka.
B. SNOWDEN, ALEXANDER TURNBULL LIBRARY, 1/2-C-014058-F

footage and numerous photographs of the launch. One of the stills, taken soon after the canoe entered the water, shows the crew standing around waiting to board as bundles of raupō — introduced for comfort — were being placed on the canoe's mānuka-stick floor. Some of the men were wearing army-style greatcoats, while others were adorned in their recently made korowai. Almost all were wearing headbands.

Once the kaihoe were seated, the kaihautū issued the first command. Three years after Maupakanga had first entered Puketi State Forest to scout for the trees, *Ngātokimatawhaorua* was embarking on its maiden voyage. Manley described the route paddled to Waitangi for a 1974 newspaper article:

> For almost five miles due east down the inlet the rhythmic paddling to chant and song and the regular call of kaituki continued steadily and a light rain fell to bless the canoe and passengers and crew on its way. On it went, past Motu Papa, Cocked Hat Island, and into the north-west corner of the Bay of Islands. Then, turning south, it travelled on through Kent Passage, inside Moturoa, and after seven miles reached the inner area of the bay.[11]

From there, Manley says, the voyage continued in a 'southerly direction across Onewhero Bay, past Brampton Shoal and across Wairoa Bay', before ending at the jetty at Ti Point, Waitangi.

Whether the crew realised it or not, when the waka left the tidal waters of Kerikeri Inlet and entered Pēwhairangi proper, they were making history. It had been at least five, perhaps six decades since a waka taua the size of *Ngātokimatawhaorua* had graced the waters of the bay, but what was more notable was the level of mana possessed by the crew. Each man and woman, and even the few children who were on board to bail, had been selected because they were direct descendants of the rangatira who had signed Te Tiriti o Waitangi a century earlier. It is almost certain that no waka had ever borne so many individuals with such bloodlines. Interestingly, given the general reluctance to allow women on a waka taua in the twenty-first century, there were several female kaihoe in the crew. Two of the women kaihoe make a brief appearance in *Mana Waka* at the 73-minute mark.

So who was the kaihautū aboard *Ngātokimatawhaorua* in 1940? Sources disagree. The Heperi family remain convinced that their ancestor, Te Hoe Pita Heperi, was the captain. To back their claim they have a letter written by Judge Acheson in February 1940 to the Waitangi National Trust Board, which acknowledges Heperi as the captain. They also point to footage in the Manley film that shows Heperi, resplendent in a feather korowai, urging the crew on during the maiden voyage.

It's pretty convincing evidence, but not conclusive, because there is also footage of Mutu Kapa — an influential figure from the north and one of Te Puea's most trusted advisers (his father was from Te Aupōuri and his mother from a senior line within Waikato)[12] seemingly performing the same role. The most likely truth is that the two men shared the captaincy of the waka.

This was supported in a private communication I received from Manley's grandson, Mel Whaanga. He told me that as he understood it, Te Hoe Heperi and Mutu Kapa were joint captains in 1940, and that 'Kapa was the fugleman responsible for keeping the paddlers in time.' That last snippet of information dovetails neatly with another piece of the story I had picked up. Talking with the vastly experienced Waikato kaihautū Hoturoa Barclay-Kerr, I learnt that the paddling technique used on *Ngātokimatawhaorua* had been taken to the north from the Waikato by none other than Mutu Kapa himself. The narratives were starting to fit together nicely.

That it would be so long before a waka of any appreciable size would be paddled in the Bay of Islands would have been unimaginable before the signing of Te Tiriti o Waitangi, and probably unthinkable right up until the end of the New Zealand Wars in the early 1870s. Coastal sailing ships began to replace large waka to transport food and other cargo soon after Europeans arrived in the country, but waka taua remained an important symbol of tribal identity, pride and power. To get an idea of how numerous such waka were in the north before the full onslaught of European colonisation was felt, we have only to read the journals of early visitors. One such record was penned by Major R. A. Cruise, who published his experiences and observations in *Journal of a Ten Months' Residence in New Zealand* in 1820. The following passage describes a fleet of 'about fifty canoes' returning to the Bay of Islands after a successful raid:

> The largest canoe we saw was eighty-four feet long, six feet wide, and five feet deep . . . It was made of a single kauri tree hollowed out, and raised about two feet, with planks firmly tied together and to the main trunk, with pieces of the flax plant inserted through them. The crevices were filled up with reeds to make the canoe water-tight. A post 15 feet high rose from the stem and stern, which, together with the sides was carved in open work, painted red, and fringed with a profusion of black feathers.
>
> The chief sat at the stern, and steered the canoe, which was impelled by the united force of ninety naked men, who were painted and ornamented with feathers; three others, standing upon the thwarts, regulated the strokes of the paddles, by repeating with violent gestures a song, in which they were joined by every one in the vessel. The canoe moved with astonishing rapidity, causing the water to foam on either side of it; and we have observed other war-canoes

cross the Bay of Islands in perfect safety, when it was thought imprudent to lower the ship's boats.[13]

By all accounts *Ngātokimatawhaorua* performed well during its maiden voyage, which doubled as a sea trial. The joins remained watertight, and no adzing was required to trim weight from the hull or to refine its balance. Poutapu and his crew had done a masterful job.

One of those on board was Eru Heperi, son of Te Hoe Heperi, and at the time of writing the last living member of the historic crew. I tracked him down in Australia and he told me he was 13 years old in 1940, and was one of the two boys tasked with bailing the canoe. When I asked him about the paddlers' timing on the way to Waitangi, he told me it was excellent and that anyone watching would have thought they were an experienced crew. He recalled how much he had enjoyed the experience, saying there was little bailing to be done because the waka was 'pretty much watertight'.[14] He also remembered the large number of pleasure boats following them all the way.

There was one particularly memorable moment for the crew during the voyage to Waitangi. As *Ngātokimatawhaorua* neared its destination, a second waka taua, the one built under Rē Kauere, was spotted powering towards them. Despite any lingering animosity between the two camps, when the smaller waka reached *Ngātokimatawhaorua* both crews threw their paddles high into the air in celebration.[15]

Despite only one waka being built under her sponsorship in the north, Te Puea's dream of seeing two waka taua at Waitangi had been realised. Whether she had hoped to provoke northern iwi into building their own waka when she sent her craftsmen into their territory is unknown, but whatever her motivation, the rival camps had both managed to complete their waka in time to launch them for the centennial commemoration. Waka taua, so nearly lost to history, were once again capturing the public imagination as their crews paddled across the calm waters of Pēwhairangi.

Nevertheless, it had been a curious state of affairs. Given Te Puea's role within Tainui, she undoubtedly understood the protocol required to undertake a project of this significance within the boundaries of another iwi (Ngāpuhi), and yet, as we have seen, she had sent Poutapu and Wirihana into Puketi State Forest virtually unannounced. Perhaps she was relying on her close ties to the north through Mutu Kapa to smooth over any ill-feeling, but that seems unlikely. Etiquette should have seen Te Puea, or at least her most senior representatives, travel north in person to seek permission. Her insistence that Ngāpuhi had no carvers of their own capable of making a waka taua only added insult to injury.

Incensed by Te Puea's slight, a number of hapū had banded together and put plans in motion to build their own waka taua. Rē Kauere, a well-respected rangatira from Ōtaua, was put in charge of the project, which was fully funded by iwi subscription.

To build the waka, Kauere had engaged the services of Toki Kingi Pangari, an experienced waka builder who built his own canoes to commute across the Hokianga Harbour.[16] Pangari, a somewhat eccentric character, was known for riding his cow into Kaikohe when his horse and cart were unavailable.

The tree Kauere and Pangari chose to build their waka from was a large kauri standing deep in the Ngaiotonga Forest, east of Russell. Tall enough to make a good-sized waka without the need for additional end sections, the tree was felled and partially hollowed out in the forest before it was dragged by a team of bullocks to the shores of the Waikare Inlet, where it was left to season.[17]

By mid-October 1939 the log had been towed by boat to Ōpua, where

'Toki Pangari and Rēnata Kauere at work on the waka *Ngātokimatawhaorua*, Opua, 1939.' The block of wood in the centre of the hull was left in situ to allow a tekoteko to be carved from it, but the innovation was abandoned after it was found to affect the balance of the waka. CAMBRIDGE MUSEUM OF ARCHAEOLOGY AND ANTHROPOLOGY, P.14030.KSL

the final shaping was completed. Pangari opted for a reasonably thin hull, which he pared down in places to a bare 5 centimetres. The lightweight hull would ensure the waka was fast, but the drawback was that it lacked some strength and rigidity. (Hec Busby told me that during the 2009 refurbishment of the waka he added bulk and weight to the hull, doubling its thickness to about 10 centimetres. He was quick to acknowledge, however, that despite the original thinness of the hull, the waka had not been at all 'tippy', which impressed him.)

It was while the waka was at Ōpua that Werner Kissling entered the narrative. The German-born scholar and diplomat was in New Zealand on a field trip when he heard talk of the waka. He visited the site having obtained permission to take photographs. One of the photos, captioned 'Toki Pangari and Renata Kauere at work on the waka Ngatokimatawhaorua, Opua, 1939', is particularly interesting.[18] It shows a large rectangular block of wood left standing inside the hull. Toto Wiremu Warena, the bullock driver responsible for moving the kauri log from Ngaiotonga Forest, was interviewed about this in 2003 by museum curator Amiria Salmond (formerly Henare). He explained that the unusual feature had been left in place so a tekoteko figure could be carved from it, but it was eventually removed because it upset the balance of the waka.[19] Warena also divulged during the interview that 'because various tapus were not correctly observed in the course of cutting down the tree, the carts between which the log was balanced went off the road as they were trying to get it down the hill'.[20] Fortunately the hull remained undamaged.

Others involved in moving the waka included Sam Maioha, Eruera Mikaka, Bob Harris and Ngawati Heremaia.[21]

When the 15.9-metre-long hull was complete, Ngawati Heremaia and Hokene Mokaraka were given the responsibility of carving the tauihu, taurapa, rauawa and other components. Local men, they had each spent three years on the East Coast learning the art of carving from tohunga whakairo and had been part of the team of carvers who worked on the

Whare Rūnanga at the Treaty Grounds. A *New Zealand Herald* reporter who witnessed the finished waka being towed from Ōpua described it as 'handsomely carved', and said it looked 'a fine picture as it was being taken to Waitangi'. After arriving at Waitangi, the waka was carried into the meeting house at Te Tii Marae, where it remained until its official launch.

Somewhat confusingly, however, this waka was given the same name — *Ngātokimatawhaorua* — as the one sponsored by Te Puea. According to Ned Peita, whom I interviewed at his Moerewa home, when the tribal elders met to discuss an appropriate name for the waka, Eka Wairere argued to call it *Ngātokimatawhaorua*, despite the fact that the waka being built by Poutapu and Heperi had been given this name as early as 1937. 'All I know,' Peita told me, 'is that when they heard the name given to *Ngātoki*, Eka Wairere said, "No. They are Tainui, they are not *Ngātoki*. My waka is *Ngātoki*." The gathered rangatira acknowledged him, and we continue to call it *Ngātokimatawhaorua* to this day.'

5

A nation prepares

IN THE DAYS AND weeks preceding the treaty centennial, Waitangi and the surrounding towns became a hotbed of activity. Rehearsals for the actors who would be involved in the re-enactment of the signing of Te Tiriti o Waitangi were held in Kaikohe, where both Māori and Pākehā performers studied faithfully recorded dialogue from the 1840 signing. Elsewhere, Māori families from all over the north were organising truckloads of fresh vegetables and eating fowl to be sent to Waitangi, while the freezing works at Moerewa processed an estimated 100 pigs and 20 head of cattle for the event.

Tradesmen from the Public Works Department arrived en masse to build a temporary village on the grasslands behind the Treaty House. They erected seven large dormitories, four ablution huts, a canteen, a butchery and a huge dining hall measuring 45 metres by 20 metres. An area was also cordoned off for hāngī pits. Purpose-built cottages were built to house government officials from Internal Affairs, the Native Department, the Health Department and Public Works. Another cottage served as a temporary hospital.

While the village was coming together on land, there was time to take stock of *Ngātokimatawhaorua's* performance. Piri Poutapu was pleased with what he saw. The waka sat well in the water and its joins remained watertight; a fact confirmed to me by Eru Heperi.

Te Hoe Heperi and the crew also had time to experiment aboard the waka. On at least one occasion they tried sitting on top of the taumanu as they paddled to see if the crossbeams could be used as seats, but by all accounts the paddlers found it taxing to reach down to the water from the elevated position and difficult to keep time with the kaituki's call. It was easier to get into a rhythm when they were kneeling or sitting on the raupō floor.

Film-maker Manley also spent time out on the waka. Sometimes hidden from view under a feather cloak, he managed to capture close-up footage of the crew in action, and also filmed a famous race between the two waka taua. The *New Zealand Herald* reported on the contest, prefacing the action by acknowledging that there was still 'a certain amount of rivalry' between the sponsors of the two craft:

> When the canoes met for the first time at Waitangi this week a friendly race was arranged and was carried out to-day. The great canoe took on board its full complement of 80 paddlers, two fuglemen to time the stroke and a number of women, all in native dress. Accompanied by a launch full of Europeans it made its way majestically down the bay to a point off Paihia, the long rows of silvered paddles flashing. The Ngapuhi crew, who, for the occasion had covered their faces and bodies with red ochre, launched their craft a little later and set off in pursuit. There were about 25 of them, something like two-thirds of the full complement, but the reduced weight appeared to be rather an advantage than otherwise.
>
> The finish of the race back was greeted by loud cries from Maoris on both banks of the river as the smaller canoe, with its crew aft and bow well in the air, drew ahead of the heavily laden larger craft, and won easily by several lengths. The moment it passed the end of the wharf the losers raised their paddles horizontally two or three times in unison to admit defeat. The victors beached their vessel, dived into the sea to wash off the ochre, and went happily away to lunch. An interesting point was that each canoe was provided with a modern bilge pump in place of the primitive wooden bailer.[1]

The film-maker and photographer Jim Manley seated behind the tauihu on the splashboard. Manley's footage would leave a priceless record of *Ngātokimatawhaorua*'s build and first days on the water. Introduced to Te Puea by Judge Frank Acheson, Manley had almost unrestricted access to the waka and its crew. COURTESY OF THE MANLEY FAMILY

Winning the race would undoubtedly have delighted Rē Kauere, whose decision to challenge the arrival of Maupakanga in the north by building another waka had not been universally supported. The performance of his waka in the head-to-head race had, however, emphatically proven his point: that Ngāpuhi could build a waka taua without outside assistance. He had publicly upheld the mana of northern tohunga tārai waka.

Te Hoe Heperi's daughter (and Eru's sister) Ani Gardam, who was six years old in February 1940, remembers the time well. Now also living in Australia, she told me she and Eru stayed in the Manley family tent, which was pitched near to where the Copthorne Hotel now stands. 'I didn't get to see much of my family at all,' she said. 'Everybody was busy. My eldest brother, my dad, my grandfather and Eru were all out practising on the waka each day, and Mum and the other women were off preparing kai. But it was all so exciting.'[2] According to Ani, the Heperi whānau were also engaged to look after Te Puea's car while she was at Waitangi. Eru's twin brother, Waka, was assigned to guard the vehicle and keep an eye on her many 'treasures and things'.

Indeed, Te Puea had arrived back in the north, having travelled with a small contingent to ceremonially gift *Ngātokimatawhaorua* to the five northern iwi. A photo from the occasion shows Te Puea and her husband, Rawiri Katipa, with members of the crew. Te Puea, under her trademark floral-print headscarf, was captured mid-hongi with a woman, possibly one of the crew members.

Te Puea's stay in the north would be short-lived, however. Events unrelated to the commemoration had soured the relationship between Waikato and the government, and they had decided to boycott the centennial commemoration. Waikato leaders were incensed at the government's insistence that the Māori king, Korokī Te Rata Mahuta Pōtatau Te Wherowhero, register under the Social Security Act of 1938 and declare his income. Based on that declaration, he was then expected to contribute to the nation's social security fund. This, while the government exempted the governor-general, consuls and vice-consuls from the tax, was seen by Waikato as further evidence of the government's continuing failure to recognise the mana of the Māori king.

As the commemoration date neared, guests from across the nation began to descend on Waitangi. While Waikato's absence was noted, Ngāpuhi were kept busy welcoming kaumātua and kuia from other iwi, many of whom had arrived at Ōpua by train and been ferried up the harbour to Waitangi on a flotilla of launches. Among the arrivals were three of the four Māori members of Parliament: Sir Apirana Ngata, the sole National Party MP of the group, and his Labour Party colleagues Eruera Tirikātene and Haami (Toko) Rātana. Paraire Paikea, the MP for Northern Māori and another Labour member, was already in camp.

All four were hard-working politicians. Ngata was the oldest by 20 years, and the 'father' of the House in Parliament. When he won the Eastern Māori seat in 1905 the other three were still children. During the First World War he was instrumental, after Gallipoli, in grouping Māori troops into a Māori battalion. Both Tirikātene and Rātana served overseas during the conflict — Tirikātene in Egypt, Rātana in Gallipoli, and both in France. Rātana was so badly gassed there that he was in poor health for the rest of his life.

The three Labour MPs were also high-ranking members of the Rātana Church, founded by Toko's father, the religious visionary Tahupōtiki

Rātana. Later, in 1940, Paikea would become the sole Māori member of Prime Minister Peter Fraser's Cabinet, overseeing the Māori war effort, including recruitment for the 28th (Māori) Battalion.

In many ways the Waitangi commemoration signalled the end of an era. Before the Second World War was over, both Paikea and Rātana — still only in their fifties — would die in office. In 1943 Ngata would lose the seat he had held for almost 40 years, making way for an all-Rātana caucus of Māori MPs, establishing a tradition that lasted until the early 1990s. Only Tirikātene would continue to hold office after the war: he was MP for Southern Māori until his death in 1967, when he was succeeded by his daughter, Whetu Tirikātene-Sullivan, the first Māori woman to hold a Cabinet position.

The launches that had been sent to ferry the kaumātua from Ōpua were called into service again on the morning of 5 February, when a contingent of 500 officers and men from the 28th (Māori) Battalion arrived at the railhead. Having spent 26 hours travelling from Palmerston North by train, they were understandably weary when they reached Ōpua, so it must have been a boost for their spirits when their launches were met by the two waka taua off Paihia. There, in the early morning light, both the soldiers and the waka crews performed impromptu renditions of Māori war songs before the waka turned to race the boats to Waitangi, the splash of their hoe contrasting with the pounding engines of the dozen launches.

Once ashore, the waka crews honoured the battalion with a stirring haka, much to the delight and admiration of the numerous visitors watching on, before the soldiers formed into platoons and marched off to Hobson Beach. There they were greeted by a guard of honour composed

Members of the 28th (Māori) Battalion march past Hobson Beach and begin the short ascent to the Treaty Grounds. Men from the north of the nation formed A Company (Northland), and along with their comrades from across the country, fought with distinction when they reached the battlefields of North Africa and Europe. P. F. NASH, *NEW ZEALAND HERALD* GLASS PLATE COLLECTION, AUCKLAND LIBRARIES, 1370-M006-5

of Māori veterans from the First World War and listened to speeches from the Māori MPs. Replying on behalf of the 28th Battalion, Major George Bertrand (Ngāti Mutunga) spoke of the obligations entered into between the two races a century earlier. If there was any question of whether Māori were honouring their obligations, he said, the answer could be seen in the men behind him. It was an apt precursor for the speeches that would be delivered by the Māori Members of Parliament the following day. The pōwhiri ended with the singing of the Māori Battalion song and the National Anthem.

Long before Captain William Hobson, consul of New Zealand and later its first governor, arrived in the Bay of Islands with his treaty in 1840, the whenua at Waitangi was under the protection of Ngāti Rāhiri, a hapū of Ngāpuhi that had a long and rich relationship with the area. Their ancestor, Maikuku, was a granddaughter of Rāhiri, the founding ancestor of Ngāpuhi, and had once lived on the land. Said to be extremely tapu, Maikuku lived apart from her people, inhabiting a cave near modern-day Hobson Beach. Early maps of the area give the name of the beach as Te Ana o Maikuku (The Cave of Maikuku).

In more recent times the land we know as the Treaty Grounds was owned and occupied by the British Resident, James Busby. Born in Scotland in 1802, Busby had dark curly hair, long sideburns and a high forehead, and was said to be a socially awkward individual. Some went as far as to consider him a prig and a bore. His appointment, taken up in 1832, had come about after 13 rangatira wrote to King William IV requesting that Britain take responsibility for the conduct of a growing number of unruly settlers in the north.

Busby's primary task as the British Resident was to act as an arbitrator between Māori and Pākehā, particularly in commercial affairs, but also in situations where Māori tikanga was being disregarded or disrespected by Europeans. How he was expected to resolve anything without any meaningful support, either political or military, has never been satisfactorily explained.

Despite the indifference displayed by his superiors, Busby still managed to play a leading role in several significant events that helped shape the country. The first was the selection of a national flag. Officials in Australia had seized a New Zealand-based ship because it had not been flying the colours of its country of origin. Busby understood the implications this would have for exporters and moved quickly to rectify the situation. In October 1834 he invited several rangatira to a hui at Waitangi to choose a flag from three designed by Reverend Henry Williams. Subsequently known as the flag of the United Tribes of New Zealand, the choice was quickly gazetted in Sydney and then acknowledged by the Admiralty in England.

A year later, with the French adventurer Charles de Thierry proposing to declare French rule over New Zealand, Busby organised another important hui. This time the assembled rangatira were persuaded to sign He Whakaputanga (a declaration of independence) to reinforce their position in international law. The document, signed by 52 rangatira, was again acknowledged by Britain. Busby's final, and arguably most important, contribution occurred after he had relinquished the position of British Resident in late January 1840. Captain Hobson, unwell but in a hurry to have a treaty executed by Māori, asked him to help write what would become the Treaty of Waitangi.

Aside from these important events, Busby is also remembered for the home he built in 1834. Overlooking Te Ana o Maikuku, it is recognised as the first government building in the country, and is now known as the Treaty House. It is one of the star attractions at the Treaty Grounds. The original four-room cottage was pre-cut in Sydney and shipped across the Tasman Sea for assembly on site. Three additional rooms were added in 1841.

The land the dwelling sat on would stay in private hands until 1932, when Busby's home and the surrounding 1000 acres (405 hectares) were purchased by the governor-general and his wife, Lord Charles and Lady Elaine Bledisloe, and gifted to the nation. Today the Treaty Grounds have become a major tourist attraction that Heritage New Zealand Pouhere Taonga calls 'the most symbolically important place in New Zealand'.

It had been several years since I had been to the Treaty Grounds, so I planned another visit. As well as spending more time with *Ngātoki-matawhaorua*, I wanted to explore the grounds themselves. I wanted to walk over the land where Te Tiriti o Waitangi had been signed, and to familiarise myself with some of the locations directly associated with the 1940 centennial commemoration.

I arrived one October morning, having driven the short distance from my hotel in Paihia. The route bisected dry inland hills and golden beaches before passing Te Tii Marae and crossing the Waitangi River bridge. From there, the turnoff to the Treaty Grounds was just a few hundred metres up the road. The site had been upgraded since my last visit, with two museums added to the already impressive menu of attractions. The first museum, Te Kōngahu, is rich with history related to the Treaty, and its stories are brought to life with a wide offering of taonga, images, maps and interactive displays. There is also a short movie re-enacting the signing of the treaty that plays on a loop. *Waitangi: What Really Happened* looks to be a good primer for anyone a little rusty on what occurred when the British met Māori here in 1840.

The other museum, Te Rau Aroha, is no less impressive. Built to acknowledge Māori involvement in warfare, from the New Zealand Wars to the present day, it is a fitting memorial to those who have sacrificed their lives for their iwi, or, more often than not, for king and country. Wandering its rooms can be an emotional experience, particularly the *He Whakamaumaharatanga* exhibition. This memorial to Māori service personnel from both world wars includes enlarged photographs of many of those who failed to return from foreign battlefields. Portrait after portrait depicted proud, strong men, intent on doing their bit, but what caught my eye was how very young so many of them were.

I could have spent a couple of productive hours exploring each of the museums, but my mind was already racing ahead to *Ngātokimatawhao-rua*. I strolled past the studio where skilled Māori craftsmen carve fine-looking taonga, and through the gift shop, before arriving at the elevated wooden boardwalk that led part of the way to the waka. Information panels on either side of the walkway gave the names and descriptions of the native trees that towered above me as I walked its length: tānekaha, kānuka, rimu, kōwhai, kawakawa, miro, tōtara and kahikatea reached up to the sky. Another set of panels listed the native birds that made their home here, tūī, kūkupa, pīwakawaka and pūkeko among their number. When I arrived at the far end a signpost pointed me down a path of golden sand mixed with crushed shell. At the bottom was the canoe house.

The scene had certainly changed since 1940. When the 28th (Māori) Battalion marched three abreast across the foreshore, there were no waka here and no building to shelter them. Instead, there were six houses lined up in a tight row facing the bay. The largest was a well-established home complete with a stone fence staking out its boundary and a number of mature trees in its backyard. Pitched among the trees were several tents. The remaining five buildings, positioned roughly parallel with the shoreline and fanning out towards the mouth of the Waitangi River, may have been those built as temporary office space for the government departments involved in the commemoration. There was nothing to suggest any permanence about their positioning: they were fenceless and lacked so much as a hint of a garden.

As the canoe house came into view, I realised it was *big* — big enough, in fact, to shelter the entire length of *Ngātokimatawhaorua*, along with two other medium-sized waka taua tucked in end to end at its side. The gable roof was held up by a series of posts, many of which had carvings of Māori ancestors affixed to them. The eight carvings on the south side of the canoe house are from iwi as diverse as Te Arawa, Ngāi Tahu, Ngāti Raukawa and Tainui, while those on the opposite side are ancestors from closer to home, including tūpuna from Ngāti Rāhiri, Ngāti Kahu, Te Aupōuri and Te Rarawa. The same shell and sand mix used for the path was spread under the waka, and a wooden boardwalk ran along one side of the shelter. Railway tracks used to move *Ngātokimatawhaorua* to and from the water led out from the front of the building.

Stepping inside, I closed my eyes briefly and listened as a recording of a kaituki's timing call — tōkihi, tōkihi — tōkihi, tōkihi — sounded out. It was almost eerie as it drifted down from the rafters. When I opened my eyes, I was struck again by the sheer presence of the giant waka. It was no wonder that so many kaihoe had been drawn here to paddle it over the decades.

Ngātokimatawhaorua is a one-off, its size and shape determined by the dimensions of the trees from which it was hewn and the eye of its designer. Seen from the raised platform at its stern it is long and sleek, but it wasn't clear *how* long until I walked its length. Sitting squarely in its cradle, it drew me in closer and closer, until I unconsciously reached out with my hand and let my fingers run along the carved surfaces. It seemed even larger than its impressive 35.7 metres.

Officially opened on 5 February 1976, Te Korowai ō Maikuku was originally named 'Te Ana o Maikuku Canoe House'.

Large enough to easily house the 35.7-metre *Ngātokimatawhaorua*, the building is also home to the stump of the kauri from which the two end sections of the waka were hewn.
ALAMY

Intent on spending as long as it took to take in all of the waka's intricacies, I began to see the waka with a new appreciation. My examination began with an inspection of the lashing used to hold the various components in place. I had studied drawings, diagrams and photographs of waka taua over the years, and tried to visualise how they had been put together — Hec Busby's explanation was invaluable — but seeing it 'in person' took things to another level.

Resting my forearms on the top edge of the rauawa, I could feel where parts of it had been worn smooth by the touch of countless tourist hands, and I could see where it had become bruised and dented by the wayward strike of paddles. Leaning forward, I looked inside the hull to see what I could of the internal lashing. Famously built without a single nail or screw, *Ngātokimatawhaorua* originally relied on natural cordage that contracted when wet. The result was a vessel whose components were pulled tight together every time it entered the water. In recent years the traditional lashing material had been replaced with nylon cord, but the pattern remained the same.

It was beautifully put together. Non-structural pieces that sat above the waterline, such as the tauihu and taurapa, were simply lashed tightly in place, while bigger components like the rauawa (30-plus metres long, 7 centimetres thick and up to 32 centimetres high) were positioned edge on edge to the piece they were to be joined to, caulking added, and then lashed in place.

The standouts, however, were the massive haumi joins. With both end sections looking like fat Vs, the joins at the bottom of the hull looked like huge scars in the process of healing, the battens covering the joins like angry welts.

After studying the lashing, I moved on to the canoe's signature pieces, starting with the large tauihu at the front of the waka. Completed in the tuere style (the one with a central quadrilateral-shaped panel standing on its side), it was beautifully carved, and its sinuous figures looked alive,

Copied after a tauihu held in the collection of the British Museum, this beautifully carved example was finished only a few days before the waka was launched.
JEFF EVANS

ready to lead the waka into battle: its black finish stunning against the red paint on the outside of the hull.

As I stood there admiring the tauihu's form, I noticed some adze marks high up on the inside wall of the hull. Made by Te Hoe Heperi and his men 80 years earlier, they were a visible reminder of the tools and skill required to build such a beautiful waka. As I ran my fingers across them, I couldn't help thinking that they were a suitable autograph for the humble builders to have left behind.

The taurapa was equally as intriguing, and when I arrived at the stern, I had to take a step back so I could take it in in its entirety. Two-and-a-half metres tall and intricately carved, it was a superb example of Māori craftsmanship. Viewed up close, the perforated spirals, termed pitau, were striking, as was the carved ancestral figure at its base. I was surprised, however, to see that the two ribs, the ones that reach up gracefully from behind the ancestral figure, remained uncarved. Like the tauihu, they are usually finished with extensive surface decoration.

The shape of the hull was an interesting feature. Among the drawings and diagrams I'd studied before coming here were several that revealed the cross-section of a typical war canoe. Making my way to the mid-point of *Ngātokimatawhaorua*, I could see that a cross-section was in the shape of the letter U, with near vertical sides and a thick belly. That heavy belly works as a sort of ballast, helping to keep the waka stable in the water. It also helps keep the hull straight as the timber dries out after use.

Some other waka taua, such as the impressive *Te Toki-a-Tāpiri*, housed in the Auckland War Memorial Museum Tāmaki Paenga Hira, have a different hull profile. Believed to have been built about 1836 on the shores of Whakakī Lagoon near Wairoa in northern Hawke's Bay, its cross-section is more V-shaped. It is a design feature which allows the rauawa to flare out rather than stand vertically, thus leaving a considerable gap between the edge of a paddle and the side of the waka when it is being paddled. It's a clever way to help eliminate paddle strike.

My time with *Ngātokimatawhaorua* was interrupted by the arrival of the day's first tour group. Couples and families with young children crowded around their guide as he talked his way along the length of the waka — explaining as he passed near me that it weighs 6 tonnes when dry and 12 tonnes when wet and fully crewed. (I have heard others say it weighs 12 tonnes even without its crew.)

The tour party hung around clicking their cameras for a few minutes and then disappeared up Nias Track towards the Treaty House. As they disappeared from view, I made my way over to the steps leading up to the platform behind *Ngātokimatawhaorua*. It had been built to showcase a series of information panels that gave a basic history of the waka, including, in general terms, where the trees for the waka's construction came from and where it was built, as well as acknowledging the contribution of Te Puea.

One panel in particular caught my attention. Forged in metal, it read: 'Te Ana o Maikuku Canoe House, officially opened by the Governor-General of New Zealand Sir Denis Blundell, 5 February 1976.' I was surprised: I had never heard the structure called by that name. It is, as far as I know, universally known as Te Korowai ō Maikuku, or simply Te Korowai. A quick check of the official signage at the Treaty Grounds confirmed Te Korowai ō Maikuku as the name in common use. Why and when, I wondered, had the name changed? I started asking around but no one seemed to know. Men in their sixties and seventies had always known it as Te Korowai ō Maikuku and could shed no light on the subject. It would take a while, but the mystery was finally solved when I asked Ned Peita.

A few weeks after first speaking to him on the phone, I drove to Peita's Moerewa home, a tidy weatherboard house on the outskirts of town. The flag of the United Tribes of New Zealand flew from a flagpole on the front

lawn. Inside, his living room was packed with mementos of a full life —
photos of family and of waka adorned many of the walls, while various
walking sticks, koikoi and taiaha leant in the corners.

Peita offered me a cup of tea and we made ourselves comfortable either
side of his coffee table. His face was expressive and his hands animated as
he recounted waka-related memories, his stories sprinkled with laughter.
Now in his sixties, he conceded that his grasp of dates is not always
accurate but that he remembered most events as if they had occurred
yesterday. When I asked him about the name of the canoe house he told me
the official name had been chosen by the Waitangi National Trust Board
without due consultation, and that in the early days it was simply referred
to as the waka shelter by the kaihoe. It wasn't until the 1990s, when Wiremu
Wiremu pointed out that the canoe house covered *Ngātokimatawhaorua*
like a korowai, that it started being called Te Korowai. From there, he said,
the name had been lengthened to Te Korowai ō Maikuku.

Our conversation ebbed and flowed and at one point Peita excused
himself, jumped up from his seat and grabbed a nearby paddle. Although
it looked as if it had been painted quite recently, he told me it was an
original 1970s paddle from *Ngātokimatawhaorua*. When he was an
active paddler, he said, he'd made a habit of holding on to his hoe after
a day on the water. There were usually more kaihoe around than seats
on the waka, so taking his hoe home ensured that he had a spot on the
waka the next day. Somehow this one never made it back.

There was also another mystery I wanted to clear up while I was visiting
the Treaty Grounds. Sitting at the back of the canoe shelter, past the two
dedication plaques, was a massive kauri stump. Largely hidden from
view, it was the one I had thought about when we were in Puketi Forest.

The question of whether it had originated somewhere near 'Canoe Track' had lingered ever since we had been unable to locate a stump to match the crown Munro had found. The information panel said it had come from Omahuta Forest, but I had my doubts.

In the months after our forest adventure, I had found a photo of this stump online. It had a different, older label attached to it. Mounted in a picture frame that was nailed to the stump, it read: 'The stump of a large kauri tree. The bow and stern sections of the waka "Ngatokimatawhaorua" came from this tree. Presented to the Waitangi National Trust Board by Mrs S. Winger of Glendowie.' I was surprised when I read it. I knew from the film footage, and from our own visit to Puketi Forest, that the tree felled for the two end sections of the waka came from the end of 'Canoe Track'. Surely, I thought, if the older label was correct, it was proof that what I was looking at was the missing stump. So why did the current information panel say it came from Omahuta Forest?

I pulled out a copy of one of Manley's photos that I had folded into my notebook. It showed the five bushmen who had felled the kauri, the one used for the bow and stern sections, standing on top of the stump. I had brought it specifically to compare the shape and markings of their stump to this one. At first it was hard to tell — Manley's photo included a thick layer of sawdust and wood chip beneath the men's feet — but after studying it for a while I could see where marks left behind by axes and the cross-cut saw on the actual stump matched those in the photograph. It was enough to convince me that this was the stump we had searched for in Puketi Forest. A small piece of the jigsaw had been found.

I was nearly done for the day, but before I followed the tour group up the path, I took a moment to stroll down to the beach. As I stood alone at the edge of the land, the sound of the tide breaking against nearby boulders seemed amplified by the absence of any man-made noise. The grey sea looked cold and uninviting and the odour of decaying seaweed, thrown up by a recent storm, assaulted my nostrils, yet somehow I felt warm and content. Spending time with *Ngātokimatawhaorua* had reminded me that the waka remains a most remarkable example of Māori art — a unique showcase of traditional Māori knowledge and skill.

I wondered, however, what the average tourist might think of the waka. To find out I walked up to a middle-aged couple who had arrived separately from the tour group and asked them. They were English expats who lived in Aotearoa and said they always made an effort to visit the Treaty Grounds when in the north, and always spent time with the waka. The first thing that struck them, the man said, was the immense length, and then the fact that it had been made from just two trees. I had watched them running their hands along the rauawa as they walked its length just as I had. *Ngātokimatawhaorua* had clearly captivated their imagination as well.

After saying our goodbyes, I turned and began to make my way up Nias Track. It was only a short walk to the top, but I made a point of stopping part-way up at the memorial seat. The plaque fixed to it said the bench was dedicated to 'Admiral Sir Joseph Nias, KCB, 1793–1879', and recalled the walk he and Hobson had taken up this track to meet Māori in February 1840.

When I arrived at the top of the track, I was greeted by a gently undulating lawn. If I discounted the hue, it looked like the smooth ocean surface you often get first thing on a summer morning. It was also big enough to accommodate several full-sized football pitches. To my left was Busby's Treaty House and the second of the new museums, Te Rau Aroha, with its moving *Price of Citizenship* exhibition, but I was heading to the carved Whare Rūnanga. The walk across the lawn took me past the flagstaff with its plaque informing me that Te Tiriti o Waitangi was signed 'On this spot on the sixth day of February 1840', then past the massive Norfolk pine Agnes Busby had planted in 1836. It was good to feel the give of the grass under my feet.

Another couple of tourists were leaving the Whare Rūnanga as I arrived. A small sign on the porch reminded visitors to remove their shoes before entering, as well as to refrain from taking food or drink into the whare. Once inside, I made my way over to one of the dozen or so leather-upholstered bench-seats and sat down, alone with my thoughts. Like other carved meeting houses, it was certainly impressive. The muted colours looked to have been chosen to allow the artistry of the carvers and weavers to stand out. The poupou — some of which were illuminated by downlights, others left in the shadows — had been crafted at the carving school Tau Hēnare had helped set up at Mōtatau, and were finished with a matt oil or stain. In this light, they looked more authentic than those carvings that were finished with that staple of protective coats, shiny polyurethane.

Equally impressive were the tukutuku panels interspaced between the poupou. Woven with kiekie strips dyed black, white or yellow, and set against horizontal slates painted dark red, they told their own stories. The poutama design, for example, illustrates genealogies as well as various levels of learning and intellectual achievement; the purapura whetū pattern represents the stars and the great numbers of people of a nation; and the pātikitiki pattern originates from the lashing of timbers for houses. Red, white and black kōwhaiwhai designs painted on the heke and tāhuhu far above completed the artists' work. The only exception to the muted palette was the inlaid pāua shell eyes in many of the carvings. Even those on the periphery of the downlights stared out with an iridescent gaze.

Back outside, I pulled out another old photo, this one of the Whare Rūnanga itself. It included a glimpse of the original canoe shed that housed *Ngātokimatawhaorua* from 1940 until it was relaunched in 1974. Built on the seaward side of the meeting house, the canoe shed was open sided like Te Korowai ō Maikuku, and likewise, its roof was held aloft by a series of posts. But up here, so far from the water, it looked more like a jail than a shelter.

When I walked over to where it once stood, there was no sign it had ever been there. Instead, trees, some of which had been planted by past governors-general, grew in its place.

When I'd finished looking for signs of the old canoe shed, I spied a bench on the far side of the lawn, near the cliffs on its eastern boundary. It proved to be perfectly positioned to look out over the waters below and I sat there for a few minutes surveying the harbour scene, enjoying the cool before the heat of the day set in. To my right lay Paihia, and then Ōpua, and directly across the harbour was Kororāreka Russell (often erroneously referred to as the first capital of New Zealand — that honour goes to Okiato or Old Russell, a spot 7 kilometres south of the town), and just to the north of Russell lay the channel between Tapeka Point and Moturoa Island, leading out into the Pacific Ocean.

It was a spectacular spot to sit and while away the day, and there was something very humbling about being here at the birthplace of modern New Zealand, but as much as I was enjoying playing the tourist, I was there to look over places connected to the 1940 commemoration. After a few more minutes, I turned and looked inland again, imagining the massive tent erected next to the flagstaff, and the speeches and haka presented in front of the Whare Rūnanga.

6

Reflection and hope: Waitangi Day 1940

THE MORNING OF 6 February 1940 dawned overcast but warm for the spectators who had made their way to the Treaty Grounds. As the focal point for the nation's commemorations, the event was well attended, with an estimated 10,000 people converging on Waitangi. An army of media, eager to report on the day for those who could not attend in person, arrived early to claim the best spots. Senior announcer Clive Drummond from Wellington radio station 2YA was among their number. Born at Marahau, near Motueka, in 1890, he was a handsome man with a confident smile, and he endeared himself to his audience by retaining his Kiwi accent when most others in his profession chose to adopt the highbrow BBC English. He was also noted for taking pride in pronouncing te reo to the best of his ability.

From his vantage point on the lawn across from the Treaty House, Drummond could see all of the important landmarks but, initially at least, his attention was fixed firmly on the waters off Hobson Beach. The sandy cove was where Hobson and Nias had come ashore from HMS *Herald* in 1840 to present their treaty to the Māori rangatira, and it was in that very bay that *Ngātokimatawhaorua* would capture everyone's imagination 100 years later.

By 8.45 a.m. a vast crowd had assembled, swarming over the Treaty Grounds and packing the then bare hillside overlooking Hobson Beach. Soldiers marched to their allotted seating and at some point in the morning, a quartet dressed as settlers rode past Manley's camera on horses.

Fully manned, with white-tipped hoe flashing in the morning light, *Ngātokimatawhaorua* looked majestic on the calm waters of Pēwhairangi Bay of Islands on Waitangi Day in 1940.

Close to 10,000 spectators were present when the waka was first put through its paces.
W. B. BEATTIE, *NEW ZEALAND HERALD* GLASS PLATE COLLECTION, AUCKLAND LIBRARIES, 1370-M010-4

Anticipation grew until someone spotted a canoe out in the bay, and then a second. Adults stood and craned their necks to get a better view; children were hoisted on shoulders to see over them. Few if any of the spectators would have seen a waka taua on the water before, and none would have seen one as large and imposing as *Ngātokimatawhaorua.*

Out in the bay, the crew aboard the giant waka revelled in the occasion, surging across the harbour as their ancestors once had, their white-tipped hoe flashing against the calm blue water. It must have made a daunting sight for the actors playing Hobson and Nias in the small pinnace as they, too, headed for shore. Watching the action on black-and-white film from across the decades, it's clear that *Ngātokimatawhaorua* was a worthy descendent of the waka taua that terrified any enemy who caught sight of them.

By the time the pinnace reached land both waka taua had landed and their crews had disembarked. Once ashore, the British party was greeted by a group of rangatira, who led them up the track to the Treaty House. Waiting patiently for them at the top was an excited crowd of spectators and the entire 28th (Māori) Battalion, immaculate in their khaki uniforms. There was also, not unexpectedly, a full complement of dignitaries, including Peter Fraser representing Prime Minister Michael Joseph Savage; Governor-General Lord Galway and his wife Lady Galway; Lord Willingdon representing the British government and his wife, Lady Willingdon; and Senator and Mrs McBride, envoys from Australia.

A ripple of applause sounded as the actors playing Hobson and Nias emerged from the Treaty House and began to make their way to the large tent for the re-enactment. Both men were dressed in period naval uniforms, buttons polished, swords swinging from their hips, bicorn hats firmly in place. Following behind them were actors representing officers from HMS *Herald*, various administrators and several of the missionaries who had witnessed the signing.

The tent itself, Drummond announced to his radio audience, was a

The two waka taua, both named *Ngātokimatawhaorua*, at Hobson Beach, 6 February 1940. Captain William Hobson's pinnace has just reached shore. It was from this beach that Hobson and Captain Joseph Nias were escorted to meet with rangatira in 1840. NEW ZEALAND HERALD GLASS PLATE COLLECTION, AUCKLAND LIBRARIES, 1370-671-11

fair representation of the original, which had been fashioned from spars and a large sail brought ashore from Nias's ship. Backed up against the flagstaff, the replica was decorated with ships' signal flags and housed a large table. Adding authenticity to the scene were numerous rangatira sitting and chatting around a low stage that reached out from the centre of the tent. Representing various hapū, the rangatira wore korowai and many were armed with period-appropriate weapons. Some had moko drawn on their faces. Completing the cast were several dozen actors playing European settlers. Beyond them a throng of spectators crammed into the few wooden bleachers that had been built, as the rest stood around the perimeter. A small number of soldiers, naval hands and civilians braved the displeasure of officials and found spots inside the roped-off lawn area. Lost in the excitement of the moment was the fate of two unfortunate men. The branch they had chosen to sit on, which overlooked the scene, broke under their combined weight, sending them crashing to the ground. Regrettably, both men ended up in hospital with broken ribs.

Before he had set sail for New Zealand in 1839, Captain William Hobson received instructions from the Colonial Office in London. He was to prepare a treaty that would gain Queen Victoria sovereignty over all, or part, of New Zealand, and have it signed by representative Māori throughout the land. The resulting document, completed with the help of Hobson's secretary, James S. Freeman, and James Busby, would become known as the Treaty of Waitangi.

The document started with a preamble in which the Queen committed to introduce law and order into the land and to protect Māori from unruly British subjects and French aggressions. It then detailed — in three articles — the conditions of the treaty. Finally, there was space set aside for the rangatira to sign. The English-language version, reproduced here, is worth a read, even if you are familiar with it:

> Her Majesty Victoria Queen of the United Kingdom of Great Britain and Ireland regarding with Her Royal Favor the Native Chiefs and Tribes of New Zealand and anxious to protect their just Rights and Property and to secure to them the enjoyment of Peace and Good Order has deemed it necessary in consequence of the great number of Her Majesty's Subjects who have already settled in New Zealand and the rapid extension of Emigration both from Europe and Australia which is still in progress to constitute and appoint a functionary properly authorized to treat with the Aborigines of New Zealand for the recognition of Her Majesty's sovereign authority over the whole or any part of those islands — Her Majesty therefore being desirous to establish a settled form of Civil Government with a view to avert the evil consequences which must result from the absence of the necessary Laws and Institutions alike to the native population and to Her subjects has been graciously pleased to empower and to authorize me William Hobson a Captain in her Majesty's Royal Navy Consul and Lieutenant Governor of such parts of New Zealand as may be or hereafter shall be ceded to Her Majesty to invite the confederated and independent Chiefs of New Zealand to concur in the following Articles and Conditions.

> **Article the first**
> The Chiefs of the Confederation of the United Tribes of New Zealand and the separate and independent Chiefs who

have not become members of the Confederation cede to
Her Majesty the Queen of England absolutely and without
reservation all the rights and powers of Sovereignty which
the said Confederation or Individual Chiefs respectively
exercise or possess, or may be supposed to exercise or
to possess over their respective Territories as the sole
sovereigns thereof.

Article the second

Her Majesty the Queen of England confirms and guarantees
to the Chiefs and Tribes of New Zealand and to the
respective families and individuals thereof the full exclusive
and undisturbed possession of their Lands and Estates
Forests Fisheries and other properties which they may
collectively or individually possess so long as it is their wish
and desire to retain the same in their possession; but the
Chiefs of the United Tribes and the individual Chiefs yield
to Her Majesty the exclusive right of Preemption over such
lands as the proprietors thereof may be disposed to alienate
at such prices as may be agreed upon between the respective
Proprietors and persons appointed by Her Majesty to treat
with them in that behalf.

Article the third

In consideration thereof Her Majesty the Queen of England
extends to the Natives of New Zealand Her royal protection
and imparts to them all the Rights and Privileges of British
Subjects.

[signed] W. Hobson Lieutenant-Governor

> Now therefore We the Chiefs of the Confederation of the
> United Tribes of New Zealand being assembled in Congress
> at Victoria in Waitangi and We the Separate and Independent
> Chiefs of New Zealand claiming authority over the Tribes
> and Territories which are specified after our respective
> names, having been made fully to understand the Provisions
> of the foregoing Treaty, accept and enter into the same in
> the full spirit and meaning thereof in witness of which we
> have attached our signatures or marks at the places and dates
> respectively specified.
>
> Done at Waitangi this Sixth day of February in the year of
> Our Lord one thousand eight hundred and forty.

So far, so good. Hobson — born in Ireland, a career sailor who was once described by Commodore Owen of HMS *Jamaica* as, 'an officer who to the most persevering zeal united discretion and sound judgement'[1] — seemed to have produced a treaty written in reasonably clear language. Determined to ensure that the rangatira understood what they were being asked to sign, Hobson then arranged for the head of the Church Missionary Society, Reverend Henry Williams, to translate the treaty into te reo Māori in order to present it to the chiefs for signing.

This is where the trouble started. Williams might have been the best option available to Hobson, but he was not fluent in te reo. Aware of his own shortcomings, Williams asked his son Edward — a competent conversationalist in the Māori language — to lend a hand. Neither man was a native speaker nor an experienced translator, and they were given only a few hours to do the job. They did their best. Their best, however, was not nearly good enough, and the translation contained critical inaccuracies. The two versions of the treaty, one in English, the other in te reo Māori, were fundamentally different in a number of crucial passages and Hobson had no idea.

To get an idea of the breadth of these inconsistencies we have only to examine a couple of lines. The English version of Article one reads that rangatira will:

> cede to Her Majesty the Queen of England absolutely and
> without reservation all the rights and powers of Sovereignty . . .

This clearly gave full authority to the Queen. The Williamses' translation, however, used the word kāwanatanga for sovereignty. This was a transliteration of an English word with which rangatira were familiar — governorship. In her 2011 book, *The Treaty of Waitangi,* Claudia Orange explains that kāwanatanga is 'derived from Kāwana (governor)', and for the gathered rangatira, that word had associations with Pontius Pilate, the Roman governor from the Bible, and with the governors of New South Wales. As Orange says, 'It tended to imply authority in an abstract rather than concrete sense.'[2] Clearly it can be rather convincingly argued that the rangatira were agreeing to cede governorship to the Queen, not sovereignty or full authority.

Article two was also problematic. In English, the treaty guaranteed Māori

> the full exclusive and undisturbed possession of their Lands
> and Estates Forests Fisheries and other properties . . .

This Williams translated as 'te tino rangatiratanga o o ratou wenua o ratou kainga me o ratou taonga katoa'. In English this means absolute sovereignty (tino rangatiratanga) over their lands (o o ratou wenua), over their dwelling places (o ratou kainga), and over all of their precious possessions (o ratou taonga katoa). When Williams used the word taonga, perhaps for brevity, in place of 'fisheries and other properties', the rangatira understood the word to mean much more than the phrase it replaced. It meant everything precious to them, including, for example, their culture and language.

William Hobson's treaty expressed the British desire for sovereignty over New Zealand, but the te reo version told the rangatira that the Queen wanted to install a governor, and that they, the rangatira, would retain their sovereignty, autonomy and self-government. Māori signed the treaty believing they retained authority over their lands, dwelling places and everything else they considered precious.

The long-term outcome of the signing of Te Tiriti o Waitangi was that it wouldn't end well. In fact, it couldn't. Hobson wrote one thing; the rangatira heard another.

The re-enactment recommenced with the meeting between Māori and the British on 5 February 1840, the day before the treaty was signed. When we join the action, all eyes are on 'Hobson' as he rises to speak. In his initial remarks he urges the rangatira to carefully consider the Treaty, and then he reads the English-language version aloud. 'Reverend Williams' narrates the te reo language version straight after. The rangatira, sitting quietly so they could catch and then make sense of Williams' imperfect pronunciation, took note of every word uttered by the Englishman. Naturally they did: theirs was an oral culture in which language is a precise tool and every word used is carefully chosen.

Once the terms of the proposed treaty had been presented in both languages, the assembled rangatira begin to debate what they had heard. Speaking with passion and eloquence, the intensity of their voices rises and falls like the waves on the beach below. Many of the speeches, including those of Te Kēmara (Ngāti Kawa), Rewa (Ngāi Tawake), Moka (Te Patukeha) and Hākiro (Ngāi Tawake), demand the return of Māori lands already taken, while others insist that Hobson take his leave and return home, stating clearly that they wished only the missionaries to remain.

It is not until Tāmati Wāka Nene (Ngāti Hao), Patuone (Ngāti Hao) and Hōne Heke (Matarahurahu) speak in favour of the treaty that the mood begins to change. Nene concedes that it is too late to stop the flood, that the north is already filled with Pākehā, and that as they currently have no power over them they should sign Hobson's treaty. His older brother Patuone agrees with him. The warrior Hōne Heke stands next to tell the assembled rangatira that he believes that without a governor they may be taken advantage of by the French or by other Pākehā, and that it would be better for Hobson to remain. Te Kēmara stands for a second time to speak against the treaty before Hobson adjourns the hui so that the rangatira might discuss the proposal at length among themselves.

When the 1940 action resumes, the re-enactment has moved forward to the day of the signing, 6 February 1840. Due to comprehensive written records from 1840, the actors were able to portray an accurate representation of the proceedings, right down to who among the British stood where and even the order in which the rangatira spoke. Newspaper and magazine articles, as well a recording of Drummond's broadcast,[3] allow us to piece together a reasonably detailed picture of what took place in 1940.

The action started with Hobson asking Henry Williams to read the Māori language version of the treaty out loud again, at which point several missionaries raise doubts as to whether the rangatira fully understand its terms. Hobson, under orders to get the document signed, dismisses their concerns and asks Hōne Heke to step forward to put his mark on the treaty. Other rangatira follow, and as each one signs, Hobson shakes their hand and repeats the now famous phrase, 'He iwi tahi tatou' — We are now one people. Barely a day after Hobson had opened the hui, Te Tiriti o Waitangi was signed.

At the completion of the re-enactment, dignitaries retired to the Treaty House for a short break. Drummond, the consummate professional, filled the gap in proceedings with anecdotes drawn from his walks through the Māori encampment earlier in the week. During one such excursion he had witnessed kuia preparing kai. 'It was interesting watching them prepare the meals,' he told his audience.

> They have an electric potato peeler here which helps
> tremendously, but still, many of the old wāhines like to sit
> down on the ground in groups of five or six with baskets of
> kumara in front of them — some using knives for peeling
> them, and others using the old traditional style of using a
> pipi shell.[4]

He also mentioned the 'huge quantities of meat and pork' that were being readied for a hāngī.

As Drummond completed his narrative, the spotlight turned on the new national Māori memorial, the Whare Rūnanga, which was to be opened by Lord Galway. The magnificent meeting house, one of the few in the north that was fully carved at the time, had had its tapu lifted in accordance with Māori protocols in the early hours of the day by Rē Kauere. Whina Cooper, who had witnessed the launch of *Ngātokimatawhaorua* just a few days earlier, completed the ritual when she was given the honour of being the first woman to cross the building's threshold.

The official opening ceremony began with Sir Apirana Ngata introducing a series of performances, including two by companies from the Māori Battalion, the second of which, performed by C Company from the East Coast, he led. A photographer captured the 66-year-old MP at the front of the group, suit jacket off and shirt sleeves rolled up, flourishing what appears to be a wahaika, a traditional fighting club.

A leading figure in Māori society during the first half of the twentieth century, Ngata had been born in 1874 at Te Araroa on the East Coast.

Sir Apirana Ngata (centre) leads C Company (made up of men from the East Coast) in a spirted haka in front of the new national Māori memorial, the Whare Rūnanga, on the Treaty Grounds at Waitangi. A tireless worker for Māori, Ngata was the member of parliament for Eastern Māori from 1905 to 1943. ALEXANDER TURNBULL LIBRARY, MNZ-2746-1/2-F

Described by one biographer as 'short like his father but immensely strong',[5] he was brought up speaking te reo and in 1893 became the first Māori to complete a degree at a New Zealand university. After graduating, he turned down the opportunity to practise law and instead chose to focus on reforming Māori social and economic status. Acutely aware that the dice were loaded against Māori — particularly when it came to retaining their lands — he sought to find remedies, working, as his biographer Ranginui Walker put it, 'within and through the law'.

> Ever alert to the possibilities of Maori land being alienated by the provisions of seemingly innocuous statutes, Ngata warned the farmers in the Waiapu Valley to beware of the provisions of the Noxious Weeds Act. If Māori land was infested with noxious weeds and nothing was done to eradicate them, the Minister of Native Affairs had the power to take the land and lease it out to a farmer who would graze the land and control the weeds.[6]

As well as his advocacy of land reform, Ngata was a patron of intertribal sporting competitions; encouraged iwi involvement in the performing arts (haka and poi); and supported the revival of carving and tukutuku work. When he helped establish the Rotorua School of Māori Arts and Crafts, he pushed for the construction of carved meeting houses across the nation, including the Whare Rūnanga at Waitangi.

By 1940 Ngata was a skilled orator and debater, and he was not one to waste the opportunity to address a captive audience during the centenary commemorations. Following speeches by his fellow Māori MPs, Ngata delivered a broadside to the assembled government representatives and the governor-general:

> Where are we to-day? I do not know of any year that the Maori people approached with so much misgiving as the

> New Zealand Centennial year. In the retrospect, what did
> the Maori see? Lands gone, the powers of the chief crumbled
> in the dust, Maori culture scattered — broken. What
> remains at the end of one hundred years after the signing of
> the Treaty of Waitangi, Your Excellency? What remains of
> all the fine things said then?[7]

Ngata paused for a moment and looked out over the assembled crowd, allowing his words to sink in. They were clear and concise and unambiguous. He was in his element. Later in his speech he addressed the acting prime minister, Peter Fraser, directly:

> Before we proceed, Mr Fraser, further with the new
> century I think the clear duty is before the Government of
> New Zealand and our European fellow-citizens to try and
> wipe out ascertained outstanding grievances of the past
> one hundred years. There are still some things that remain
> over, and I have been asked by the assembly here to say
> to the Government: When the Taranaki confiscated land
> problem was settled, the Taranaki people ceased to look
> backward; they looked forward. When the Arawa lakes
> claim was settled, that tribe ceased to look backward, they
> looked forward. Will the Government assist Waikato to
> close their eyes to the past and look forward with the rest
> of the tribes of New Zealand? Our South Island friends the
> same; the Natives in the Bay of Plenty also.[8]

Ngata's measured attack continued, citing injustices specific to the north that related to the confiscation of land, as well as the unexpected consequence of the Crown protection guaranteed by the Treaty of Waitangi: rates and taxes.

Fraser took the microphone next. Always well-dressed, his receding hairline and small, round, wire-framed glasses were hallmarks of the man who would soon lead the country. Standing in for the terminally ill Prime Minister Michael Joseph Savage, his voice was confident and clear, and there was little evidence to be heard of his native Scottish accent. He began by delivering messages of congratulations from across the Commonwealth and around the world, before addressing the Māori citizens of the nation directly.

Fraser acknowledged that there had been mistakes and misunderstandings during the past century,

> but step by step in recent years over a considerable period, when there has been successive sympathetic administration, efforts have been made to obliterate the bad effect and, we hope, the memory also of those mistakes through which the Maori people often suffered, and suffered unjustly.[9]

Then, in a comment perhaps designed to lift the mood, Fraser noted that as far as he knew, Pākehā were not particularly fond of paying government taxes either.

Speeches from Lord Willington, representing the government of the United Kingdom, and Senator McBride, representing Australia, followed, before the governor-general read a message from King George VI. In his address, the King congratulated New Zealand for having 'established a vigorous and progressive community on a basis of mutual understanding', and then acknowledged the nation's 'generous and valued contribution' to the ongoing war effort.[10] Finally, in declaring the Whare Rūnanga open, Lord Galway noted the historic site on which it had been built, acknowledging 'the work done by the Maoris themselves in building this meeting-house which has an honourable place alongside the Treaty House of the past'.[11] The commemorations finished late in the afternoon with the unveiling of memorials to William Hobson, James Busby and the many rangatira who signed the treaty. The last of the memorials read:

New Zealand Centennial, 1840–1940

This tablet commemorates those chiefs, leaders of the Maori
People, who in the year 1840 affixed their signatures to a
voluntary treaty, afterwards called the Treaty of Waitangi,
and thus forged an indissoluble link between the British
people and the Maori. Dedicated and unveiled in this Treaty
House, 6th February, 1940.

After the ceremony a large crowd made its way down to the wharf to
farewell the dignitaries. They also witnessed the crews of the two waka taua
farewell the Māori Battalion with a rousing haka, and the soldiers answer
with their own, as their launches set off for Ōpua. If the sight of two waka
taua being paddled on the waters of Pēwhairangi Bay of Islands earlier in
the day had seemed like a vision from the past, the sight of this massed
haka must have made it feel as if the ancestors had materialised once again.

The following day Sir Apirana Ngata was invited to a hui hosted by
Rē Kauere and others at Te Tii Marae, where the *Auckland Star* reported
that Kauere gifted his waka taua to the politician. The newspaper
reported that Ngata

was received regally, and as a gesture of mourning for Tau
Henare, chief of this section of the Ngapuhis, rare kiwi and
pigeon feather mats comprising the dressings of the canoe,
and the canoe itself, were offered to Sir Apirana. In accepting
these gifts Sir Apirana signified his intention of preserving
the equipment and decoration of the canoe by depositing
them in the Dominion Museum, Wellington.

However, the waka would never make it to the nation's capital. Instead, it would languish for a decade at Te Tii Marae, before being moved to Ōtiria, near Moerewa, where it was exposed to the elements for another decade. It was finally moved to Pukerata Marae, Ōtaua, southwest of Kaikohe, in about 1960, where it was housed in a shed. More recently, a purpose-built shelter, Te Whare Whakaruruhau, has been erected for the waka on Pukerata Marae.

As the crowds departed Waitangi, Hohepa Heperi and the other kaumātua charged with looking after the larger *Ngātokimatawhaorua* met to discuss their own pressing question: what to do with the waka now that the commemoration was over? It was impractical to paddle it any appreciable distance to where it might be stored, and it would be expensive to truck it anywhere. Various options were debated until a consensus was reached. The waka would remain at Waitangi, to be held in perpetuity by the Waitangi National Trust Board subject to its ownership remaining with the five original iwi. There were stipulations: the waka needed to be available for use on important ceremonial occasions such as royal visits or the return of Māori soldiers from the war, and a canoe shed, designed in keeping with Māori aesthetics, was to be built to house it.

Ultimately, a site for the shelter was chosen alongside the Whare Rūnanga, and the Public Works Department, which had set up much of the infrastructure for the commemoration, was contracted to build it. In preparation for its eventual housing the waka was dismantled and moved up the hill from Hobson Beach. The majestic waka, a little over three years in the making, had been in the water for less than two weeks.

142 NGĀTOKIMATAWHAORUA

There's no doubt that the two waka taua had kicked off the festivities in spectacular style, and the larger waka's involvement in particular garnered considerable favourable comment in the nation's newspapers. The *Auckland Star*'s account was typical:

> Many who went to Waitangi, both Maori and pakeha, had heard that they would see there a Maori canoe, but until they arrived they did not realise the beauty, grace and even majesty of this craft, nearly 120 ft long, in the building of which the best of Polynesian culture found expression. As for the Maoris themselves, though they had always admitted the place of the war canoe in their history and sentiment, until they actually saw Nga-tokimatawhaorua they had not fully understood what the canoe had meant to their race. Evidence of this came in a peculiar way. As each Maori party left what one speaker, with the innate poetry of his race had called the 'sacred courtyard of Waitangi,' their last and most intimate farewell was to the canoe. As Waitangi fell from sight, as civilian and soldier alike departed, they called in greeting and in pride, 'Farewell to the canoe! Canoe, farewell. O, farewell.'[12]

The centennial had been a focal point for the country during a time of escalating anxiety across the globe and, despite the Waikato boycott of the festivities, it was still a triumph of sorts for Te Puea. *Ngātokimatawhaorua* had captured the imagination of everyone who saw it and the many who read about it. More importantly, the building of the four new waka taua, two in the north (both named *Ngātokimatawhaorua* — one under the sponsorship of Te Puea, the other by Kauere), and two in Waikato (originally named *Aotea* and *Takitimu* and later renamed *Tumanako* and *Te Rangatahi* respectively), had saved the art of the tohunga tārai waka from drifting into oblivion.

So why did these waka appeal to so many? Undoubtedly, they were awe-inspiring in the true meaning of the word. Few, if any, of the spectators would have seen a waka taua before, and surely only a handful of them at most would have seen one being paddled. Waitangi was also the perfect location to showcase them, with warm days and calm waters allowing the waka to be appreciated in their natural setting.

Waka taua had graced the waters here for centuries: this had been a meeting place for northern waka before they departed on trading voyages, as well as on their feared southern raids. The hope now was that Pēwhairangi would once more become known for its waka, and that in time a fleet of them would grace the waters below the Treaty Grounds.

The odds were quickly being stacked against any immediate resurgence in waka culture, however. The war raging in Europe would soon engulf northern Africa and then spread to the Pacific, and the focus of the nation returned to providing fighting men and provisions for the conflict. *Ngātokimatawhaorua* was quietly retired to its new home.

7

An icon is relaunched

IF TE PUEA HAD hoped for a revival in the art of waka taua construction after the triumphs of 1940 she would have been greatly disappointed. Although Waikato would launch *Taheretikitiki II* in 1972, it would be 50 years before there was any widespread activity — when a fleet of waka taua was commissioned for the government-sponsored Sesquicentennial Celebrations in 1990.

As for the great waka *Ngātokimatawhaorua*, it did not leave its house for 34 years, and only then after considerable debate. Somehow the terms of the original agreement between the five northern iwi and the Waitangi National Trust Board had been lost or forgotten. When iwi representatives wrote to the trust in late August 1973 to ask that the waka be relaunched in time for the 1974 visit of Queen Elizabeth II, their request was summarily dismissed. The trust put up a reasonable argument: they believed it would be risky to refloat the waka after it had been out of the water for so long, and also pointed out that the canoe house would need to be dismantled in order to move the canoe.

But their reply missed the point. The decision wasn't theirs to make, and their refusal to cooperate led to a heated running battle. It was only resolved after several months of negotiation when the Tai Tokerau District Māori Council accepted responsibility for the seaworthiness and competent crewing of the waka during a hui at Ōtiria Marae.

To gain an insight into the waka preparations for the visit of Queen Elizabeth, I visited the South Auckland home of the waka's current kaihautū, Joe Conrad. A confident, proud and strong-willed leader, I once watched him guide *Ngātokimatawhaorua* expertly through a maze of moored yachts as it returned to shore after welcoming a voyaging canoe into Pēwhairangi Bay of Islands. Conrad's orders, clear and concise, ensured the waka slipped comfortably through what looked like impossibly tight gaps.

Now in his sixties and with hair that is transitioning from black to a distinguished silver-grey, Conrad is a tall, handsome man who grew up on a family dairy farm in Te Kao, an hour north of Kaitaia. He is affiliated with Te Aupōuri, Ngāti Kuri and Te Rarawa. His mother, Kerewai, juggled looking after her own 15 children with the duties of a midwife, and his father, Nicky, managed the farm and worked as a bus driver. He was also a respected holder of Te Aupōuri tribal knowledge and an active member of the Tai Tokerau District Māori Council, and was heavily involved in the decision to relaunch the waka in 1974. Conrad was 15 years old when *Ngātokimatawhaorua* was returned to the water.

Relaxing at his kitchen table with a coffee one weekend morning, Conrad began our talk by entertaining me with stories of a recent visit he'd made to the west coast of the United States and Canada. He had gone there as a guest of the Confederated Tribes of the Grand Ronde to participate in the annual Tribal Canoe Journey, a coastal voyage made in traditional First Nations vessels. Conrad described being among 'ninety or a hundred indigenous canoes' originating from the coastal settlements of Alaska, British Columbia and Washington as they paddled to the host settlement of the Swinomish Nation. They made for a truly inspiring sight, he said, and he would love to organise a similar event in Aotearoa.

When the conversation turned to waka taua, I asked him what he remembered from the relaunch of *Ngātokimatawhaorua*. He told me his father had been the joint captain of the waka in 1974, along with Alan Karena, and how he and three of his brothers had been there on a wet morning as the waka was moved from the canoe shelter alongside the

Whare Rūnanga down to Hobson Beach. He recalled — with a grin — how they tried to use a truck to winch the waka down the tricky descent, but the truck ended up being dragged down the hill by the weight of the waka. It was 5 January 1974; the Queen would be arriving in a month.

I was about to ask another question when Conrad called out to his adult daughter, Waimirirangi, asking her to bring him something from a nearby room. She was also a kaihautū — she captained the ceremonial waka *Te Whānau Moana* — and had a growing reputation for leading by example and for working selflessly for others.

Waimirirangi handed an off-white tote bag to her father. Inside was a large Warwick Guard book that had been repurposed as a scrapbook. Conrad carefully took it out of the bag and placed it on the table, adjusted its position slightly, and then opened it. It felt as though I was about to be shown something special. I was.

Sheathed in a light-brown cloth cover, the scrapbook was a unique record of the 1974 waka relaunch and royal visit. Photographs, some in colour and others in black and white, provided glimpses of the waka, its crew and many of the essential support staff. Elsewhere, ephemera in the guise of official New Zealand Day invitations and sundry newspaper clippings filled the gaps between photos.

Conrad began to leaf through the book, stopping just a few pages in to gaze at a wonderful caricature. Drawn in black ink, the cartoon depicted a full-length figure facing out from the page, a hoe in one hand, cat o' nine tails in the other. On one arm was an armband bearing the word KAPITANE. There was no name attached to the image and I asked him if it was his father. Conrad smiled. 'Yes. Yes, it is.'

As he turned the pages, the faces, names and events recorded in the book triggered memories from his childhood. Sometimes it took a few seconds before he could tell me the story behind an image, sometimes his words were instantaneous. A photo of *Ngātokimatawhaorua* tied up in the Waitangi Estuary, near where Kelly Tarlton's sailing ship *Tui*

Pēwhairangi Bay of Islands, February 1974. The kaituki, standing directly behind the tauihu, controls the timing of the crew by lifting and dropping his taiaha. The role is made considerably more challenging in rough or windy conditions by the waka rolling from side to side. NZME/NEW ZEALAND HERALD

once housed the Museum of Shipwrecks (before it was converted into a restaurant), prompted memories of sleeping out under tarpaulins stretched between car doors, and the condensation that dripped throughout the night. 'Sometimes,' he said, 'it got so that you didn't know if you were sleeping under the tarpaulin or in the rain.' Another photo reminded him of his own involvement during the waka's refurbishment. He was old enough to be enlisted to help the raupō gatherers.

> Instead of having seats, we had ti-tree slats that went along the length of *Ngātoki* and the paddlers sat or kneeled on those. We put raupō on top of the slats so that the knees didn't get dinged up. One of the places we used to get our raupō was up by Puketona, and my job was to help the raupō crew cart all the raupō to the trailers, because the cars couldn't get through the paddocks.[1]

The scrapbook was an immensely valuable historical record. If Manley's film and photos had left a priceless account of the build and launch of *Ngātokimatawhaorua*, then this book would prove indispensable when it came to looking back at the relaunch of the iconic waka for the 1974 New Zealand Day celebrations. A highlight was the inclusion of several lists, carefully typed out on A4 sheets of paper and taped in place, containing the names of everyone involved, from the cooks to the medics, the canteen staff and the women who made the uniforms. Remarkably, there were also the names of each of the 162 men who had vied for positions as kaihoe. (The lists are included in this book as appendices.)

Observing the scrapbook from across the table, I could see that it had been well thumbed over the years, and I could also see that its compilation had been a labour of love. Detailed pencil sketches decorated page corners seemingly at every turn: swordfish, shells, owls and whales, kōwhai, mamaku, kōtukutuku and more.

I moved around the table to sit next to Conrad so I could better see what he was looking at. My notes, initially ordered and tidy, quickly turned near illegible as I tried to keep up with his memories. At one point he stopped at a black-and-white image of *Ngātokimatawhaorua* dated 13 January 1974. Caught by strong currents while trying to make its way out of the estuary and into the bay, the waka had been pushed broadside against the bridge spanning the Waitangi River. Someone, either the captain or a steersman, had badly misjudged the approach and the anxious crew were left trying to hold their precious waka off the concrete pillars with outstretched arms.

A rope lassoed around the stern of the waka hints at how it was eventually rescued. Aside from capturing the incident itself, the image is interesting for showing the outlet pipe for the bilge pump, set midship and exiting through a hole cut into the bottom of the rauawa on the port side of the waka. A stream of water was being pumped out when the photo was taken. The pump's effectiveness would come into question within a few short days, when the crew were subjected to another embarrassing lesson. Just days before they were to feature centre stage for the Queen's arrival at Waitangi, the waka foundered while out on a training paddle. Like the bridge incident, it was a very public affair, and the scrapbook's author cut straight to the bone with this written comment:

> Did you know a submarine was born?
> Captained by FREDRICK AUGUSTINE CONRAD.

Hec Busby had told me about this episode several years earlier. The agreed plan, he said, had been to bring Piri Poutapu up to Waitangi to look over the waka before it was relaunched, so he could judge whether it was seaworthy. But the inspection never happened. Instead, over-eager locals began taking the waka for short outings before Poutapu could make the trip, and then, with time running out, the training sessions started in earnest:

Ngātokimatawhaorua's crew fight to keep the waka off the Waitangi River bridge pillars, 13 January 1974. Caught by unseen currents, the waka was in a precarious position until help arrived. In a precursor to a more serious incident that occurred just a few days later, the bilge pump was employed to help empty water from the hull.
COURTESY OF JOE CONRAD

It was leaking a bit from the outset, but we figured it would be okay because we had a reliable bilge pump on board. Then one day, while we were going across to Russell from Waitangi with a full crew, we found ourselves in trouble. The weather was fine, and the water was flat, but about halfway across the waka started to fill up and before we knew it the water was up to the gunnels.[2]

Busby continued, telling me that while a few of the younger crew members were initially anxious, as soon as everyone realised that the waka wasn't going to actually sink they calmed down. A passing boat was hailed and managed to tow the swamped waka to shore.

Busby then recalled that once the waka was safely back at Waitangi, and with the Queen's visit just 10 days away, Tom Munu was summoned to help repair the waka:

He started from the prow and walked right around the canoe feeling it, and then he stood in front of it as though he could see the other end and said it was crooked. He was as blind as a bat and couldn't see the other end, but he could feel the joins and he knew it wasn't quite right. He showed us how to replace the muka and make sure the haumi joints were really tight. He started by lashing the top two holes on each side of the hull, before lifting the end section of hull up so he could pack fresh muka into the joint. When he had the required amount of muka packed in, he eased the end back down, which crushed the muka in position, and then we finished lashing it. I saw straight away how effective that way of doing it was, but it was one of those things you might not work out without a lot of trial and error.[3]

Ngātokimatawhaorua was seaworthy once again.

Elsewhere in Conrad's scrapbook were images of the crew training on land, portraits of crew members and, of course, photos of the Queen taken during her visit. Close-ups of the waka also provided a few surprises. One photo of the prow showed four slender branches, each with a few feathers tied to its end, affixed to the tauihu to act as the ihiihi instead of the standard circular karu atua. They were perhaps a makeshift substitute attached prior to the completion of the ones used during the commemoration itself.

Interestingly, there was a series of photographs taken on 3 February showing a group of women on board *Ngātokimatawhaorua*. Representing the five iwi affiliated to the waka, they were there under the protection of the tohunga Rae Tana, and had been escorted to the waka by a guard consisting of two flanking lines of kaihoe. A pair of colour photos also showed the women being escorted back to Te Tii Marae after the trip, and on the next page was a list of their names for the most part organised by iwi:

> Te Aupōuri: Mei Matiu, Hemowai Brown and Margaret Conrad.
>
> Te Rarawa: Maraea Brown and Mei Motu.
>
> Ngāpuhi: Mata Moon, Mereana Kuru, Teresa Mutu and Hoana Rapatini.
>
> Ngāti Whātua: Bella Clarke and Emily Latimer.
>
> Ngāti Kahu: Rere Moana Rutene.

Three additional names, added without tribal affiliations on the side of the page — Rachael Windsor, Agnes Jack Leefe and Ellen Murray — complete the list.

According to one caption in the scrapbook, wānanga to train the crew started in earnest on 19 January 1974. Joe's father, Nicky, one of only three original kaihoe from the 1940 launch to return, was given the task of preparing the crew alongside Alan Karena, who had a military background and was there to instil some discipline. With enough men to make up two full crews, the competition for seats was fierce. At any time one crew might be training out on the water while the other was being put through their paces with land-based drills. And when they were finished with their waka training there was always kapa haka practice.

Those out on the waka often faced challenging workouts; sessions scheduled for two hours routinely stretched to three or four as demanding taskmasters sought perfection. Given the short lead time it was perhaps fortunate that an early suggestion — that the waka be manned by senior students from Northland colleges — was dismissed by Nicky Conrad, who pointed out that 'custom and tapu dictated the waka should be handled by adults only'.[4]

Ultimately, the crew was drawn from communities right across the region, and the list of their names was sent to the Minister of Internal Affairs for final approval.[5] Any men who failed to make the grade were drafted into the kapa haka group to perform for the Queen at the Treaty Grounds.

As expected, there was significant media coverage during the leadup to the commemoration, and *Ngātokimatawhaorua* and her crew were a natural focus. One unidentified kaihoe gave a reporter an insight into what it meant to be part of the crew:

> When I first climbed into the canoe and settled myself down I had the strangest feeling. It seemed as if I was surrounded by the spirits of my ancestors. I felt at one with all those who had lived here in the past. A part of the history of my people. The emotion welled up inside me and I felt tears coming into my eyes, and the man in front of me turned and looked at me. 'You're sweating too,' he said, and the tears were running down his cheeks. It was an extraordinary feeling and something I shall never forget.[6]

One of the ongoing challenges facing the organising committee was how to feed the paddlers during the wānanga weekends. To help alleviate the financial burden, families from across the north contributed to the communal pantry, and Conrad remembered digging up sacks of kūmara and potatoes from his family's garden to take to Waitangi.

> We had a red Mark II Zephyr at the time and an old trailer
> that probably shouldn't have been able to take the weight
> that it did, and we would fill it up for each wānanga. We'd
> butcher a lamb, and my older brother Bullu would drop a cow,
> and we'd go out fishing, you know, and bring back three or
> four hundred fish, mostly netted mullet, and we smoked most
> of them because we never had much storage or refrigeration.
> And I remember that we used to bring cabbages from home
> that were half eaten by caterpillars and all that sort of thing,
> but we ate it all.[7]

Most of the food ended up being cooked in an old-fashioned kāuta at Waitangi Marae. Conrad remembered helping his mother unload the trailer on one trip and seeing all the kuia sitting around the fire with iron rods holding their pots over the flame. They were, he said, special times.

The scrapbook also recorded inconveniences we don't have to deal with today. A typed notice to participants, for example, encouraged all drivers to bring a two-gallon tin of petrol in reserve. 'The garages close at 12 noon and the nearest police station is at Kawa Kawa [sic], roughly 18 miles from Waitangi, if a permit [to buy petrol after hours] is required.'[8]

Page by page the scrapbook continued to release its memories. As I watched Conrad study each photo, I began to get a feel for what

Ngātokimatawhaorua meant to him. He told me he hadn't been interested in getting involved with waka when he was young, and it wasn't until he returned from a decade spent working in Australia that he felt the pull. Even then, he said, he didn't want to join the crew of *Ngātokimatawhaorua*. Instead, he signed on as a crew member of *Mataatua-Puhi*, a waka taua built by Hec Busby. He chose that waka, he told me, because the protocols weren't as strict as they were for the crew of *Ngātokimatawhaorua*. His elders were far from happy with his decision, however, and took Conrad aside to explain to him that he had an obligation to follow in his father's footsteps, and that a position was waiting for him aboard *Ngātokimatawhaorua*.

Circumstances would save Conrad from disappointing the kaumātua group for much longer: it was decided to rest *Ngātokimatawhaorua* for several years immediately after the 1990 sesquicentennial. When the waka was returned to the water, in 1996, Conrad finally joined the crew, bringing with him five years' experience captaining *Mataatua-Puhi*. By then he already carried a detailed chart of the many features found within the Bay of Islands seascape in his mind. In a moment of self-reflection he told me that by 1996 he felt as if he knew the rhythm of the sea and the moods of the harbour. 'It was in my DNA. I had a feel for the tides and for the wind, and I had the experience leading men, both professionally and on the waka.'[9]

On joining the crew, Conrad was immediately fast-tracked into the ihu section commander's role, before becoming the kaihautū of the waka in 2009. His promotion coincided with a refurbishment of *Ngātokimatawhaorua*, a task that took 18 weekends and included re-lashing the entire waka.

By the time we'd finished looking through the scrapbook, I'd gained a fairly good idea of what had transpired during the days and weeks leading up to the Queen's arrival in 1974. It was a magical period, but not one entirely without controversy.

The 1974 commemoration again attracted a massive crowd — estimated at over 20,000. There had been a hopeful request from the Waitangi Māori Committee that the Queen might ride to shore in *Ngātokimatawhaorua* from the royal yacht *Britannia*, but this was rejected. Instead, the waka ferried Prime Minister Norman Kirk and the Minister of Māori Affairs, Matiu Rata, out to the *Britannia* to have the Royal Titles Act (which changed the official title of Elizabeth II to 'Queen of New Zealand'), signed by Her Majesty. Before the waka embarked on its mission, the prime minister's wife, Ruth, was heard to cheekily ask her husband whether all of his insurance premiums were up to date. Once the document had been executed, the waka escorted the royal barge to the jetty at Waitangi, from where the Queen was driven to the Treaty House. Waiting for her there was the Māori Queen, Dame Te Atairangikaahu, and her official party, who walked Queen Elizabeth to her seat.

Those who made the trip to Waitangi were greeted by a fine summer's day and given the opportunity to sit through a two-hour-long pageant depicting New Zealand's development. The spectacle was reported to have thrilled the crowd and entertained Queen Elizabeth.[10] Māori performances were led by the Tai Tokerau Cultural Group, which welcomed the royal party with a karanga, a pōwhiri and a haka. Later, groups representing numerous communities took the stage, including the Wellington Tokelau Islands group, the Auckland Samoan group, the Auckland Niuean group, and a Cook Islands group from Porirua.

It was evening by the time the prime minister stood to speak. Illuminated by powerful lights, Kirk acknowledged the Queen and the Duke of Edinburgh before touching on his government's recent controversial decision to change the name of the commemoration from Waitangi Day to New Zealand Day:

The caption accompanying this picture in Joe Conrad's scrapbook of the 1974 relaunch states: 'Our greatest moment of the whole celebrations. Berthing Ngatoki-mata-whaorua alongside the Royal Yacht. The Prime Minister is about to go aboard the Britannia.' COURTESY OF JOE CONRAD

> For over a century this most important day in our history
> has been celebrated by the people of Northland alone, but
> from 1974 onwards Waitangi Day is to be New Zealand's day
> and will be observed as a holiday throughout the country . . .
> We have chosen the anniversary of the signing of the Treaty
> of Waitangi as New Zealand's day, and as we do, I wonder if
> we all realise the special meaning of this choice. Some other
> nations celebrate on their national day acts of violence, a
> revolution, a coup, or perhaps a war. But we achieved our
> independence and our nationhood gradually and peacefully.
> We have had no desperate revolution as the focus of New
> Zealand's day. We remember no martyrs who fought to
> overthrow a tyrant or to drive out an alien power. We were
> the lucky country.[11]

What the prime minister could not have known is that just two years later, on the election of a new government, the name of the commemoration would revert to Waitangi Day.

When the Queen stood to speak, she focused on the recent Commonwealth Games in Christchurch and the 'spirit of mutual respect' evident within New Zealand. The sovereign said she did 'not believe that any country can claim to have made a greater effort than New Zealand to work out a lifestyle acceptable to all sections of a multi-cultural community'.[12]

Away from the stage, the sharp-eyed may have noticed that for the first time New Zealand's flag was enjoying pride of place at the top of the Treaty Ground's flagstaff — replacing the Union Jack — and that the flag of the United Tribes of New Zealand was also hoisted high.

This special envelope commemorates the relaunch of *Ngātokimatawhaorua* in 1974, and was among the letters carried in a mail bag aboard the waka on New Zealand Day, 6 February 1974. In a nod to the 'VIA AIRMAIL' stamps used at the time, a 'VIA CANOE' stamp was ordered especially for the occasion. COLLECTION OF THE AUTHOR

The dispersal of the New Zealand Day crowds from Waitangi ushered in another period of conflict between the Tai Tokerau District Māori Council and the Waitangi National Trust Board. As summer rolled into autumn and then winter, the fate of *Ngātokimatawhaorua* was once again a cause for discord. The board insisted that the waka be returned to the upper Treaty Grounds as originally agreed, but instead the council, fearing that the waka might suffer irreparable damage if it were hauled back up the hill, moved *Ngātokimatawhaorua* to nearby Waitangi Marae. They also petitioned the Minister of Māori Affairs, Matiu Rata (a member of the Waitangi Board at the time), requesting that the canoe shelter be relocated from alongside the Whare Rūnanga to Hobson Beach.

After several tense meetings, the Waitangi National Trust Board finally agreed to build a new canoe shed at Hobson Beach. By October 1974 the design had been approved and funding secured, in part from Auckland industrialist Luke Fisher.

While the negotiations were dragging on, tribal elders began to put in place measures to ensure the longevity of the vessel. Crucially, in early 1975 Hec Busby was named kaitiaki of *Ngātokimatawhaorua*. If the building of the waka taua for the 1940 centennial was responsible for saving the tohunga tārai waka lineage 35 years earlier, his appointment would usher in the involvement of the most important figure in the renaissance of waka taua since. Busby would become a driving force behind the use of *Ngātokimatawhaorua* for important events at Waitangi for several decades, and in time help keep the art of waka taua construction alive by building several himself. To say he would become a colossus of waka culture in Aotearoa is no overstatement.

One of Busby's first tasks was to undertake a detailed examination of the waka. He hadn't forgotten Tom Munu's assessment that the hull was crooked — a fact confirmed when the crew reported that they were having trouble turning in one particular direction. With the help of some builder's string, Busby determined that the stern was in fact 200 millimetres out of alignment. The remedy was straightforward: all it would take to straighten the vessel out was to shave 6 millimetres off one side of the front haumi. This was not a difficult operation by any stretch of the imagination, but conscious that the waka was a taonga that belonged to the five iwi of the north, Busby sought reassurance from Munu. He needn't have worried. Not only did Munu agree with Busby's suggested course of action, but he also reiterated to Busby that he had the authority to do whatever needed to be done.

Once the refit was complete, the waka was moved into the Waitangi Estuary, where it remained anchored until the new canoe house was ready. Te Ana o Maikuku Canoe House, an open-sided shelter, was officially opened by the governor-general on 5 February 1976.

A period of learning and innovation followed. To understand what happened during those years, I talked with several individuals who were involved with *Ngātokimatawhaorua* from 1974 onwards. The first was Stanley Conrad, Joe's younger brother. We'd first met in the late '90s when I went to see *Ngātokimatawhaorua* one Waitangi Day, and then again a few weeks after that when we were both on board *Te Aurere*, Hec Busby's voyaging canoe. The waka-hourua was part-way through a circumnavigation of the North Island and Busby allowed the odd interested person to join the crew for a leg. I had managed to talk my way aboard for the overnight sail from Tāmaki Makaurau Auckland to Tutukākā.

It was a pleasant, largely uneventful trip. We passed America's Cup yachts in Tīkapa Moana Hauraki Gulf as we departed Auckland, and later watched dolphins race our prow at sunset. While on board I tried to imagine what it must have been like to voyage for weeks at a time through the Pacific on such a vessel. Leaning against the railing as night fell, I suddenly became acutely aware of just how small the waka was. I tried not to dwell on what it would be like for a confirmed landlubber like myself to be on it when the waka was hundreds, if not thousands, of miles from shore.

Stan Conrad knew that feeling better than most. His father was at one time a commercial fisherman and relied on Stan to help on the family boat on weekends and during school holidays. When Stan left school he moved to Whakatū Nelson to study for his commercial skipper's ticket before returning home to captain the family fishing boat for five years. He was also one of the pioneers of contemporary Māori voyaging, having joined the crew of the Hawaiian double-hulled waka *Hōkūle'a* in 1985 for the Rarotonga–Waitangi leg of the Polynesian Voyaging Society's 'Voyage of Rediscovery'. He became the captain of *Te Aurere* in 1992 and has since sailed extensively throughout the Pacific. In 2018 he was capped in the Micronesian Pwo ceremony for his commitment and services to voyaging.

We arranged to meet at the Birkenhead home he shares with his wife, Kelli, and their son, Kiwa. Now in his fifties, Conrad is unassuming and carries the calm expression of a person who has everything under control. Nothing seems to bother him overly, and when he spoke about *Ngātokimatawhaorua* he did so not with the jaded response of a 45-year veteran, but with the wide-eyed enthusiasm of someone recently introduced to the waka.

His relationship with *Ngātokimatawhaorua*, he told me, began when he was 11, in 1974. From then on he accompanied his father to Waitangi every February, initially to meet up with friends and have fun exploring the Treaty Grounds and surrounding area from sunrise to sunset. His interest eventually turned to the waka, and he joined the crew as a bailer before progressing to a paddler and eventually to a section commander.

He may well have become captain if his older brother Joe had not held the position.

When I asked him about those early years at Waitangi, he said a tight group of elders were in charge and ensured that things ran smoothly. Typically, one or two of them would be charged with organising the training wānanga, which were held at marae in locations across the north, such as Ōtiria, Mitimiti, Panguru and Rāwhiti. The first two or three wānanga were always scheduled prior to Christmas.

> We'd get there and be straight into our lines, practising
> our kaihoe drills, or straight into our kapa haka training. I
> remember we'd spend hours perfecting our tutungaru, our
> rākau haka. We used to do the old Ngāpuhi one, *Kai ke te*
> *weewee, kai ke te waawaa,* and Alan Karena would be there
> swinging his koikoi at our legs, encouraging us to all jump at
> the same time. If you did it wrong he would hit your legs until
> you fell over, and then he'd make us all do it again.[13]

A smile crept over Conrad's face as he recalled the meals provided for the hard-working kaihoe. It was simple kai, he said: mince, kūmara and potatoes often featured, as did roast meat, boiled brisket, cabbage and watercress. And he fondly remembers the plates of boiled fish, kūtai and pipi. 'The ladies made sure we were well fed. We were never hungry.'

Then, part-way through our conversation, Conrad said something interesting. He told me that he didn't actually pick up a hoe until 1978 or 1979, and that back when he was starting out, they had to learn 'all sorts of stuff' before they were given the opportunity to paddle. You learnt the basics, waited for an opportunity, and then you were invited to join the crew when the time was right.

> So by the time we got to paddle we knew that they leave
> water in the bottom of the hull so the wooden joints could
> swell and tighten up; that the thickest part of the hull was

> down below so it could act as the keel; and that the paddles have a sharp end so that when they go into the water you can hardly hear them.

They were also taught from the start that their paddle was the equivalent of a life-vest, that it would always float. 'It was drilled into us. If you lose your paddle, you find it. If you drop your paddle at sea, you jump over the side and get it.'

These days, Conrad is a vocal advocate for crew members getting involved in the maintenance of the waka. He says the hours spent helping refurbish a waka pay dividends, and those who regularly get involved learn its capacity, how far it can be pushed and what stresses it can withstand. That insight led me to a question I had about the structure of the waka. I was interested to learn about the weakest points of a hull, the two haumi joins. I had seen footage of a waka in heavy seas with the prow momentarily suspended in mid-air, several feet above a trough, and I thought that it looked like a pretty good way to damage a vessel.

'Well, you have to try to take the swell slightly on an angle,' Conrad explained, 'because if you come off a swell and the kaihoe are out of the water above a trough, that's a lot of weight on that front join, especially if you have a heavy crew. The other thing is that when you take it out in swells, you have to try not to pound into the swell, because that also puts a lot of stress on the joins.'[14]

Our conversation continued for another quarter of an hour or so, during which he told me about a few of the personalities that dominated the waka in the 1970s and '80s; then he gave me the names of some retired kaihoe I might contact to add to the story. As we said goodbye, Conrad promised to introduce me to a few key people next Waitangi Day weekend. It was a good six months away, but I began to make arrangements to be there.

8
Dissent and protest

WAITANGI HAS always been a special place. From its status as the home of the ancestor Maikuku through to the signing of Aotearoa New Zealand's founding treaty, Waitangi has been a focal point of regional and national attention. In modern times it has also been the main focus for media during Waitangi Day commemorations, and that has made it a prime destination for protesters challenging successive governments on their failure to uphold the terms of the Treaty of Waitangi. If you want to slap the government in the face, why not slap them when the nation is looking?

The 1980s was a particularly turbulent decade at Waitangi. Protests initiated by the activist group Ngā Tamatoa had started peacefully enough in 1971, but had become increasingly confrontational as their demands were repeatedly ignored. I witnessed the protesters' anger and frustration first hand in the 1990s. Standing on the footpath as the demonstration made its way from Paihia to the Treaty Grounds, I was subjected to a torrent of abuse that caught me off guard.

What I didn't realise at the time was that the house I was standing in front of was being used by the police as a supposedly covert command centre. The protesters knew it, and I suppose with my short haircut and camera I looked a lot like a plain-clothed police officer taking evidential photographs. Even so, I was taken aback by the venom behind the words. In retrospect, the heightened emotions of the day were understandable — Māori had suffered for long enough and it seemed that no one in power was listening to them — but the verbal volley had frozen me in place. In that moment it felt to me as though Waitangi was ready to explode.

I wasn't the only one caught off guard by the ferocity of the protests. A young and impressionable Stan Conrad was initially confused by the presence of protesters at Waitangi.

> We were caught up in this turmoil of Māori against Māori, and some of us were thinking, 'Why are you yelling at us?' I think that was the hardest thing, because we were getting abused when we were walking down to the water, and we got abused for flying the New Zealand flag from the taurapa. They'd yell at us to 'Take that fucking flag off our waka' — stuff like that. Later it became, 'We're going to cut that bloody waka up.' And one night, soon after, we heard a chainsaw starting up down by the beach. It put the fear into you, you know.[1]

In response to the threat against *Ngātokimatawhaorua*, a ring of kaihoe were stationed around the waka at night, and two more hid under a tarpaulin on the waka itself, ready to defend it if required. Fortunately, for all concerned, the chainsaw never returned.

'There was a little bit of argy-bargy from time to time,' said Stan Conrad, 'but we never actually got involved in fist fights. Our elders and our leaders at that time taught us that our job was to look after our wāhine, to look after the kaupapa, and to look after the waka.'

Ned Peita, the kaumātua who had explained to me how the name Te Korowai ō Maikuku had evolved, told me that if they had fully understood the protesters' agenda there would not have been such a standoff — it would have been more of a gathering of minds.

> But because Ngā Tamatoa was anti-establishment, they brought their grievances and dumped them on people who had no idea what they were [on about]. It could have gotten nasty. We were pretty much locked up in the marae just

to save them from us, because that was the potential. The
kaihoe were mostly young and up for a fight, and these
people were corrupting our point of view.[2]

The only real physical confrontations Conrad saw occurred up at the
Treaty Grounds.

These bloody Pākehās came running across the field to chain
themselves to the flagpole or to climb up the Norfolk pines,
but the problem was they were running too close to our
wāhine, so Alan Karena started swinging his taiaha — and
whack! On the deck. And the cops came out and dragged
them off. So when that started we acted as spotters, and
no sooner did we say, Watch out!, then there'd be another
whack! And the cops came in and picked them up too.

Demonstrators supposedly protesting against the government were
instead sparring with Māori. 'Back then the radicals were radicals,'
Conrad explained.

All they wanted to do was come and disrupt the Waitangi
celebrations, and it didn't matter if the celebrations were for
kaupapa waka or whatever. For the likes of us, we went to
celebrate the waka, to celebrate *Ngātoki*, because back then
there was no other waka that could draw such a crowd; no
other waka that could bring two people, Māori and Pākehā,
together like it could.[3]

It was an uncomfortable period for many of the crew and supporters
of *Ngātokimatawhaorua*, and a number of them, upset by the conflict,
left and never returned. Most stayed, however, including Stan Conrad.

We were lucky that we had the kaumātua we had in those
days. They helped a lot of us get through it. Without them

Waitangi Day has seen its fair share of confrontations over the years. High on the agenda is a demand that the government honour the terms of the Treaty of Waitangi.
STUFF LIMITED

> reminding us why we were there — to celebrate our waka,
> to celebrate having *Ngātoki* out on the water. I think their
> reinforcement helped a lot of us get through it.

The kaumātua also offered some advice to the protesters, suggesting that instead of attacking the waka and its crew, they put on their best suits, head down to Wellington and fight the government down there.

If regular run-ins with the protesters had taken the shine off the Waitangi Day commemorations for some, the opportunities to participate in a number of one-off events throughout the 1980s kept drawing kaihoe back to *Ngātokimatawhaorua*. One of the most memorable was when the Prince and Princess of Wales, Charles and Diana, climbed aboard the waka in 1983 for the short ride from the wharf at Waitangi to Hobson Beach. Photos from the day show the couple sitting mid-waka, the Princess in a canary-yellow dress and high heels, and the Prince in a light-grey suit. They made for a beguiling, if unusual, sight.

Scarcely noticed sitting nearby were Hilda Busby, Elsie Rakuraku and Marlene Moranga, three women who had been assigned to accompany Princess Diana on the waka. It was the second time in two years that women had been invited onto the waka.[4] Hec Busby told me special karakia were recited to clear the way for Prince Charles and Princess Diana and their escort, and he thought that they both enjoyed the experience. He smiled when he told me he got to shake their hands, but when he had leaned in to touch cheeks with the Princess she had quickly backed away.

That wasn't the entire story of the day, however. Given the level of protest at Waitangi and the media focus on the couple, security for the royal visit was at an all-time high. Aroha Harris, the author of *Hīkoi: Forty years of Māori protest*, noted that the police in attendance were suited up in full riot gear and that 'Almost one hundred protestors, Māori and Pākehā, were arrested before any protest even occurred.'[5]

Indeed, the police were taking no chances. They had demanded a full list of *Ngātokimatawhaorua*'s crew prior to the royals' arrival, and when looking through the names their attention was drawn to one kaihoe in particular — that of a gang leader who had only recently joined the crew. Busby told me that as soon as the police recognised the name, they put a cross against it. 'His commitment was faultless', Hec Busby recalled, 'but he was well known to the police and they told me they didn't want this guy on the waka'. Rather than bow to official pressure, Busby stood up for the man and declared that if he wasn't in the crew then the waka wasn't going to be launched.

> I told them that I had enough faith in this guy and I was
> sure he wasn't going to play up while we were on the canoe.
> I knew he was trying to get back on the straight and narrow,
> and that if I had to remove him from the crew that it would
> ruin him.[6]

Busby's stance was non-negotiable, and the eventual launch of the waka with the gang leader among its crew was indicative of the high standing Busby had within his community. That *Ngātokimatawhaorua* was the catalyst for change, even for one man, was significant, and would have delighted Te Puea. Her strategy to use waka taua to uplift Māori was still delivering results four and a half decades after the centennial commemoration.

Prince Charles and Princess Diana seem to be enjoying their ride on *Ngātokimatawhaorua*. Accompanying them are Heke-nuku-mai-ngā-iwi (Hec) Busby (standing, left) and his wife, Hilda Busby, who is sitting directly in front of Princess Diana. NZME/NEW ZEALAND HERALD

Another noteworthy event occurred in 1987, when *Ngātokimatawhaorua* participated in Whangaroa County's centennial celebrations.

Early on I had learnt that the best place to find stories about *Ngātokimatawhaorua* was directly from crew and support staff, and unlike the original 1940 crew and, to a lesser extent, the 1974 crew, there were still a good number of participants from the 1987 voyage alive to interview.

To uncover some of their stories I contacted Karen Williams, whose husband, David, had been in the waenga section during the 1987 voyage. She was volunteering for her iwi when I first contacted her in early 2021, furnishing homes for people moving out of transitional housing and into rentals. When a second wave of Covid-19 struck Northland and the region began to undergo lockdowns, Karen added the delivery of food packages to vulnerable families and kaumātua to her busy daily schedule. A woman who gets things done, she had organised a hui within a week of my phone call so I could meet several ex-crew or, in some cases, their surviving families. She also offered me a place to stay.

I travelled to Kaeo, a small town on State Highway 10 some 80 minutes north of Whangārei, and met Williams outside Te Rūnanga o Whaingaroa office. She was in her mid-sixties, fashioned her hair in a bob, and was wearing jeans and a mustard-coloured top. Our first day together would be full. Taking her 4 × 4, we'd start by visiting the Adams whānau at Pupuke, a few minutes up the road from Kaeo. Then we were to go sightseeing: first to Penia, near Waitaruke, where *Ngātokimatawhaorua* had finished its 1987 voyage, then to view Whangaroa Harbour. Finally, we'd return to Kaeo, pick up my car and head over to her home, where her husband David would be waiting.

The Adams home was a comfortable single-storey dwelling with a wraparound deck and the whānau meeting house just a few metres away. The matriarch, Anne Adams, greeted me before explaining over tea and biscuits that her late husband, Hakopa, had been running a te reo and

DISSENT AND PROTEST 173

tikanga class in Kaeo at the time of the voyage, and that he had joined the crew to encourage his students to do the same.

She soon produced some scrapbooks and photo albums that had been pulled out in anticipation of my visit. As we thumbed through the pages, Adams reminisced about how all the local whānau had come together to support the crew, and how seriously the kaihoe had taken their preparation for the voyage. There was training at Waitangi most weekends, and a couple of additional evening sessions during the working week in Kaeo. On the nights when they weren't training, the men were lacing up long-retired running shoes and hitting the roads. Anne's daughter Charlene, a teenager at the time, recalled the effort required. 'Our father would run all the time, and make us run with him. He was a big man but lost so much weight because he was dedicated. All of them were. These old men, some in their seventies, like Uncle Joe Poata, they were all out running.'[7]

It was a fascinating look into the drive and dedication these men had shown, and I was thankful to hear their story. After a generous cooked lunch, Williams and I thanked our hosts before continuing north to Penia. Dodging cowpats, we walked across an empty farm paddock to where she could point out where *Ngātokimatawhaorua* had been anchored. There was a memorial plaque — a sister to the green ceramic plaque under the shade of Te Korowai ō Maikuku — on the shoreline. A two-tier concrete base incorporated the plaque and a mauri stone brought from Waitangi.

I took a couple of photos and we made our way back to Whangaroa township, where we parked beside the harbour. Just out from us, seemingly within throwing distance, sat Motu Wai Red Island. It was near this small island that the sailing ship *Boyd* sank in 1809, after being assailed by local Māori further up the harbour, off Ohauroro Peach Island. Seeking utu after the mistreatment of a young chief on board, local Māori attacked and killed up to 70 of the *Boyd*'s crew and passengers. While the ship was being pillaged its cargo of gunpowder ignited, triggering a massive explosion. Drifting on the tide, the burning ship must have made quite a sight before it finally succumbed to its fate.

After a few short minutes we headed back to Kaeo to pick up my car, and then headed to Karen's home. When we arrived, Karen's husband, David, was waiting for me. He had recently been diagnosed with Alzheimer's disease, and during the course of our chat he would occasionally hesitate while he searched his memory for an image from the day we were discussing. He usually found something. He told me, for instance, that the weekday training sessions were held at Whangaroa College, the Kaeo Community Hall or the old courthouse by the police station. And he recalled how senior crew members would acknowledge individual kaihoe when the waka was passing their tūrangawaewae — their homelands — and how they 'had a good way of making you feel proud of yourself when they talked to you about the effort you put in'.[8]

He also remembered that by the time they were nearing Motueka Flat Island, not far from the entrance to Whangaroa Harbour, the swell had begun to build, so they decided to cut between nearby Motuekaiti Little Flat Island and Pakuru Point on the mainland, rather than paddle between Motueka and Motuekaiti. That was when Williams was called to the back of the waka to help the kaiurungi, the steersmen, because as a keen diver and fisherman he was familiar with the coast.

> The tide was out as we were approaching the gap, which was pretty narrow. There were rocks all around, and we could see the seaweed when we looked down into the water. When they asked for more speed, we could feel the whole waka just lift out of the water.

Joanne Hona later added to the story, telling me she had heard her dad, Acey, talk about surging through the gap.

Dad talked about this one time when the waka just lifted and shot through the gap, and he said he could hear the karakia happening and all that sort of stuff. Dad said it skimmed. It lifted and skimmed along. He said it was just them, the log, and the water.[9]

The drive to Wainui Marae the next morning took us in convoy past a series of beaches, each seemingly more spectacular than the last, before we turned inland along a short unsealed road into the heart of Wainui Valley. Karen led the way onto the grass reserve, and I parked next to the fence as her truck disappeared behind the marae buildings.

It was a beautiful setting. The grounds were well tended, the coast was a short stroll away, and mature native trees covered the hills to the north. Even though we were in a valley there was a feeling of openness. Nestled among a dozen or so homes, the marae was well positioned to excel in its role as the beating heart of the community.

Responding to the karanga, I made my way up the concrete path, past a huge phoenix palm that had been planted to commemorate the ninetieth birthday of a kaumātua in the 1970s, and stepped up onto the porch of the compact weatherboard building that served as the meeting house. I took off my shoes and entered. Like the grounds, the whare was spotless, and the still air was warmed by the sunlight streaming through the windows. A bench-seat had been placed in the middle of the room, anticipating my arrival. Dozens of ancestors watched over the pōwhiri from their photographs on the wall.

Over the course of the morning, I listened as Rusty Porter, Morgan Hemi, Arena Heta and Harry Te Awa shared their memories of the 1987 voyage, as did two of their Pākehā crewmates, Tony Shepherd and Rodger Borman. I also heard about the role of the kaikaranga from Tahua Murray, one of the women who drove the coastal route ahead of *Ngātokimatawhaorua*, so they could call to the waka as it made its way north. And at the end of the session, after they had finished preparing our lunch in the whare kai, Rauaroha Heta and Joanne Hona joined us to share memories of their fathers' experiences on the waka, as well as some of their own memories of supporting the kaihoe from shore.

Together, they painted a vivid picture of the men and women who had helped make the voyage a reality, including local police officer Paddy Whiu, who opened the old courthouse in Kaeo when it was needed for practice; and the women who cooked for the crew while they were training. I learnt the names of the kaumātua who paddled on the waka, including Joe Poata, Mita Hape, Te Uru (Eru) Heta and Simon Snowden — all of them gone now.

What I heard most often, however, was how proud they were to have been selected for the voyage. Tony Shepherd spoke for many when he said it had been a privilege to be part of the crew, and three decades later the experience was still a highlight for him. Rodger Borman told me he had felt so protective of his place on the waka that he slept with his hoe so he would have it with him each morning. 'I wasn't going to lose my place. I fought hard for it. I went to every training, every marae stay, and I wasn't going to give it up.'[10]

The voyage had been set in motion in October 1986, when a group of kaumātua from Whangaroa, including Te Uru Heta, Kira Williams, Joe Poata, Sid Kira, Mita Hape, Joe Everitt, Ned Peita, Ani Bosch and Turoa Tepania, sought and gained permission from the kaitiaki of *Ngātokimatawhaorua* for the waka to feature in Whangaroa County's centennial celebrations. It was a request that would not only allow the waka to venture out of Pēwhairangi Bay of Islands for the first time, but would also attract dozens of new kaihoe to waka.

Preparations for the voyage began in earnest the following month, when notices were sent out inviting people to put their names forward for the crew. Organisers also visited the Kaeo Rugby Club, and later announced the call for crew over Northland Radio. If the organising committee were at all nervous about finding 80 enthusiastic kaihoe to fill the waka, they needn't have been. More than enough men were keen to get involved.

It had been 14 years since the relaunch of the waka for the Queen's visit in 1974, but *Ngātokimatawhaorua* had been taken out for Waitangi Day commemorations every year since. There was now a solid leadership group in place, and they had a good understanding of the challenge facing the Whangaroa group: how to prepare for a huge voyage in a few short months. The key was to assign leadership roles to experienced men, and chief among those chosen was Wiremu Wiremu.

Stocky, strong and with an authentic parade-ground voice (he was a regimental sergeant major), Wiremu had spent time on Waikato's waka taua at Ngāruawāhia and brought that experience to the weekend training sessions at Waitangi.

Supporting him were a number of experienced kaihoe and kaumātua, including Alan Karena, Joe Everitt and Ned Peita. There was also Jake Puke, one of several soldiers who travelled up from the Waikato to paddle with Wiremu Wiremu.

With a significant number of the kaihoe being first-timers, initial training sessions were land-based and focused on basic paddling techniques. It wasn't long, however, before a water-borne training regime was introduced, with ever longer distances introduced during weekend wānanga. Session by session, week by week, the crew improved. Their timing tightened as paddles entered and left the water, and they became more adept at responding to the instructions issued by their section commanders. No one wanted to let down the kaihoe next to him.

When Harry Te Awa sat down at the small table where I was recording the interviews, he started by explaining to me how the captain managed a tiring crew. It wasn't, as I had imagined, as simple as resting the whole crew together. Instead, the crew was split into three groups, with a large group in the middle and a smaller group at each end:

> So the order would go out, and everyone went flat out, until
> it was time for two of the sections to rest, leaving one group
> to carry on paddling. Then, when the waka started to slow,
> everyone started paddling together until we got back up to
> speed again, and then the next groups would rest.[11]

It proved to be an effective strategy, although another crew member later described paddling while two sections rested as 'paddling in quicksand'.[12] Despite the hard work, there were still occasional moments to remember with a laugh. According to Stan Conrad, kaumātua Alan Karena was a tough drill master who particularly disliked seeing any kaihoe take an unscheduled break. During one punishing outing Karena noticed a hoe lying across a rauawa while the waka was being paddled. Conrad remembers the moment vividly:

> I was the leader of the ihu section at the time and I had this
> old fella paddling right behind me. We were going along, and
> I heard Alan yell out, 'Stanley, hit that person on the head.'
> I looked around and I'm looking at him and he goes, 'It's all
> right, boy. Hit me on the head.' I started to say I wouldn't hit
> him, but he said, 'No. I deserve it. I shouldn't have had a rest.'

So I went, 'I'll give you a little donk.' And I hit him softly on the head, and he went, 'No, harder!'[13]

It wasn't only the kaihoe who travelled to Waitangi for the weekend wānanga. Whānau accompanied many of the paddlers to support them, and they brought food for the collective pantry. 'We took what we could,' Karen Williams told me.

> Especially the ones in Kaeo. When you are coming from not-rich families, we still made sure that our paddlers were fed. There was a well-organised routine: breakfast at six. Then the waka boys would be out doing their practice. We'd be getting lunch ready. They'd come in for lunch and then be back out doing waka, and we'd get tea ready. Then after tea it would be time for kapa haka, which would go for hours. It was nice kai, and it had to keep them sustained so they could do what they had to do. Fuel the body.[14]

One of the lasting memories from the wānanga for Charlene Adams was the sound of the column of kaihoe — 120 strong — out running barefoot. 'You could hear them coming from miles away; all the way down the hill and then all the way along the beach. You could hear the stamping of their feet from inside the whare.'[15]

Final preparations for the voyage to Whangaroa began in earnest the afternoon of the Waitangi Day commemorations. Once the regular crew's obligations at Waitangi were finished, *Ngātokimatawhaorua* was paddled to Te Tii Bay and handed over to the new crew. There, the waka was checked for water-tightness and then checked again.

180 NGĀTOKIMATAWHAORUA

Lashings were examined, paddles tallied. Later in the evening the kaihoe selected for the voyage listened as kaumātua spoke to them about the exploits of their ancestors and what was expected of them the following day. Karakia were recited throughout the night.

The crew's final meal was served around 11 p.m., and it would be the last food they were permitted to eat until the end of the voyage the following afternoon. All they would have to sustain them on the voyage was a supply of fresh water, some of it carried on a barge that would shadow them, the rest carried on its escort vessel, HMNZS *Takapu*, which would also carry a number of reserve paddlers.

According to Stan Conrad, the crew followed established protocols and traditions before the voyage. 'No alcohol or drugs were consumed in camp, and we were not allowed to sleep with our wāhine the night before the voyage. We were also forbidden from taking tobacco, watches, food or money onto the waka.'

The strict protocols were to cause discomfort for some. Rauaroha Heta recalled the anguish of not being able to sleep beside her husband the night before the voyage:

> The men slept by themselves because of the whole tapu and
> noa around the mahi that they had to do. They had a kai
> and then went to their marquee to prepare themselves. But
> it was hard for us, because even though they had trained,
> anything could have happened out there. It was a long way to
> Whangaroa.[16]

She was not wrong. The 65-kilometre voyage to Whangaroa was a daunting challenge, but *Ngātokimatawhaorua* was well designed and had a solid core of experienced leaders. It was also fast. I had been out on a support boat when the waka had been launched to welcome the double-hulled voyaging canoe *Hōkūle'a* to Waitangi and been surprised by its pace. For a man-powered vessel, it seemed to move with deceptive speed. Once, in optimal paddling conditions with the tide and breeze in its favour, *Ngātokimatawhaorua* had been clocked at 9 knots by the captain of a support boat during a run down to Ōpua. It was an impressive feat for a waka weighing 12 tonnes.

Had there been more time to prepare for the 1987 voyage, the waka may have moved even faster — Hec Busby had toyed with the notion of rigging a sail for the voyage. He told me that he had had a mast and sail ready, but ultimately thought better of it. None of the crew had *sailed* a waka taua before, and Busby decided that it would be dangerous to introduce such a major adaptation at the last minute.

The alarm echoed off the wooden walls of the whare and out to the marquee at 3.30 a.m., and any crew who had managed to fall asleep amid the excitement and anticipation were soon woken from their slumber. Within minutes the kaihoe and their kaumātua had begun to ready themselves for the day ahead, and by 5 a.m. they had assembled down at the foreshore to take part in the pre-voyage rituals. Surrounded by family and well-wishers, the kaihoe listened to speeches and karakia. The bright lights of a Japanese film crew, one of a handful to capture footage of the voyage, illuminated a corner of the scene.

Once the formalities had concluded, pairs of kaihoe, barefoot and wearing black shorts, walked into the shallows, climbed onto the waka and made their way to their allotted positions.

At 5.20 a.m., a little over two hours after high tide, Hec Busby, carrying his taiaha and adorned in a feather cloak, issued the command, and 80 hoe were plunged into the still water. The waka inched forward, the grip of the dark seawater below stretched but not yet broken. Another stroke followed in quick time, and then another, and another. Only then did the ocean begin to loosen its hold. By the time the count had reached a dozen the waka was moving freely.

Spectators, huddled in groups against the cold, watched on in near silence as a karanga followed the waka out onto the tide. Karen Williams, one of the many wives there to farewell their husbands, remembered it as a tough time.

> The emotion was huge, just watching them go. I don't think there was one of us standing on that beach who didn't have a tear in their eye, and they were tears of fear. It was the not knowing. Were they going to make it? We were all very anxious.[17]

In a matter of seconds the huge waka had melted into the darkness, the kaihautū's call the only indication that *Ngātokimatawhaorua* was still in the bay. 'It went so fast,' Williams recalled. 'I drove over to the waka house but they had already passed Te Korowai when I got there. It wasn't until I got up to the top of the golf course that I could make them out.'

The waka followed a course roughly parallel to the coast before turning out into the harbour proper once they were below the golf course. From there it made for Cape Wiwiki, the headland on the northern side of the entrance to Pēwhairangi Bay of Islands. Rodger Borman, a diesel mechanic by trade, will never forget the day. 'It was amazing. It was like we were floating on a cloud. When you have 80 men all paddling at the same time — it's just amazing.'[18]

The experience for the 40 kaihoe who were not required to paddle initially was memorable for another reason. Sitting down the centre of the waka in a pair of shorts and a light T-shirt, they were soon shivering in the chill of pre-dawn. Senior crew weren't immune to the cold either. Marty Bercic, a section commander during the voyage, recalled temporarily commandeering one kaihoe's position so he could warm up. It wasn't long before others followed his example.

DISSENT AND PROTEST 183

As well as being tracked by a small convoy of whānau in cars, kaikaranga Akamiria Rose, Hera Richards, Iwa Alker, Nellie Paora and Tahua Murray travelled along the country roads to call to the waka from pre-selected locations. They started at Hobson Beach before moving to the cliffs by the golf course. Their karanga were then repeated as the waka passed Tākou Bay, Matauri Bay, Te Ngaere and Mahinepua. According to Murray, they called to the men 'because they were carrying the wairua of their tūpuna, the ones who came from Hawaiki'.

As the sun began to climb, another film crew, this one following the waka in a pleasure boat, began to pick out details on *Ngātoki-matawhaorua*. The hull was painted much as it is now: darkish red with the puhoro design painted under the tauihu, but the rauawa were still unpainted, left in their natural wood state. Up front, the pure white feathers of the ihiihi reflected the sun's rays, while the feather streamers trailed theatrically from the taurapa. The camera then focused in on the kaihoe. Still relatively fresh, and no doubt enjoying the warmth of the sun, they leaned their backs enthusiastically into their work as the New Zealand flag fluttered from a pole attached to the taurapa.

Rusty Porter completed the picture for me when he described how a rope tied to the back of the taurapa and knotted along its length was used to estimate the vessel's speed. 'This long rope [dragged] behind the waka, and the faster we went, the more knots came out of the water. So if you looked back at it, you'd look for the last knot on the surface of the water, and if it was the fifth knot, then we were doing 5 knots.'[19]

By the time *Ngātokimatawhaorua* had navigated the inside gap at Cape Wiwiki and entered Tākou Bay, a wide and open stretch of coastline bordered by Taronui Bay in the south and Waiaua Bay in the north, the morning wind had arrived and a low swell was beginning to build — but not near the waka, according to Porter. 'The funny thing about it was that after we came around the Nine Pins the water all around us was choppy. It was getting light, and we could see the support boats around us bouncing around, but there was a flat patch about 20 metres wide that we were on.' The path was there, he said, due to the power of the karakia that had been chanted throughout the night.

It was about then, once they got out of Pēwhairangi, that the whole wairua of the waka changed, added Arena Heta. 'That's when the rhythm got going — when the sun was up.'[20]

Waiting for *Ngātokimatawhaorua* at the southern end of Tākou Bay were the travelling supporters and the carload of kaikaranga. Anxious for the first sign of their loved ones, they strained to see out across the bay from Otaha headland. When the canoe was finally sighted a karanga pierced the silence, calling to both the kaihoe and their waka.

Further along the coast, as *Ngātokimatawhaorua* approached the midway point of the bay, the order was given to stop paddling. There, at the mouth of the Tākou River, a karakia was recited, the words drifting landward to acknowledge the resting place of the migration waka *Mātaatua* and to pay tribute to the ancestors who crewed it to Aotearoa. It was an emotional experience for many of the paddlers.

By midday the euphoria of the early morning departure had begun to wear thin. The crew had already paddled further than they had during any of their training sessions, and for some kaihoe the energy reserves from their last meal were beginning to dwindle. Paddle strokes, so crisp and efficient earlier in the day, were becoming less so with every passing hour. Once upright backs were starting to round, shoulders were slumping. Salt deposits began to bite into parched lips.

By 2.30 p.m. the waka had negotiated the shallows between Motu-ekaiti and the mainland and was met by a flotilla of 30 vessels at the entrance to Whangaroa Harbour. Fishing boats, pleasure craft and kayaks made up the mismatched fleet that surrounded the massive waka taua. A helicopter hovered above. It was about then that Stan Conrad and his long-time friend and accomplice Marty Bercic got themselves into a spot of bother.

We'd sung our traditional waiata all the way up, repeating them several times, and as we came into Whangaroa Harbour we were trying to think of another waiata to sing. We needed something fresh to lift morale because we were getting pretty tired by then, so we started to sing 'Row, row, row your boat'. And of course just as we did, we noticed the reporter for the *Northern Advocate*. We were on the water for something like 11 hours and in the five minutes the reporter was there she caught us singing 'Row, row, row your boat'. Well, that went into the paper, and all I remember was a fuming Hilda Busby. 'Who the bloody hell started it? Martin! Stanley!'[21]

It was just the first of a number of notable occurrences near the harbour entrance. According to Ned Peita, once inside the harbour the waka was enveloped by a peculiar headwind. He described it as a warm, swirling wind that started at the front of the waka and made its way through the crew. 'And as soon as it had passed, we saw the figure of a warrior doing a haka up on a hill near Totara North. We asked about him when we landed, but no one had sent anyone up there.'[22] Several of the crew wondered whether it was a spiritual encounter, perhaps an ancestor urging them on, but the figure would later be identified as a local man, Buzzy Gates, who had scrambled up the hill with his taiaha on his own initiative to urge the crew onwards.

As the waka surged past familiar landmarks within the harbour, the excitement on board grew. Morgan Hemi described it as a particularly emotional experience. 'I was really hyped up when we came down the mouth of Whangaroa, because this is where we were from — well, the majority of us. The feeling of coming back home in such a significant waka was something really special.'[23]

The emotion was different for the waiting wives and whānau. Karen Williams recalled the anxiety felt by many of those on shore.

The emotion side of things is hard to explain. It's taken how many hours? And you've counted the hours waiting and still nothing — and you have to remember there were no cell phones back then, so we had to wait for someone who had actually seen the waka to tell us where it was. It wasn't until someone turned up at Penia and told us they were nearly here that we realised the waka was among the boats we could see in the distance.[24]

One by one, the spectator vessels dropped back as *Ngātokimatawhaorua* approached Penia, allowing it to arrive alone and triumphantly. The epic voyage ended with an emotional pōwhiri. Onlookers, cordoned off by a farmer's fence, leaned forward as kaikaranga, holding green leaves, called the crew to shore. Charlene Adams was particularly taken by the wairua of the karanga. She said the feeling coming from the voices of the kuia was surreal. 'We could *feel* the wailing.'[25]

Once ashore, there were whaikōrero and waiata. The *Northern Advocate* reporter, by now back on land, described the crew: 'Stiff walks, red, salt-sprayed backs and heavy eyelids revealed the weariness of the paddlers.'[26] Footage from the documentary of the voyage, *Rere Ki Uta, Rere Ki Tai (The Journey)*, backed up her observations, capturing numerous exhausted kaihoe asleep with the speeches still in progress.

The voyage to Whangaroa was a significant event in the history of *Ngātokimatawhaorua*, as well as being a milestone in the revival of waka culture in Aotearoa. It also added to contemporary knowledge around the capability of waka taua on coastal expeditions, serving as an important reminder that such voyages were achievable. An untested crew, pulled together from interested locals, had defied all probability and successfully paddled the 65 kilometres at an average speed of a touch under 3.25 knots. It was a remarkable achievement.

What no one foresaw, however, was the upswell in demand for waka taua that would follow the voyage. Sitting with Arena Heta at Wainui Marae, I listened as he told me that after the voyage Whangaroa decided that it wanted a waka of its own, and turned to Hec Busby to make their dreams a reality. 'Mātaatua was Hec's first waka, the first he built, so I suppose in a way the voyage brought the waka kaupapa to life. It really came to life after that trip.'[27]

Joanne Hona also acknowledged what the voyage did for the wider community during our conversation:

> It was a journey, and I guess that's an easy thing to say, but for a lot of the crew they were on different paths in their life journeys. But on board it didn't matter if you were the richest man in town, or the guy who was in constant trouble with the police. They had each other's backs. They saw each other at their rawest. They saw each other at their happiest. They saw each other when they were down. It didn't matter in that specific moment, because there was that brotherhood, or that whakawhanaungatanga — knowing they would always have your back.[28]

9

The Year of the Waka 1990

THE DEAL WAS straightforward. Any iwi interested in participating in the 1990 Commission's Kaupapa Waka event could apply for a $50,000 grant to help them build a waka. If they needed a log or two, they could apply for those as well. All they had to do was ensure their waka would be ready for the sesquicentennial commemoration. On the face of it, it seemed like an attractive offer, but in reality the funds available would prove to be only a fraction of what was needed. Any shortfall was to be made up by iwi, and in one case that would amount to several hundred thousand dollars.

And when it came to deciding how they would create their waka there were options available for iwi. They could build a new waka, renovate an existing one, or rescue an ancient hull from a swamp or riverbed and rebuild that. Nearly all chose the first option, leading to 20 new waka being built. Waikato were the only group to choose to renovate, refurbishing *Taheretikitiki II*, *Tumanako* and *Te Rangatahi*. None of the iwi who signed up chose to resurrect an old waka.

In addition to these waka, Ngāi Tahu also built their own canoe, which they named *Kōtukumairangi*. Constructed without government funding, it stayed in the South Island to commemorate the sesquicentennial.

Of the new waka, most were built from tōtara or kauri logs, following traditional practice, although a handful of iwi, unable to source the size of tree they required, chose instead to construct their hulls from laminated timber. One or two other groups, hindered by the lack of experienced tārai waka, opted for fibreglass hulls.

This innovative use of modern materials was often accompanied by imaginative paint jobs and contemporary carvings. Ngāti Maniapoto's waka, *Tuhi Mata Kamokamo*, for instance, was finished in a striking combination of blue hues and featured heavily stylised tauihu and taurapa. Likewise, the tauihu on *Te Awatea Hou*, a waka built by Te Runanganui o Te Tau Ihu o te Waka a Māui (the confederation of the nine Marlborough and Nelson tribes), sported a modern interpretation of the traditional prow piece. It featured a patu-wielding Kupe and Te Wheke-o-Muturangi, as well as the celebrated dolphin Pelorus Jack, all on a background of traditional spirals. To complete the transformation, the usual representation of Tūmatauenga affixed below the tauihu was replaced by a bird spearing forward in full flight.[1]

Not all of the tohunga tārai waka had dispensed with tradition however, and there would still be a number of waka for the purists to admire. In February 1989 Lyonel Grant began planning Te Arawa's waka. Like Poutapu, he had studied carving in Rotorua, at what is now called Ngā Kete Tuku Iho New Zealand Māori Arts and Crafts Institute, and he was a skilled carver with 16 years' experience to draw on when the project began. Asked to build a traditional waka taua in the local style, he took inspiration from a canoe built in the Rotorua region in the 1840s, as well as from Te Arawa-style tauihu and taurapa held in a German museum.

The resulting 20-metre waka was a masterpiece. Named *Te Arawa* and built from wind-felled tōtara that had lain in Whirinaki Forest for more than 60 years, its construction phase proved to be a revelation for the carvers. Skills scarcely used outside of the north or Waikato in a century or more were rediscovered and revived. At one point, Te Arawa carvers had to go as far as reshaping some of their precious adzes in order to replicate particular cuts.

During an interview filmed for the documentary *Waka: The Awakening Dream*,[2] Grant admitted that as far as he was concerned, modern-day carvers had not yet reached the heights of their ancestors. To do so, he continued, he and his contemporaries would have to become totally immersed in the art.

When the waka was finished, tribal history adorned every carved surface. The eight beating hearts of Te Arawa iwi were represented in the tauihu, and the numerous hapū descending from the crew of the ancestral migration waka (also named *Te Arawa*) were depicted in the rauawa carvings. One particular feature that made the waka stand out was the finish given to the inside of the hull. Oftentimes completed with a smooth surface, it was instead painstakingly carved with a stunning scallop finish.

When I arrived at Te Tii Bay to see where the waka had been beached for the sesquicentennial, I parked my car before scrambling down the boulders to the beach. Glancing north I could make out the masts of Kelly Tarlton's *Tui*, and, a little further around, the Treaty Grounds themselves. My only companions were a few flighty seagulls. It was a far cry from the overwhelming number of spectators that had been here 30 years earlier, crowding around the waka and almost suffocating the kaihoe.

Indeed, the scene that greeted anyone rounding the Bluff as they departed Paihia for Waitangi must have been spectacular. A total of 22 waka dominated the long, sweeping sands of Te Tii Bay, filling the beach and shallows. Some had been paddled at least part of the way to Waitangi (Ngāti Pāoa's *Te Kotūiti Tuarua*, for example, was paddled 52 kilometres from Kaiaua to Auckland), but most had been moved by truck. Sadly for one iwi, their waka didn't survive the road trip. Faulty brake linings on the transporter caused a fire, destroying its precious cargo. Another waka wasn't finished in time.

Nevertheless, 1990 was, Ned Peita told me, a reawakening for waka.

> When Te Puea came north to Waitangi she had a dream,
> and that was for the Waitangi harbour to be covered in waka.
> That was her dream. People laughed at her when she said waka
> shall cover the beach, but that dream came true in 1990.[3]

The travelling waka arrived during the week preceding Waitangi Day, coming from as far south as the top of Te Waka a Māui South Island and as far north as Doubtless Bay. In the close environment of Waitangi, relationships between the various crews strengthened, allowing for an exchange of waka knowledge between the sometimes competitive iwi.

That sense of manaakitanga was tested just three days out from the start of the commemoration when the hull of the Ngāti Kahungunu waka *Tamatea Arikinui o Te Waka Tākitimu* was damaged after running aground on a submerged sandbank, just along from Te Tii Marae. After moving the waka around to the calm waters of the estuary behind the marae, the anxious crew carefully inspected the hull. They were shocked by what they found: a massive crack had appeared, severely compromising the integrity of the hull. Unless a solution could be found fast, there would be no possibility of the waka taking part in the proceedings. Months of fundraising, construction and training lay in the balance.

Despite the seriousness of the situation, the crew were lucky in one respect: it turned out that local kaihoe had access to construction-grade equipment, and the suggestion was that steel plates and several massive bolts might be strong enough to hold the hull together. Karen Williams, who was present as this work got under way, said the entire Ngāti Kahungunu crew stayed with their waka through the night as work progressed, accompanied by six or seven kuia, who

> never left the waka. They sat there all night while my
> husband and a couple of others worked on their waka. We
> offered them food and cups of tea, but they wouldn't eat, they

wouldn't drink. They just sat there the whole night in the freezing cold. They sat on the bank singing while they were fixing the waka.[4]

Elsewhere the daily routines continued. Daylight hours were spent training on the harbour or interacting with the thousands of spectators who crowded the beach. There were also group runs for many of the crews to endure.

Evenings were a different matter. Fires lit along the beach illuminated the scene as kaumātua conversed with their crews, sharing traditions and talking of the ancestors who would surely protect and support them when they climbed aboard their waka. In the background, tohunga quietly chanted karakia. Later, guitars materialised and waiata sprang up as pockets of kaihoe settled in to guard their waka through the night — protesters were back and passions were running high. None of the crews were willing to leave their waka unattended.

What wasn't widely reported was the opportunity for several wāhine to ride aboard *Ngātokimatawhaorua*. In an echo of the 1940 maiden voyage, those selected represented the northern iwi. Sharon Edwards, May Davis, Peka More, Karen Williams, Rauaroha Heta, Rosie Toetoe, Ani Hape, Mere Poata, Linda Wiremu and Kate Pinkham were the chosen few.

Hosting the kaihoe and their supporters over these few days was once again an immense undertaking. This time Wiremu Wiremu stepped to the fore. Calling on his contacts in the armed forces, he arranged for army marquees and tents to accommodate hundreds of guests, and organised catering for 6500 visitors over the course of the week. Buddy Mikaere, who wrote an enthralling article about his 1990 experience at Waitangi for *New Zealand Geographic*, went up in a helicopter and viewed the military precision of the encampment from above. He credited Wiremu's 'underlying order' for the fact that 'events at Waitangi seem so natural and relaxed'.[5]

Tamatea Ariki Nui from Ngāti Kahungunu was severely compromised after hitting a sand bank just days before the sesquicentennial in 1990, celebrated as the Year of the Waka. The crew, seen here relaxing after taking their waka out, are oblivious to the near-heartbreak that is just days away. ARNO GASTEIGER

When Waitangi Day dawned, the wind was calm and the water flat. For the crew of *Ngātokimatawhaorua*, the morning started with a march in the half-light of pre-dawn to the beach, from where they launched their waka. Once out on the water and silhouetted by the low sun, the waka seemed even longer than usual.

Sitting among the kaihoe was Haare Williams. A respected radio journalist, Williams had previously interviewed several northern elders, including Hec Busby, for Radio New Zealand.

> My work was essentially to archive the stories of our kaumātua. Hec wasn't quite a kaumātua at that stage, but I realised that he was a fount of knowledge in relation to the history of navigation and waka and their construction and the narratives that accompany waka. So I got to know him in my interviews and broadcasting in that area.[6]

Williams said there were about 17 waka on the beach and three or four on the water when *Ngātokimatawhaorua* was paddled out to HMNZS *Canterbury*. As they came alongside they heard a whistle and then all the officers and crew who were lined up on the deck saluted them.

> Then the waka crew hit the paddles on the bottom of the waka and we glided right along the side of the *Canterbury*, and the only voice talking was my hushed reporting. When we got to the other end of the ship they blew the whistle again and finished their salute, their tribute, to the waka. Wow, what a moment.[7]

THE YEAR OF THE WAKA 1990 195

While *Ngātokimatawhaorua* was being honoured at sea, excitement and anticipation were growing among the hundreds of kaihoe still on shore. Up and down the beach they began lining up to receive their elaborate marker-pen moko while kaumātua and kuia watched on quietly.

The sharp-eyed among the spectators might have caught glimpses of many different custom-made hoe as the kaihoe assembled. Te Ati Awa's paddles, for example, were finished with an upoko carved into the top of the handle, while some paddlers from Ngāti Whātua's *Mahuhu o Te Rangi* had intricate surface patterns carved on their unpainted blades.

As with previous benchmark commemorations, the official programme for the sesquicentennial began with a re-enactment of the signing of Te Tiriti o Waitangi. This time invited guests were seated in towering stands erected at the top of Nias Track, from where they could see both the performance and the fleet of waka arriving in the bay far below.

Towards mid-morning the last of the crews dragged their waka down the beach and into the tide. Friends and whānau watched on, iwi flags and banners fluttering in the gentle breeze. Declared seaworthy once again, *Tamatea Arikinui o Te Waka Tākitimu* bobbed on the tide 40–50 metres from shore. The waka's leadership group had decided it would be safer to anchor the waka out at sea rather than risk beaching it. Nevertheless, there must have been some nervous kaihoe sitting above the repair when the order was given to start paddling.

By 10.45 a.m. all of the waka were out in the bay below the Treaty Grounds and positioning themselves to form a guard of honour for Queen Elizabeth and the Duke of Edinburgh. When the royal barge arrived 40 minutes later, *Ngātokimatawhaorua* escorted it to the Waitangi jetty, with *Tinana* and *Te Rangimata*, representing Muriwhenua and the people of Rēkohu Chatham Islands respectively, following close behind. Further back still were several waka-ama representing Niue, the Cook Islands and Tokelau.

With the royal party ashore, the kaihoe turned their waka and headed back to land. One thousand hoe dug into the water. One thousand kaihoe, driven by the spirit of their tūpuna, strained to get the nose of their waka ahead of the rest.

When the first of the waka reached the beach their crews leapt into the tide — for those at the front it was up to their waists, for others further back it was over their heads — before making their way up onto the warm sand. Once all of the waka had landed, the assembled kaihoe formed up for a mass haka. Ned Peita, who was among *Ngātokimatawhaorua*'s crew, recalls glancing down the beach and seeing it packed with kaihoe in lines four, five or six deep.

> We lined the whole beach, each crew differentiated from the others by their outfits. And all the waka crews did the same haka. We were like one voice right along the beach, with all the hoe moving at the same time — flashes of white and red.[8]

Kaupapa Waka — the Year of the Waka — had been a success. Participation in the event enabled many iwi to make a powerful statement about their place in the nation and their aspirations for the future. Some had revived the tārai waka skills of their ancestors; others had harnessed modern technology to meet their requirements.

Despite the positives, it was of course still disappointing that in 1990 it would take a government sponsored (but still grossly underfunded) project before the public could see more than a single waka taua at Waitangi or three at Ngāruawāhia. That aside, the 22 waka that made it onto the water at Waitangi formed what was undoubtedly a fitting tribute to the dreams and aspirations of Te Puea and those who shared her vision.

Thousands of spectators flocked to experience the waka at Te Tii Bay in 1990. Te Tii Marae, with two red-roofed buildings, is on the left. Just below the marae are the army tents organised by Wiremu Wiremu. The Waitangi River bridge that leads to the Treaty Grounds can be seen at the top right. ROBIN MOORE

There was one unintended consequence for *Ngātokimatawhaorua*, however. Now that waka taua were once again a widespread symbol of iwi mana, it seemed that every iwi had its own, and kaihoe who might once have eagerly travelled to Waitangi to crew the giant waka now stayed closer to home and focused on crewing their own. *Ngātokimatawhaorua* no longer had the pulling power it once had, and sadly there were years when it was not taken out at all. Ominously, there were also years when it was taken out grossly undermanned.

10
Lessons given, lessons learnt

THE DRIVE TO Waitangi was long and slow: the roads choked with families fleeing Auckland for the long weekend. I'd been lucky enough to find a motel room after a last-minute cancellation, so had decided to travel up for Waitangi Day. It would be an opportunity to renew acquaintances as well as to explore the location of one of *Ngātokimatawhaorua*'s most infamous episodes. For a couple of weeks prior to the trip north, my thoughts had been fixated on an incident that had occurred 20 years before, on New Year's Eve 1999. Undermanned and caught by strong winds, the waka had been dashed against rocks while attempting to leave Wairoa Bay, a few minutes' drive to the north of the Treaty Grounds. Television footage of the aftermath made for unsettling viewing.

It was unquestionably the darkest day in the storied history of the waka, and I had hesitated to bring up the incident in several interviews with crew members. But I had eventually come to terms with the fact that it was part of the canoe's history and could not be ignored, even if discussing it might make people feel uncomfortable. Before leaving home, I reread the newspaper reports: they all mentioned the atrocious weather, the shortage of adult paddlers on the waka and the resulting hyperthermia among a handful of the crew.

In the end I decided the best option was to see if I could get a few senior kaihoe together to talk about the day. But before I did that, I wanted to head over to Wairoa Bay to look over the landscape for myself. What little I knew about the grounding came from the mainstream media, and I felt I owed it to anyone who agreed to speak to me to have at least visited the place.

I drove up past the Treaty Grounds, past a few greens belonging to the Waitangi Golf Club, then pulled over into the lookout carpark near the top of the hill. I got out of my car and looked north, to where a sizeable bite had been taken out of the coastline. Wairoa Bay stretched out below me.

The most likely location for the grounding, I reasoned, was somewhere near the end of the headland I was parked on. That's where the waka would have turned south as it headed back to Hobson Beach. I considered trying to walk down there but the route looked distinctly unappealing. The foreshore was obscured by what looked like a wide strip of mangroves and thick scrub. I decided instead to take a sweeping video of the bay so I could ask if anyone at Tent City, where *Ngātokimatawhaorua*'s crew ate and slept, could point out where the incident had occurred.

When I had finished filming, I took a minute to soak in the view. Yachts and motorboats were out in force, and a single kayak was making slow progress on the far side of Wairoa Bay. Undoubtedly families with children were splashing in the warm afternoon water all along the coast — it was a summer holiday destination for thousands. There were also dozens of small islands in view, and somewhere in the distance, out beyond the end of the peninsula where the township of Russell had been built, was an island I had once visited. A haze made it difficult for me to see where one island ended and the next started, but I knew that Moturua Island was not too far distant. I had been there with a group of archaeologists, and accompanying us had been Ngāti Kuta kaumātua Matu Clendon, who had grown up on the island.

We had arrived at Mangahāwea Bay on the west side of the island by water taxi, having motored past Rangiātea (a well-known island name across Polynesia) and Motuoi, before making our way up the sandy beach. A ring of hills looked down on the grassy flat where we assembled. After a karakia from our kaumātua to clear our presence on the island, archaeologist James Robinson stepped forward. He was the archetypal tall, lean, floppy-hat-wearing professor, and wore his long-sleeved shirt buttoned to the wrists. We, as it turned out, were his clueless but eager students. When he began to talk we moved in close, forming a tight semicircle in front of him, and listened intently as he spoke. His inclusive nature quickly made us feel we were all part of what he was describing.

He told us that he had conducted four digs on the island since 1981 and been part of teams that had unearthed some extraordinary taonga in the fertile soil. There was evidence of hāngī pits, and gardens that once grew kūmara, taro and yam, and they had found tools made from volcanic glass and shell, as well as a number of fishhooks made from moa and seal bone. But one find was especially important — a fishing lure made in a distinctly Polynesian style from a native New Zealand shell species. It had, Robinson said, undoubtedly been fashioned here in Aotearoa by very early arrivals. Moturua Island was an exciting portal into the past, and one that readily captured our imaginations.

On the boat ride back to Russell, Robinson told us that carbon dating suggested the site was first inhabited about 1300CE, a date that is supported by the discovery of Cook Strait limpet shells (*Cellana denticulata*) in some middens on the island. Along with moa bones, Robinson called the limpet shell an early settlement marker, as both species had been eaten to extinction in this location early on in the period of human settlement.[1]

I arrived at Tent City in the early afternoon and went looking for Marty Bercic. We'd spoken briefly about the waka grounding years earlier and I hoped he could help me identify the exact location. I was nervous. No one really likes to be reminded just how close they had once come to disaster, but that was exactly what I was about to do. After introductory pleasantries I handed him my phone with the video footage of Wairoa Bay. I asked him if it showed the place where *Ngātokimatawhaorua* had gone aground. He told me it didn't, but that he was willing to take me to a spot from which I would be able to see it. It was more than I had hoped for.

The worst of the sun's heat had already passed when Bercic and I jumped into his car. Our route took us up into the hills far behind Waitangi, and along an unsealed back road that twisted and turned at every opportunity. As we neared the coastline Pēwhairangi began to reveal itself to us. From high above the harbour the water was mesmerising in its myriad blues, and the occasional white triangle of sail in its midst seemed to shimmer like a distant star. A border of vibrant green clung to the harbour's edges. It was stunning.

As the car rounded another corner, I seized the moment and asked Bercic why he thought the waka had grounded. He hesitated for a moment, then said the reason was basically twofold: they were unfamiliar with the conditions in the bay and the waka was grossly underpowered. In my mind I added that it wouldn't have helped that it was unseasonably cold and wet on the day in question, with a howling easterly pummelling the coastline.

I felt for Bercic. He had been a senior member of the crew on the day of the grounding, but what transpired was none of his making. All the same, he seemed to be carrying the weight of the incident on his broad shoulders, and whenever we talked about it a sadness entered his eyes.

We left the main road and turned down a lane that dropped towards the foreshore. When we reached the bottom of the hill Bercic slowed and took a sharp right into the Wairoa Bay Recreation Area. This was where the kaihoe had camped in late 1999.

It was easy to see why the spot appealed. The reserve lay directly behind the beach and was big enough to accommodate several large

Looking anything but dangerous, Wairoa Bay was the scene of *Ngātokimatawhaorua*'s worst day. The Wairoa Bay Recreation Area, where the kaihoe set up camp, is mid-frame on the left, hidden by trees; the waka went aground after rounding the headland to the right. AERIAL VISION

marquees, with easy road access for support vehicles. A hill covered in mature trees sheltered the reserve from both southerlies and westerlies, and the foreshore itself was lined with a row of trees that formed a decent enough windbreak from all but the worst easterlies. We exited the car and wandered down to the beach.

The bay was semicircular, with the opening facing east, towards the Pacific Ocean. The beach consisted mainly of coarse sand, pebbles and stones, and the water was clear and shallow. It was high tide when we arrived, and 30 or so metres out, running more or less parallel to the beach, a collection of dark jagged rocks pierced the water's surface. A little further past them the blue of the inner bay abruptly turned darker, signalling deep water. Off to our right lay the deep channel where *Ngātokimatawhaorua* had been anchored between excursions.

When I turned to Bercic, he was looking out across the water towards a low headland that reached out from the southern end of the bay. I followed his gaze to where brown grass merged with thick bush and then the darker green of the mangroves I'd spied from the lookout. He pointed to where barely visible whitecaps were breaking over a submerged rocky shelf that jutted out from the end of the headland. That, he said quietly, was where it happened.

In normal circumstances it should have been an easy paddle from Wairoa Bay around to Hobson Beach. There was a short leg of about 500 metres from the beach to the end of the headland, and then, turning south, a couple of kilometres of easy paddling past the golf course before the route skirted the rocks below the Treaty Grounds. Instead, undermanned and understrength, the crew struggled from the outset.

Standing in the warmth of the afternoon sun I asked Bercic to describe what had happened. This time there was no hesitation.

> The wind was strong, and we had to hug the headland to
> even make it out of the bay. I knew we were in trouble when
> we came around the point. The wind caught us straight away

and started to drive us sideways. We had gone out with too
few paddlers for the conditions and most of the crew were
teenagers. We didn't have enough weight in the waka or
enough manpower.[2]

Bercic described the chaos on board when the waka went aground and then rolled on its side. Seats that normally sat snugly but unfastened on cleats, as well as recently introduced footrests, were sent surging through the waka as the ocean swell began to fill the vessel with freezing water. Anything loose became a missile, including dozens of hoe let go by numb hands. It was a miracle that no one had been badly injured.

Soon after Bercic had finished describing the scene, he turned and began to make his way back to the car. I paused only long enough to grab a couple of hurried photos and then followed him back along the path. It was hard to get a handle on his emotions as we drove back to Tent City. He had once told me that the night following the grounding was one of the worst of his life, as he tossed and turned in his car waiting for first light. Left to the mercy of Tāwhiri-mātea, he had no idea whether the waka would survive the night.

Conscious not to push Bercic for more information than he was willing to divulge freely, I sought out others who had been involved with the grounding. Robin 'Rabbit' Moore, a senior crew member, and Hoani Tuoro, who had been a kaiurungi on the day, both agreed to talk to me.

Moore was a 27-year waka veteran. Pākehā by birth, he was introduced to the waka whānau after driving his army truck north to help Wiremu Wiremu transport the marquees and tents needed over several Waitangi weekends, and he loved being involved. Supremely fit during his service years, he gained his nickname for his athletic prowess, particularly long-distance running. By 1999 he was the kaituki, his role to stand just behind the tauihu, lifting and then dropping his paddle to set the timing for the kaihoe.

Moore's Kiwi accent rang out clearly when I spoke to him over the phone at his Brisbane home. 'A lot of activities were cancelled that New Year's Eve because of the weather,' he told me, 'so when word came back that we were still going out, a few of us older experienced crew were quite surprised.'

As he stood peering out across the bay through sheets of rain, Moore became increasingly uneasy. The wind was being whipped up by a storm out in the Pacific, and the conditions on shore were unpleasant enough. What, he asked himself, would it be like out in the bay? 'I was timekeeper on that day,' Moore continued,

> and I had the feeling before I even got on to the waka that it was going to be a struggle, because the wind and swell were blowing straight in on us, and when we went out, it was probably in the worst of it. It was cold, it was blustery, it was raining — squally rain with near gale-force winds. I couldn't even stand up on my little platform at the front because of the wind. It was unsafe. We were probably looking at 60–70 km/h gusts or something like that.[3]

As the waka inched away from its anchorage, the crew struggled to turn the bow into the wind. Moore recalled that te ihu (the front section of the waka) was not well manned, and neither was te kei (the back section), and that te waenga, the central section, often referred to as the engine room, was filled with kids and teenagers. The problem, he explained, had been that a significant number of experienced kaihoe were busy preparing to paddle waka at other locations, or to perform in kapa haka groups for the millennium celebrations. Without the weight of a full crew the waka sat considerably higher in the water than usual, and that meant there was a larger than normal surface area for the wind to push against. Even as they tried to leave their anchorage, the waka was being shunted sideways. It wasn't until they made it into a pocket of cover near the southern shore of the bay that they were able to make any appreciable headway.

No one could have been comfortable on the waka. The rain assaulted their faces as the salt water, flicked up by the paddles, dripped down their foreheads and into their eyes. Moore was luckier than most, having his back to the weather once they'd managed to turn the waka.

At about 4 p.m., just as they were rounding the headland to turn south, the waka was caught broadside to the howling wind. When the kaihautū needed to call on a strong and experienced crew to power the waka to safety, there weren't enough mature men on board to meet the challenge. As Moore witnessed first-hand from his position just behind the tauihu, the ring-ins, largely untrained and untested, were barely dipping their paddles into the ocean.

Concern turned to alarm as the waka was blown closer and closer to the shore. Every time the kaihoe lifted their paddles out of the water to get into position for their next stroke, any forward momentum was lost. 'At one point I looked around and there was only about a foot and a half of water [under us]. I could see that we were going to hit the reef,' said Moore.

At the critical moment, Moore continued, just as *Ngātokimatawhaorua* looked set to hit the reef, he threw the forward anchor out into deep water. 'I analysed the situation and knew that we were going to be in dire straits if I didn't do something quickly, so I made the decision to pick up the anchor and I threw it out.' Had he not done so, it's likely the waka would have been dashed onto the rocks side on, sustaining damage along its entire length.

'I had to make a choice and I had only a split second. Wiremu had his head turned away to te kei at the time, so if I had waited until I could get his attention it would have been too late.'

At the very moment Moore heaved the anchor into the ocean the crew felt a sickening shudder make its way along the hull. *Ngātokimatawhaorua* had hit the reef. More drama was to follow. With the ihu anchor now holding the front of the waka in place, the taurapa end was pushed across the reef and up onto the rocks. Sitting partially out of the water, the waka began to pitch from side to side and fill with ice-cold seawater. Moore, as one of the old hands on board, leapt into action.

> For me it was about keeping the younger ones from panicking. That was the key element, because they were starting to feel very uncomfortable. Hyperthermia was fast approaching because it was a very, very cold day. I know I was cold to the bone, so I know what the kids were like.

Somehow in the chaos, everyone made it to shore. 'Even though it was mostly shallow,' Moore said, 'there were some deep parts, so the bigger guys back in te kei section carried the kids over to the shore, and we all helped to guide the teenagers — hold their hands so to speak.'

By the time the first kaihoe had made it to shore, frantic whānau and supporters were already trying to get down to them from their vantage point on the road above. When they realised that the route to the waka was blocked by an impenetrable thicket of vegetation, they made the decision to call in a rescue helicopter.

Hoani Tuoro was among those who were air-lifted to safety that afternoon. Now a thick-set man in his fifties with a penchant for wearing a black leather vest over T-shirts and for keeping his greying hair in a top knot, we met at a café near his Tikipunga, Whangārei, home to discuss the day.

An experienced kaihoe at the time of the grounding, Tuoro had

Low tide, the morning after the grounding, shows the bed of rocks that *Ngātokimatawhaorua* floundered on. Remarkably the only damage was some bruising to the hull. NZME/NEW ZEALAND HERALD

first climbed into a waka when he joined the crew of the Ngāti Whātua waka taua, *Māhuhu ki te Rangi*, in early 1990, before transferring to *Ngātokimatawhaorua* two years later. Most of his memories from the day mirror Moore's, but he was able to add that they had been short of paddlers when they launched *Ngātokimatawhaorua* from Hobson Beach a few days earlier. 'Even when we paddled up to Wairoa Bay from the Treaty Grounds we had to ask tourists if they wanted to paddle with us. Lots of our kaihoe were away, so we were really short-handed.'[4] The number of available kaihoe hadn't improved by New Year's Eve, and Tuoro had also been unsure whether they should have launched.

When he had finished describing what he remembered of the day for me, he turned to the media attention that the incident attracted. His opinion was that too much had been made of the handful of crew members who had required medical attention. Tuoro explained that the injured were all senior crew who had stayed on board to ensure that the rest of the crew got off safely, and that was why they needed treatment. What no one commented on at the time, he pointed out, was that their emergency training had worked: despite the potential danger, everyone got off the waka safely and made it to land.

He had a valid point, and in fact it's questionable whether the incident would have made quite the headlines it did had the TV cameras not been in situ to film the voyage. When I looked up from taking notes, Tuoro was staring into the middle distance with a downcast expression. It was clear that he felt there had been more than a hint of Māori-bashing going on.

Another participant who was able to shed some light on the aftermath of the incident was Ned Peita. He had been part of the team that helped refloat *Ngātokimatawhaorua* the morning after. He had also been at Wairoa Bay early on New Year's Eve and was surprised to learn later that the waka had been launched. Several other experienced kaihoe had also left Wairoa Bay when he departed that morning, convinced the waka would remain anchored for the day. He was extremely upset when he heard the news that *Ngātokimatawhaorua* had been launched and then gone aground.

The storm had passed by the time Peita arrived at the scene the next morning. The tide was out and *Ngātokimatawhaorua* was sitting on the rocks, held in place by the anchors. He surveyed the scene and then drove to the Treaty Grounds, where he arranged for groundsman Ross Perrin to truck over as many large plastic drums as he could find, and several lengths of rope to help with the recovery operation.

> We tied four drums to the front of the waka, four where the waka was wedged on the rocks, four in front of a big rock, two behind the big rock, and two at the stern. We tied them all nice and tight so they were just sitting under the hull, maybe two feet apart. Then we waited for the tide to lift the waka. First the front started to float a bit, then the middle lifted. By then the coast guard had arrived and after another 10 minutes the tide was high enough for us to have it towed off the rocks and back down to Hobson Beach.[5]

It had been a distressing incident for everyone involved, and a wake-up call for the wider waka community. The Year of the Waka, nearly a decade earlier, had marked the beginning of a boom period for waka culture in Aotearoa, and now with numerous waka on the oceans, rivers and lakes, iwi found themselves responsible for the wellbeing of hundreds, if not thousands, of kaihoe.

If there was one positive outcome from the grounding, it was the fast-tracking of a much-needed review of waka safety protocols. The Ngā

212 NGĀTOKIMATAWHAORUA

Waka Federation moved quickly to take the lead, calling for a national hui on water safety to be held at Tuteao Marae, Te Teko, on 14 January 2000. Kaumātua and politicians were invited to attend, as were representatives of the Maritime Safety Authority, which led the government response.

The outcome was a set of robust guidelines for the operation of all types of traditionally designed waka. Included in the document were outlines of the roles and responsibilities for training requirements, operational and emergency procedures, and equipment, design and construction.[6] Among the long list of conditions introduced for *Ngātokimatawhaorua* was the need for a minimum of 60 mature paddlers to be on the waka when it is taken out, at least three nominated bailers, at least six flotation tubes, and for spare life jackets to be carried on a dedicated support vessel.

Ngātokimatawhaorua had survived the night and been returned to its shelter more or less intact, but there were still questions to be asked. First and foremost, given the conditions, what possible motive could the leadership group have had for giving the order to take the waka out? The storm brewing out in the Pacific Ocean was funnelling straight into the Bay of Islands from the east and directly into the belly of Wairoa Bay. Rain was falling near-horizontally, the swell was building, and the winds were gusting dangerously. By mid-afternoon, as the understrength crew were preparing to launch, the storm was approaching its peak.

There is a suggestion that there was an agreement in place with one of the television networks, which wanted to lead its coverage of the millennium celebrations with live footage of *Ngātokimatawhaorua* in action. Whether it was a desire to see their waka feature on national television that swayed what were usually more cautious heads remains unknown. Whatever the reason, the decision had lasting consequences.

11

Tent City

ANOTHER YEAR, another trip north. Not that I was complaining. Waitangi is a magical destination that delivers year after year — it's just that the drive from Auckland can get a little stale after a while: Warkworth, Wellsford, Te Hana — tick. Up the winding Brynderwyns, bisect Whangārei, escape past Hikurangi — check. Arrive at Kawakawa, then decide whether you're going to turn left and drive through Moerewa and Pakaraka, or go straight and pass through Ōpua and Paihia — check/tick. Either way, you reach Waitangi 30–40 minutes later.

I arrived at Tent City on a Thursday afternoon, two sleeps before Waitangi Day. The view from the road approaching Bledisloe Domain showed the extent of the camp. Four large white marquees set aside for kaihoe, and a fifth, larger marquee that did duty as both the whare kai and a place to welcome visitors. A sixth marquee, much smaller than the others, stood 30 metres away, to shelter manuhiri waiting to be welcomed. A portable shower block and some portable toilets stood in one corner, as did a pair of shipping containers filled with mattresses and other necessities. Behind the single-storey clubrooms were two walk-in chillers, brought in for the week to store fresh meat and vegetables. To complete the picture, several dozen family-sized tents and caravans were dotted along two sides of the domain. Tent City was aptly named.

Driving across the field, I spied a small gap in the tent line that looked like a suitable place to pitch the pup tent I'd borrowed. It was in the corner of the reserve and far enough away from the hustle and bustle of the marquees to allow me to hope for a good night's sleep. It also featured a natural windbreak — kānuka, tarata and other trees formed a barrier from any northerly or easterly winds. My car would play a similar role against any breeze coming in from the west.

Having secured my campsite, I went looking for my host. I had rung Joe Conrad to ask if I could stay here, with the kaihoe, soon after I visited his brother Stan, and he had graciously agreed. I found him sitting at a table on the veranda of the clubrooms talking with a group of kaumātua. As it happened, I knew most of them. They were men who had been around waka most of their lives, and in time I would lean on each of them as I tried to piece together the history of *Ngātokimatawhaorua*. At one end of the table Joe and Stan Conrad were talking with Marty Bercic. I also recognised Robert Gable, who had been involved with waka in one role or another for decades, and Tamahou Temara from Toi Māori. I gave my regards, then left them to it. I had arrived as they were planning for the imminent arrival of the prime minister, Jacinda Ardern. She had become a regular visitor to Tent City over the past few years.

When Ardern arrived late in the afternoon with her entourage of Māori MPs and her security detail, she was greeted by a thunderous haka before being called into the largest marquee by a pair of kaikaranga. When she stood to speak she began with a short mihi and then continued her speech in English. Visiting Tent City, she said, was one of her favourite parts of Waitangi Day when in the north — she enjoyed being away from the politics that dominated elsewhere on the day. Then she issued a challenge. The government was investing in a new education syllabus, and an important part of it would be based on waka culture. The history and relevance of waka — from the migration canoes up to today's waka — was going to be taught in schools, and she wanted those with the knowledge to contribute to the curriculum. It was an overdue announcement and one that received enthusiastic applause.

Listening, I wondered what Te Puea would have thought if she were here. Surely she would have shed tears of joy to hear a prime minister announce to the kaihoe of *Ngātokimatawhaorua* that the history of waka would be taught in the nation's schools.

The prime minister's visit was only a short reprieve for the dozens of kaihoe in attendance. Training filled their days, on shore and on the water, and they were soon being put through their paces to the hypnotic refrain of the kaituki's call: tōkihi, tōkihi — tōkihi, tōkihi. As much as it was same again, they were all taking it seriously. No one wanted to travel to Waitangi and miss out on a seat in the waka.

I watched on from a comfortable distance as sweat began to stain the earth beneath the feet of the kaihoe. Mostly energetic teenagers and twenty-somethings, they had the energy to carry on long after others might have wilted. A handful of water bottles lay on the ground alongside them, ready to be drained during a break. Young boys, bare-chested and wiry, stood to the side, imitating their seniors.

Waimirirangi Conrad's all-female crew were also there, sharpening their reactions to her orders and perfecting their paddling technique. They were the only women I would see on a waka this year.[1]

Around the corner of a marquee, detached from the main group of kaihoe, a number of first-time paddlers were being put through their paces. Lined up in columns, eyes focused forward, they were being subjected to a training regime that seemed designed to get them up to speed in a hurry. An experienced kaihoe was drilling them in a never-ending cycle of the commands they would need to respond to when they got on a waka. As the minutes ticked by their reactions seemed to tighten and there were fewer and fewer hoe lagging as they moved from one position to the next. It looked like tiring work and I was glad to be watching from the margins.

After a few minutes observing them, I walked over to a pile of hoe and picked one up. As I had suspected, it was nowhere near as fancy as one you might find for sale in a tourist shop — there was none of the fine surface carving you often see embellishing them. Instead, the plain wood had been finished with a thick layer of paint, and the edge of the blade had been sheared off at some point. All the same, it was comfortable in the hand and felt well balanced.

Dinner, an hour or so later, was a brief opportunity for the kaihoe to re-fuel tiring bodies and soothe parched throats. Plates full to overflowing with boil-up, mince on toast and potatoes were quickly emptied, and 25 minutes after sitting down the kaihoe were back practising. There was no room for the uncommitted here.

It was a scene that could have been witnessed any February since 1974, albeit not always here. In the early days kaihoe stayed and trained at Te Tii Marae, and it wasn't until a pair of marquees were donated to them that they moved out and set up in an adjacent field. Tent City grew from there, becoming an institution by the mid-1980s, when Wiremu Wiremu brought in the army to help with the logistics. A further move took Tent City to the campground on nearby Tahuna Road (now the Waitangi Holiday Park) for a few years, before a short, ill-fated stint at Wairoa Bay. The camp then returned to Tahuna Road, before finally moving here to Bledisloe Domain.

Waitangi week hasn't always been solely dedicated to waka. In the early days, one keenly anticipated event for the kaihoe was a version of the popular television game show series *Top Town*. The day's competition included hotly contested waka races between sections of *Ngātokimatawhaorua*'s crew (competed in two smaller waka), a

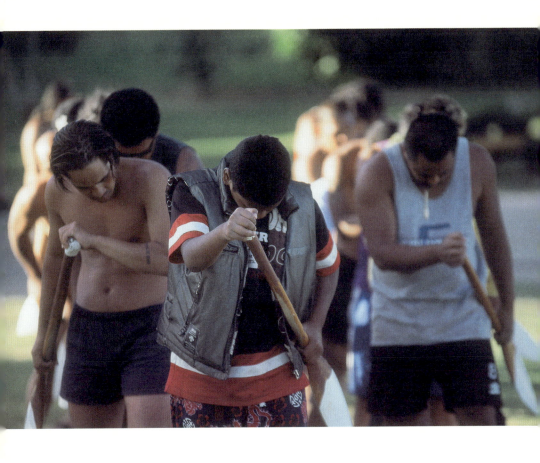

Hours of in-camp training, both in the waka and on land, fill the days of kaihoe, who hone their responses to the calls of their kaihautū. JEFF EVANS

wood-chopping competition, touch rugby and cricket matches. There was also a hotly contested tug-of-war competition between teams from Affco Moerewa, several northern forestry depots (including Te Aupōuri, Te Kao, Omahuta, Puketi and Waitangi) and three teams from *Ngātokimatawhaorua*.

The location of Tent City may have changed frequently over the years, but the value of an experienced head cook who could prepare a meal suitable for hungry paddlers has remained a constant. The current cook, Bess Conrad, has been in the role a decade. Her mother, Kerewai, had been a driving force in the kitchen on Waitangi Day in the 1970s. Bess's shock of grey hair was a beacon visible from a distance and when I found her she was taking a rare break on the veranda, teatowel scrunched in one hand, cup in the other. She chatted with me between sips of milky tea. I started by asking her where she had learnt to cook for such large numbers. She told me she started her apprenticeship at the apron strings of her mother and that from an early age she and her siblings were recruited to help peel the potatoes, kūmara and carrots for weddings and other big events at her home marae.

It was obvious that Bess was a savvy operator. She had to be, given the amount of food that needed to be prepared. On a busy day the camp would devour up to 100 loaves of bread and 20 two-litre bottles of milk. Then there were vegetables by the box-load, bowls of fruit and boxes of cereal, as well as all the other ingredients needed for a varied menu. On top of all that, Bess also oversaw a weekly meat order of one beef and five mutton.

When I asked her if she had any secrets to share about running a kitchen this size, she told me the main thing was to try to get on with everyone. This, she confessed with a smile, ensured there would be willing helpers when she needed them. After another sip of tea, she told me she also tried to instil confidence in her helpers.

> When someone asks how I want something done, say they are making egg sandwiches, I ask them how they do it at home, and then tell them they can make them exactly the same way here. It really doesn't matter if it's not the same way I would do it, as long as it tastes okay.[2]

When I retired to my tent later that evening, I pondered the community that was Tent City. From what I could gather, there were several waka crews in camp this year, and the vessels were all, as far as I could tell, from the north. Everyone had a role — as kaumātua, kuia, ringawera, kaihautū or kaihoe — and everyone was respected for their place within the group. It was a community held together by a common purpose and, in many cases, by a shared whakapapa.

It was still dark when I got up the next morning, woken by the raspy vocal attack of an all-too-close rooster. A heavy fog had rolled in overnight, enveloping everything with an insidious dampness, and the chill air seemed to be pulling my throat tight from within. By the time I'd made my way over to the kitchen and loosened it with a cup of tea, Tent City was beginning to stir.

Once the fog had burnt off we found ourselves witness to another glorious summer's day. The only downside was the oppressive heat that accompanied a cloudless day here in the north. With the cooling late-afternoon breeze hours away, I decided against heading down to the Treaty Grounds and instead arranged to chat with Marty Bercic and Stan Conrad. I was especially interested to hear about *Ngātokimatawhaorua* from these two experienced kaihoe. I also wanted to get a description of the paddling technique used to propel the multi-tonne waka.

We found a quiet corner in the largest of the marquees, smoothed down the paper tablecloth covering our table and settled in. Having made themselves comfortable, Bercic and Conrad explained to me that the crew is split into three sections: te ihu at the front, te waenga in the middle, and te kei at the rear, and that with a full crew the sections are manned by 10, 58, and 12 kaihoe, respectively. Then there are the specialist roles. The kaihautū, the captain, is responsible for the welfare of the whole crew and the waka itself, and he often doubles as the section commander of te waenga section. Then there are two other section commanders, the kaiurungi, the kaituki or timekeeper (because of its length *Ngātokimatawhaorua* sometimes has a second timekeeper positioned mid-waka), and finally three kaihoe assigned as bailers.

I then asked about the seating. I had heard about the raupō flooring used in 1940 and again in 1974, but I had no idea when the current seating arrangement — wooden 4 × 2s that fitted crossways below, and just in front of, each taumanu — had been first used. Conrad explained:

> They were introduced in 1983 for Lady Di's visit. Before that we had tried all sorts of things to see what worked. We tried sitting on the taumanu at one stage, but the centre of gravity was too high so that didn't work, and we even experimented with sitting on the inside paewai.[3]

He was referring to the battens that run the length of the waka, inside and outside, covering the join between the hull and the rauawa. I couldn't quite imagine it — paewai are typically only about 7–8 centimetres thick. When I asked him how it was sitting on one, tight against the inside of the hull, Conrad said it had been extremely uncomfortable, and that nearly everyone had to swap from side to side in the waka to ease cramping gluteal muscles.

Getting the seating right had clearly been a case of trial and error, and I wondered if it had been the same for the paddling technique. In my youth I paddled and raced waka-ama — sleek six-person canoes with an outrigger — and was curious whether there was any similarity in the strokes. The answer was yes, but those similarities were mostly superficial. The hectic action of a race saw the paddlers of a waka-ama stretch further forward and pull their paddles through the water appreciably faster.

Having not paddled on the waka myself, I sought some video footage of *Ngātokimatawhaorua* so I could study the kaihoe's paddling technique. I was quickly captivated — there was something mesmerising about the repetition of their stroke. The lower hand, the one holding the hoe nearer to the blade (and the water), seemed to move in a smooth, almost circular motion, and maybe it was the efficiency of that movement, combined with the timing call, that drew me in. The other hand (the one closer to the centre of the waka) was placed at the top of the long handle — sometimes holding the top of the shaft, sometimes wrapped over the end.

When the crew were preparing to paddle they held their hoe horizontally above their lap, the blade end pointing out from the waka. On the kaihautū's command they moved as one, pushing the hand closest to the blade forward and slightly out from the side of the waka while tilting the tip of their hoe into the water. The top hand then pushed the blade down until all but the top few centimetres of the blade was submerged. As the top hand was pushing down, the lower hand was pulling the hoe back along the side of the hull. Then, just as the blade passed the hip of the kaihoe, it was lifted out of the water and pushed forward for the next stroke. Each stroke, necessarily broken down into a series of movements to describe it here, was completed in what appeared to be a near effortless cycle. Watching the film, I had begun to mimic the call of the kaihautū to try to internalise the timing. It was one stroke for every two calls of 'tōkihi'.

Bercic confirmed that the top hand pushed the hoe down into the water while the bottom hand was where your power came from, as it dragged the hoe back. He imitated the stroke from his chair and, to

Willing hands hoist a young kaihoe skyward so he can attach the feather puhi to the taurapa of *Ngātokimatawhaorua*. JEFF EVANS

ensure I got the entire picture, began to chant the timing call as he paddled his imaginary waka. When he was sure that I understood the gist of his lesson, Bercic leant forward, rested his forearms on the table, and explained that the crew got up to speed in the first seven or eight strokes, and then focused on keeping up the momentum. There were a number of other strokes for the kaihoe to master, he added, mostly for turning the waka one way or the other, or for stopping it quickly.

As Bercic's tutorial finished, Conrad joined the conversation. His eyes focused in on me, as if to ensure that I took in everything he was about to tell me. He was, I was about to find out, not at all happy with the amount of noise being made by kaihoe while on the water these days.

> We were taught never to knock our hoe on the waka. We
> never used to go Tōkihi, clunk! Tōkihi, clunk! Instead, we
> let our bottom hand hit the rauawa. We're on a waka taua
> — they're meant to be stealthy. You don't come up a river or
> into a harbour making a hua of a racket!

Before I could ask him what he thought had prompted the change to allow excessive noise on the waka, Conrad lifted his hand and motioned towards the practising kaihoe. He told me to listen to the tempo of the commands issued by the kaihautū. Even to my uneducated ears there was a definite rhythm to their calls. They were spot on, he said, before commenting that some other kaihautū sometimes vary the rhythm of the commands they gave. He had mentioned this frustration in an earlier interview, saying that there was a good reason commands were called with a specific rhythm, and nothing should be left to the whim of the kaihautū on the day.

Bercic, who began his waka career as a kaihoe in 1979 and graduated to section commander alongside Stan Conrad and Felix Davis in 1983, jumped in to explain that the reason they give commands in a certain rhythm is that the delivery of these initial instructions helps to set the timing for the paddlers. He began to tap out the rhythm with his forefinger while he recited the call used to get the attention of the kaihoe prior to paddling. (The first bold letter in the lines below signals the initial movement of a stroke, the second the hesitation before the next stroke commences.)

Te ihu,	kia rite,
Waenga,	kia rite,
Te kei,	kia rite,
Taringa	whakarongo,
Tena	whakataua,
Anana	koia hoki,
Rite,	kia rite,
Tōkihi,	tokihi

Conrad again:

> You have some kaihautū who speed the call up and run words together: Te ihukiarite, or waengakiarite. How the hell are you supposed to get your timing off that? It is all out of whack, eh. We're the guardians of the knowledge. It's not ours. This knowledge and this tikanga and these skills, they've come down from those fellas who are not here today. They come down from our tūpuna, and that is what we tell these young fellas. 'This is what it is.'
>
> The knowledge and the kaupapa have to carry on. You know, if they don't think like that, then I think they are on the wrong waka. They are on the wrong kaupapa if they are coming with the frame of mind of doing what they want to do. The main thing here is the waka, not the self.[4]

His tone was almost schoolmaster-ish with either frustration or perhaps slight anger. It was hard to tell, given his underlying calm demeanour.

As if to emphasise the importance of doing things correctly, Conrad then spoke about the wairua of the waka.

> I tell the young kaihoe coming through that a lot of old fellas have been on this waka. They've been and gone and they've left a good wairua. You can feel it. You feel it when you get on board. You feel the people who have been on it before. The spirit is there, and that is what makes that waka what it is today. Some other waka that are parked up, they've got no wairua in them anymore. They are just sitting there, and it's because they have been treated wrong . . . If you treat the waka wrong the wairua goes, and you can't get it back.
>
> So I tell the young guys that if they're coming on here to look good, then it's not for them. You come here to give the mana to *Ngātoki*, not to yourself. You earn that later. That's what I was taught. You keep giving. I'm glad to just sit there and bail the waka, or to stand on shore and throw the anchor, or catch the waka when it comes in. I'm fine with any of that.

His brother Joe had said something similar on another occasion when I'd asked him what it took to be a good kaihautū. He told me that when you captain *Ngātokimatawhaorua*, you don't do it to look good, you do it so the waka looks good.

> When you are given the honour to look after a national treasure you have a responsibility to all those who went before and all the ones who are following on. When I stand on it, I am standing on thousands of years of history.[5]

Kaihautū, Joe continued, had a responsibility to teach their crews where they came from and how they were connected to the waka. 'We know that [the ancestral migration waka] *Ngātokimatawhaorua* came to this land with karakia, with whakapapa and with all the tapu stuff;

so I need to remind the boys who paddle *Ngātokimatawhaorua* about this history.'

Not long after Conrad and Bercic left the tent I met the first of a couple of long-time crew who I was fortunate to be introduced to. Joe Everitt agreed to share some of his memories from the 1970s and '80s. It was a lucky break meeting him: he had the time and inclination to chat, and plenty to tell.

Now in his late seventies, Everitt was wearing a straw cowboy hat and a grey short-sleeved plaid shirt when he sat down opposite me. He rested his bone-handled cane in his lap and smiled. His speech was slow but sure when he began to tell his story. He told me about spending time with Tom Munu at Waitangi in the mid-1970s and learning a bit of the canoe's history from him, and then about how kaihoe Pita Hepi had travelled down to Whangārei to secure some railway track so they could launch *Ngātokimatawhaorua* on bogies rather than roll it over logs. 'We got some young fellas to come and help put the tracks in, and the guy from the railway led them. So we got that all done, and when the bogies arrived the waka was raised on timber jacks, and lowered down onto them, and we were set.'[6]

Next he recalled future MP Dover Samuels wanting to take photos of *Ngātokimatawhaorua* with his underwater camera and asking Everitt to guide the waka above him during its voyage. That was back in 1987, when the waka had been paddled up to Whangaroa. 'I still haven't seen the photos,' he said with a smile.

Then he stopped talking and looked into the distance for a minute before turning to me and asking if I wanted to hear about the time he sat on the waka's tauihu. It wasn't something I had heard mention of, and I nodded to let him know that I did.

Everitt looked away again and shifted in his seat, in that way someone might if they had instantly regretted mentioning something. Although he had a long and distinguished career on the waka, as both a kaituki and a kaiurungi, he conceded that he was perhaps best remembered for straddling the tauihu of *Ngātokimatawhaorua* during a trip from Waitangi to Ōpua.

> It was a rough day and the swell was coming at us from the side. It was really rocking the waka, and the kaituki standing at the front got thrown overboard. Well, the first thing he heard when he surfaced was me calling to the crew to keep paddling. I knew we had to keep moving because the swell was quite dangerous. Anyway, they grabbed hold of him and managed to get him into the waka, and then he made his way back up to the front, sat by me and said, 'Well, you get up there and do the job.' Then I looked at him and said, 'Okay then.' Well, just behind the tauihu there is a tiny platform — about the size of two A4 sheets of paper — that the timer has to stand on. It's small. So I looked at that — and we were still rolling — and I decided that I needed to straddle that tauihu and sit on it if I wasn't going to follow him into the water. Afterwards I got some stick, and some of the people said 'Oh, he thinks he is on a horse!' but they never told me off about it.

It was a role I hadn't really thought a lot about, and it wasn't until I talked to Robin Moore, another long-time kaituki, that I realised just how challenging and important the job is.

> There are usually only about four or five of us standing on the waka, so you have to show that you are a leader. You're standing up the front, keeping time to 80-odd paddlers, so you feel the pressure. If you are busy looking elsewhere

> and not focusing on your job then that's it; you get that
> spider effect of paddles all over the show, and it doesn't
> look good from the shore. For me, I took great pride that my
> coordination was reflected through the rest of the crew. The
> whole time you're balancing with your legs, and timekeeping
> with your upper body — and you are very mindful of the
> balancing, but you still have to show that you have strength.[7]

Soon after I farewelled Everitt, Brian Wiki, a spritely 73-year-old, arrived for a late-afternoon ceremony. He was impeccably turned out in an aubergine-coloured merino jersey over a dress shirt, and pressed grey trousers; his moustache was turned down at the corners. It was yet another fortunate opportunity for me to spend time reminiscing about the waka with one of a diminishing number of older kaihoe.

I asked Wiki if he remembered anything from the training wānanga back in the 1970s, and he told me there were often 200 or more men vying for the 80 seats, so competition for a place was fierce. Looking around as he spoke, he seemed surprised at the number of young paddlers in attendance, telling me that when he started paddling there were no school-aged children to be seen anywhere near the waka. 'And in those days they insisted that we practise our paddling close to the water, not this far from it. Times have changed. It's different now.'[8]

As we were chatting, the call of several kaihautū began to drift up from nearby Haruru Falls. A number of crews had paddled around to the basin to work on their technique and sharpen their timing. The falls were a little way away from the hustle and bustle of Waitangi and afforded some privacy. It was also where *Ngātokimatawhaorua* was taken when they needed to clean it in fresh water and perform the requisite karakia before returning it to its korowai.

After I thanked Wiki for sharing his memories he made his way slowly to the front of the marquee to pay his respects and gaze on the portraits of three kaihoe who had passed away during the previous year. I watched him for a moment, then turned away.

There was no sign of the previous day's fog when the sun rose on Waitangi Day, nor had there been a single squawk from the rooster to wake me. By the time I crawled out of my sleeping bag it was already 6 a. m. — the kaihoe had eaten, washed their dishes and were preparing to head to the Treaty Grounds. I sensed a nervous excitement in the air, something similar to the atmosphere before a sporting match. Groups of kaihoe hurried over to the buses that would carry them to their waka, while I hitched a ride with Bercic. He was driving his car down to Hobson Beach so the kaihoe would have somewhere secure to leave their belongings while they were out on the water.

When we arrived at the beach we could see from the car that the conditions were perfect for taking the waka out: the bay was calm and there was barely any breeze.

But what of *Ngātokimatawhaorua*? It had been confirmed. Its kauri hull wouldn't be tasting salt water this year. Instead, it would be moved out from under the shade of Te Korowai ō Maikuku to sit above the waterline. For a while I had entertained hopes of joining the kaihoe on the great waka — not today, but during one of the training paddles earlier in the week. I wanted to be able to describe what it was like to be on the waka from a first-person perspective, to feel the hoe in my hands as the ocean's spray soaked me, but circumstances derailed my hopes before I could even broach the topic. With the Covid-19 pandemic gaining momentum, there were not enough adult kaihoe here to launch the waka. Instead, I was restricted to watching on as five 15- to 18-metre waka were manhandled down from the grassed foreshore above the

The fleet of waka depart Hobson Beach. On average about half the size of *Ngātokimatawhaorua*, the waka shown here are more easily transported from site to site and don't require as many crew members as the larger vessel. JEFF EVANS

beach and into the tide. As it happened, witnessing these waka on the water was an experience worth travelling for.

As soon as each crew was settled in, their kaihautū issued the command and one by one they departed for deeper water. Watching as they sped from shore, I was momentarily mesmerised by the swirls of bubbles left behind by each hoe stroke — they looked like miniature whirlpools before they dissolved into the blue-grey of the bay. By the time the waka were 100 metres or so offshore the only noise we could hear from them were the commanders' overlapping orders arriving as whispers on the breeze.

In truth the waka made an exceptional sight, and if you could block out the tourists and the pleasure boats at anchor in the bay, it wasn't hard to imagine this scene belonging to a time before the arrival of Pākehā. The illusion was amplified by the presence of the voyaging canoe *Ngāhiraka Mai Tawhiti* sitting at anchor offshore.

We weren't the only spectators to appreciate them. Crowds lined vantage points for as far as I could see along the coast. Even offshore, the waka made for arresting viewing.

I followed the fleet's progress until it was out of focus, and then turned to leave. With no appetite to join the throngs of people heading to the stalls to buy souvenirs and food, I decided to cut the day short and went to look for a shuttle bus back to Tent City. My Waitangi trip was coming to an end.

Had I enjoyed my stay among the kaihoe in Tent City? Most definitely. The organisation within the camp was first rate, as were the facilities provided. Toilets, showers and shelter were available to all, and three square meals each day had been served up to an army of warriors. The atmosphere in camp, as far as I witnessed, was caring and supportive. But what impressed me most was the conduct and commitment of those in attendance. Everyone seemed focused on being part of the waka whānau, and there seemed to be a general sense of honouring the traditions and knowledge of those who had gone before. For some, Tent City and *Ngātokimatawhaorua* continued to provide a much-needed opportunity to reconnect with their tūpuna, especially for those who live in cities and lack that valuable link in their day-to-day lives. For others it seems to be part of an attempt to reclaim a more traditional, healthy lifestyle.

As my bus wound its way back to Bledisloe Domain, I wondered what Te Puea would have made of the last few days. I think she would have been delighted at the number of young kaihoe in attendance, learning the ways of their tūpuna, and thrilled by the number of waka on display. I like to think she would also have been heartened to see so many Pākehā enthralled by the canoes. As she had hoped all those years ago, waka taua had indeed become a symbol to make Māori proud and for Pākehā to admire.

Appendices

1974 CREW LIST AND SUPPORT STAFF OF *NGĀTOKIMATAWHAORUA*

These lists come from a scrapbook in the possession of Joe Conrad. The two crew lists are labelled 'Practice purposes only'.

First list

Christopher Beazley	Alan Karena	Mutu Karena
Rev. M. Marsden	Harry Mane	Conrad Conrad
Brian Wiki	Abe Karauti	Paki Para
Harry Marsh	Clem Marsh	Gilbert Paki
Fred Robson	Selwyn Kaihe	John Mihaka
Joe Mutu	George Rameka	Tim Wiki
Joel Anderson	John Tipene	Hohipere Erueti
Walter Whiu	Jack Thompson	Wati Hetaraka
Charlie Wilson	Jack Crallan	Harry Apetera
Haupeke Piripi	Pae Rangi	Teretiano Henare
Hugh Percell	Paul Kaihe Jnr.	Cameron Pou
Mathew Wihongi	Jim Heemi	Daniel Nopera
Wiki Karena	Maurice Brown	Joseph Marsh
Toi Marsh	Tom Paku	Billy Conrad
Colin Harris	Paehere Brown	Karena Karena
Billy Waa	Jack Nelson	Selwyn Wilson
Bob Howard	Ted Bird	Ranga Peita
Lou Hohaia	Eru Taurua	Paora Mano
Ivan Toia	Te Kii Ashby	Victor Moon
Brownie Bristowe	Renata Tane	Raymond Pomana
Whata Wairua	Tuhiwai Eruera	Cedric Culham
Tuhi Davis	Hector Rakena	Mita Stewart

Tai Rakena
John Whiu
Brian Watts
Graham Alexander
Walter Ngawati
Harding Mutu

Joe George
Ace Hona
Ken Alexander
Maurice Cassidy
John Thompson
Allie Wiki

Edward Stewart
John Beazley
Eddie Pia
Christopher Beazley
Sam Kereopa

Second list

Wiremu Rudolph
Haki Repia
George Edwards
Martin Parata
Peter Hauraki
Simon Tuara
Murray Heta
Tauhia Te Tai
Jacob Te tai
Mervyn Tatana
George Murray
Mita Kemp
Kerry Claridge
Young Wihongi
Patrick Burling
Hira Tua
Don Ngawati
Arapata Wharemate
Bruce Graham
Maru Brown
Bill Davis
William Blair
Eru Henare

Bill Conrad
Joe Bristowe
Hohepa Kauwhata
Mukai Hura
Hau Tipene
Walter Mountain
Sid Rudolph
Hector Rakena
Menehia Tahana
Rua Paul
Peter Hepi
Fred Williams
Toi Hepi
Glass Murray
William Parkinson
Phillip Hakaraia
Bruce Cherrington
Selwyn Whiu
Willy Pou
Neville Rudolph
Ope Heta
Steve Hansie
Monty Martin

Haukaha Tipene
Peter Cherrington
Michael Mackie
Tahu Henare
Percy Beattie
Gabriel Manukau
Dave McClean
David Simon
Dick Motu
George Leefe
Peter Leefe
Harry Mane
Hekenuku Busby
Raymond Parkinson
Hau Tipene
Lance Harris
Rex Gibson
David Davis
Thomas Warmington
Bob Frew
Tiwi Honetana
Ray Heta
Hector Busby Jnr.

Tim Motu
Ian Gregory
Raymond Cooper
Ian Cormack

Herbert Murray
Jack Cherrington
Murray Munroe
Marsh Murray

Walter Busby
Manuel Reihana
Alvin Ryan

Women to support paddlers

Martha Moon
Dicky Bristowe
Agnes Leefe
Kume Gregory
Pia Munroe
Rina Ngaika
Hine Rua
Ann Murray
Nancy Karena
Josephine Rameka
Hoana Rapatini
Hilda Wilson

Kataraina Kauwhata
Viv Watts
Emily Marsh
Rachael Windsor
Margaret Conrad
Fay Silvester
More Matu
Ann Mane
Mei Motu
Georgina Repia
Nana Cassidy
Pauline Davis

Raihia Ngawaka
Roberta Tobin
Mary Brown
Janet Marsh
Ellen Murray
Margaret Puriri
Gladys Karena
Mia Wiki
Janie Te Tai
Hira Murray
Hannah Cherrington

Raupō gatherers, rippers, sponge rubbers

Hohipere Erueti
Conrad Conrad
Ranga Peita
Tuhiwai Eruera
Cedric Culham

Charlie Wilson
Billie Conrad
Ivan Toia
Billie Waa
Walter Whiu

Phillip Hakaraia
Joe Mutu
Harding Mutu
Colin Harris

Waitangi sewing factory

Kaikohe

N. Beazley
Y. Parker
M. Moon

G. Repia
M. Perkins
H. Robson

F. Rameka
C. Wihongi
M. Cooper

Kawakawa

L. Cooper
V. Davis
Phyllis Tureia

Ngāwhā Springs

M. Harris
Jenny Cross
Hine Adlam

Otiria

M. Brown

Ōtaua

R. Rewa
M. Rogers
M. Phillips
W. Tarawa

Moerewa

H. Cherrington
M. Cherrington
L. Harris
M. Kuru

Whangārei

B. Peita

Other names mentioned with no locations given

A. Murray
M. Motu
Nancy Karena
V. Paul
H. Brown
Joy Hohaia

H. Murray
Rongo Pene
Mahera Nathan
M. Paul
Hira Murray
Mereana Perkins

M. Busby
Maia Wiki
Gladys Karena
D. Motu
Rere Rutene

Ringawera (Kitchen staff)

Mere Davis
Mana Peita
Glenda Anderson
Bella Tipene
Budgie Davis
Hotu Kuru
John Davis
Peter Tipene

Bonny Conrad
June Whiu
Margaret Puriri
Rona Nathan
Mathew Davis
Tupi Puriri
Buddy Wiki

Teresa Mutu
Harriet Mutu
Sophie Cook
Shirley Cormack
Paul Kaihe
Puhi Nathan
Charlie Cook

Medical and first aid

Dr Bruce Gregory	Ted Bird	Andrew Moon
Martha Moon		

Kaikaranga

Mate Toia	Susan Tohu	Fanny Rameka
Doris Rameka	Aida Davis	Arihia Taurua
Rewa Moioha	Moengaroa Moon	Kohe Whiu
Kerara Maaka	Atawhia George	Taka Takimoana

Canteen staff

Meremere Paitai	Belle Clarke	Hazel Paul
Mary Toia	Ngamako Brown	Ritihia Brown
Dot Pivac	Mary Tipene	Peggy Winiata
Rita Cherrington	Emily Cherrington	

Some names were, unfortunately, illegible. I apologise for any oversights or omissions from this list.

1987 CREW LIST AND SUPPORT STAFF OF *NGĀTOKIMATAWHAORUA*

Collected and compiled by Karen Williams and Charlene Adams for the thirty-fifth anniversary reunion of the 1987 voyage, held on 4 June 2022.

Kaumātua

Nicky Conrad	Sir James Henare	Te Uru Heta
Tarawau Kira	Winiata Morunga	Pita Paraone
Tom Parore	Tupe Puriri	Simon Snowden
Turo Tepania	Kira Williams	

Kaihautū

Martin Bercic	Hector Busby	Stan Conrad
George Edwards	Joe Everitt	Alan Karena
Wiremu Wiremu		

Kaihoe

Hakopa (Jacob) Adams Snr	Jacob (Jayk) Adams Jnr	Peter Algar
Edward Baker	Shelton Atkinson	Richard Avery
Johan Bosch	Greg Barron	Rodger Borman
Felix Davis	Allan (Bimbo) Bramley	Phillip Bramley
David Greg	Cheyne Foley	Dene Fowler
Wattie Haare	Michael Halliday	Jayjay Haare
Mervyn Hape	Darryl Hape	Herbie Hape
Wikaio Hape	Mita Hape	Tuaru Hape
Rodney Heke	Arthur Harrison	Adrian Heke
Allen Heta	Tim Heke	Morgan Hemi
Kelvin (Kina) Hikuwai	Eru Heta	Charlie Hikuwai
Aceford (Acey) Hona	David Holland	Shane Holland
	Shepherd Hona	Wiremu Howard

Mukai Hura Snr
Martin Kaka
Kevin Langman
Soloman Manuel
Kingi Marsh
Malcolm Masiutama
Robin (Rabbit) Moore
Rod Morey
William (Bill) Nepe
Billy Pawa
Robert Petera
Joe Poata
Hakopa (Jake) Puke
Robert Reynolds
William (Beany) Saies
Allan Smith
Donny Stevenson
Richard Takimoana
Peter Tawhi
Rima Te Awa
Shane Thorley
Thomas Tua
Moana (Munz) Waikato
Robyn Te Kaha
   Whaanga
Arthur Williams
Henare Williams
Willy Williams

Jofe Jenkins
Mohi Kara
Jeremy Lepper
Steve Marr
Te Hura Marsh
James (Jim) McClutchie
Raina More
Phillip (Tata) Morgan
Alister Paul
Ned Peita
Whetu Pihema
Jason Pomana
Robin (Rob) Reed
Taiapo (Bambam) Riwhi
Alex Sanderson
Derek Smith
Marty Stevenson
Robert Takimoana
Harry Te Awa
Willie Te Awa
Steven Toetoe
Hemi Tukaaki
Paddy Walker
Sydney Whaanga
Patariki Wihongi
David Williams
Iwa Williams

Jofe Jopson
Roger Kingi
Arthur Mahanga
Albie Marsh
Pere Marsh
Tyrone Minhinick
Willie More
Scott Murray
Howard Paul
Joe Petera
Peter Pinkham
Rusty Porter
Wairongoa (Magoo) Renata
Tema (Timbo) Rudolph
Toni Shepherd
Wally Smith
Moana Stewart
Gary Tatana
Nick Te Awa
Hamu Te Hame
Mike Townsend
Nathan (Nat) Tuwhangai
Dean Whaanga
Paddy Whiu
Fred Wikaira
Eugene Williams (Toka)
Tony Williams

I apologise for any oversights or omissions from this list.

Glossary

haka (v) to perform a haka; (n) performance of the haka

hāngī earth oven

hapū kinship group, clan, tribe, subtribe

haumi a section of hull added to lengthen a waka

heke rafter in a whare

hiwi hull of a waka

hoe paddle

hongi to press noses in greeting

hōrirerire grey warbler

hui to gather or meet

ihiihi feathered rods projecting from the front of a waka

ihu front of a waka

iwi extended kinship group, tribe, or people

kai food

kaihautū captain of a waka

kaihoe crew, paddler

kaikaranga woman (or women) caller who has the role of making the ceremonial call to visitors onto a marae or other venue

kaimahi worker

kaitiaki guardian

kaituki fugleman, time caller

kaiurungi steersman

kapa haka cultural group performances

karakia prayer

karanga ceremonial call of welcome

karu atua eye/s of god

kaumātua elderly man or woman with status in the community

kaupapa agenda or programme

GLOSSARY 241

kāuta cooking shed or lean-to
kāwanatanga governorship
kiekie thick native vine
kōauau a cross-blown flute
koekoeā long-tailed cuckoo
koikoi a long spear pointed at both ends
kōkako endemic New Zealand wattlebird
korowai cloak
kōwhaiwhai painted scroll ornamentation
kuia elderly woman
kūkupa New Zealand pigeon
kura huna important knowledge
kūtai mussels
mahi work
mana prestige, authority, status, spiritual power, charisma
manaakitanga hospitality, support
manaia stylised figure used in carving
Māori indigenous person of Aotearoa New Zealand
Māoritanga Māori culture, Māori practices and beliefs
marae the open area in front of a wharenui
maunga mountain
mau rākau to wield weapons
mauri the essential quality and vitality of a being or entity
mihi to greet, pay tribute, acknowledge, or thank
miromiro white-breasted North Island tomtit
moko Māori tattoo
muka prepared flax fibre
noa ordinary; free from the restrictions of tapu

paewai batten lashed over the join between the hull and the rauawa

Pākehā person of European descent

patu club, weapon

pitau perforated spiral carving

pīwakawaka fantail

poi dance where a light ball on a string is twirled rhythmically

poupou upright slabs forming the framework of the walls of a
meeting house

pōwhiri formal welcoming ceremony onto a marae

pūhā perennial sow thistle

puhi plume, plumed rods, feather ornaments on a canoe

puhoro traditional kōwhaiwhai pattern, often painted onto the underside of the prow of a waka taua

rākau haka posture dance performance with weapons

rangatira chief

rauawa top boards, attached sides of a canoe above the hull

raupō bulrush

ringawera kitchen hand

rohe region or area

taha tangata human element

taha wairua spiritual element

tāhuhu ridge pole of a meeting house

taiaha two-handed weapon

tangata whenua local people, born on the land

tangi funeral

taonga anything precious

tapu sacred, prohibited, restricted

tārai waka waka builder

tauihu figurehead of a waka

taumanu thwart of a waka

taurapa sternpost of a waka

GLOSSARY 243

te kei stern section of a waka

te reo Māori language

tikanga customary system of values and practices; correct procedure

tī kōuka cabbage tree

tohunga tārai waka master waka builder

tohunga expert or master

toutouwai North Island robin

tukutuku panels, ornamental latticework

tūpuna ancestors

tūrangawaewae a place where one has the right to stand through kinship and whakapapa

upoko head

utu vengeance

waenga middle section of a waka

wāhine women

waiata song

wairua spirit or soul

waka-ama outrigger racing canoe

waka-hourua double-hulled voyaging canoe

waka taua war canoe

wānanga seminar, training conference

whaikōrero formal speech or address

whakapapa genealogy, lineage

whakawhanaungatanga process of establishing relationships

whānau family or extended family group

whare house, building

wharekai dining hall

whare nīkau house or building constructed from the nikau tree

whare waka canoe house

whare wānanga place of higher learning

Notes

Introduction

1. *Auckland Star*, 2 March 1940, 12.

1. Puketi, a forest of giants

1. Michael King, *Te Puea: A Life*, 2nd edition (Auckland: Hodder & Stoughton, 1982), 182.
2. Ibid., 182.
3. Ibid., 189.
4. Frank Acheson, Letter to Waitangi National Trust Board, 12 February 1940: www.facebook.com/Ngatokimatawhaorua
5. Isabel Ollivier, *Extracts from Journals Relating to the Visit to New Zealand in May–July 1772 of the French Ships Mascarin and Marquis de Castries under the Command of M.-J. Marion du Fresne* (Wellington: Alexander Turnbull Library Endowment Trust and Indosuez NZ, 1985), 24.

3. Tradition and ceremony

1. Māori Land Court, *Bay of Islands Minute Book*, vol. 16, 13 October 1937, folio 108.
2. Ibid., folio 108.
3. Ibid., folio 109.
4. Ibid., folio 110.
5. Ibid., folio 110.
6. Ibid., folio 111.
7. Ibid., folio 111.
8. Māori Land Court, *Bay of Islands Minute Book*, vol. 16, 31 January 1938, folio 246.
9. Jim Manley, untitled, undated photograph. Waitangi Museum Archive, Waitangi.
10. Frank Acheson, Letter to Waitangi National Trust Board, 12 February 1940: www.facebook.com/Ngatokimatawhaorua
11. Ibid.
12. Kaata, 'The last Maori war canoes', December 1938, photocopy of newspaper article (source unknown).
13. Ibid.
14. *A Report on the Motion Picture Film.* Photographic Equipment and Material in the Estate of the late Princess Te Puea Herangi. R. G. H. (Jim) Manley, Ngā Taonga Sound & Vision, Deposit 0574, Box 2, Folder 2.
15. A Summary of the Origin of and Proposal for Action on Films of Building, Launching and Voyaging of Ngatokimatawhaorua & Waikato Canoes. R .G. H. (Jim) Manley, Ngā Taonga Sound & Vision, Deposit 0574, Box 2, Folder 2.
16. Peter Calder, 'Mita's troubled waters', *New Zealand Herald*, 21 December 1989, 1.
17. Isabel Ollivier, *Extracts from Journals Relating to the Visit to New Zealand in May–July 1772 of the French Ships Mascarin and Marquis de Castries under the Command of M.-J. Marion du Fresne* (Wellington: Alexander Turnbull Library Endowment Trust and Indosuez NZ, 1985), 165.
18. Elsdon Best, *The Maori Canoe*, 2nd edition (Wellington: Government Printer, 1976), 77.

19. Calder, 'Mita's troubled waters', 1.
20. Frank C. Jones, 'War canoe', *Auckland Star*, 20 December 1937, 5.
21. Ibid.

4. Reviving lost skills

1. *Auckland Star*, 7 August 1937, 8.
2. Michael King, *Te Puea: A biography* (Auckland: Hodder & Stoughton, 1978), 183.
3. 'Kerikeri craft delayed', editorial, *New Zealand Herald*, 16 February 1939, 14.
4. Jeff Evans, *Waka Taua: The Maori war canoe* (Auckland: Reed Publishing, 2000), 28–29.
5. Heke-nuku-mai-ngā-iwi (Hec) Busby, interviewed by author, 31 August 2013.
6. Himiona Kāmira, 'Kupe', *Journal of the Polynesian Society* 66 (1957): 221.
7. Elsdon Best, *The Maori Canoe*, 3rd edition (Wellington: Te Papa Press, 2005), 55.
8. 'Plans for centennial', editorial, *New Zealand Herald*, 29 December 1938, 12.
9 Frank Acheson, Letter to Waitangi National Trust Board, 12 February 1940: www.facebook.com/Ngatokimatawhaorua
10 Michael King, *Whina* (Auckland: Hodder & Stoughton, 1983), 143–444.
11. Jim Manley, 'Canoe is symbol of reverence for brave ancestors', *New Zealand Herald*, 4 February 1974, 6.
12. Manuka Henare, 'Kapa, Mutu Paratene', Te Ara — The Encyclopedia of New Zealand, https://teara.govt.nz/en/biographies/4k2/kapa-mutu-paratene
13. Richard Cruise, *Journal of a Ten Months' Residence in New Zealand* [1820], 2nd edition (Christchurch: Pegasus Press, 1957), 193.
14. Eru Heperi, interviewed by author, 17 March 2020.
15. 'War canoe afloat', editorial, *Auckland Star*, 31 January 1940, 8.
16. 'HAERE KI O KOUTOU TIPUNA', *Te Ao Hou* 14 (April 1956): 3.
17. Amiria Henare (Salmond), 'Te Hokinga Aria Mai: The Māori photographs of Werner Kissling', *Journal of Museum Ethnography* 17 (2005): 215.
18. Ibid., 215.
19. Ibid., 214.
20. Ibid., 213.
21. From the caption of a photo sent to the author by Amiria Henare (Salmond). Four other men are unnamed.

5. A nation prepares

1. 'Victory to Ngapuhis: Smaller craft superior', editorial, *New Zealand Herald*, 3 February 1940, 13.
2. Ani Gardam, interviewed by author, 27 March 2020.

6. Reflection and hope: Waitangi Day 1940

1. A. H. McLintock, 'Hobson, William', from A. H. McLintock (ed.), *An Encyclopaedia of New Zealand* (1966): https://teara.govt.nz/en/1966/hobson-william
2. Claudia Orange, *The Treaty of Waitangi* (Wellington: Bridget Williams Books, 2011), 48.

3. Clive Drummond, 6 February 1940. Ngā Taonga Sound & Vision: https://ngataonga.org.nz/collections/catalogue/catalogue-item?record_id=221231
4. Ibid.
5. M. P. K. Sorrenson, 'Ngata, Apirana Turupa', from A. H. McLintock (ed.), *An Encyclopaedia of New Zealand* (1966): https://teara.govt.nz/en/biographies/3n5/ngata-apirana-turupa
6. Ranginui Walker, *He Tipua: The Life and Times of Sir Apirana Ngata* (Auckland: Viking, 2001), 114–17.
7. 'Whare Runanga', editorial, *New Zealand Centennial News*, 1 April 1940, 26.
8. Ibid., 27.
9. Ibid., 28.
10. 'Centennial messages from the wide world', editorial, *New Zealand Centennial News*, 1 April 1940, 8.
11. 'Whare Runanga', 31.
12. 'Maori symbolism', editorial, *Auckland Star*, 2 March 1940, 12.

7. An icon is relaunched
1. Joe Conrad, interviewed by author, 1 April 2016.
2. Heke-nuku-mai-ngā-iwi (Hec) Busby, interviewed by author, 31 August 2013.
3. Ibid.
4. 'Canoe must be manned by adults', editorial, *Northern News*, 15 November 1973, 3.
5. 'Paddlers will be chosen soon', editorial, *Northern News*, 21 January 1974, 1.

6. 'New Zealand Day introduced in royal style', editorial, *Northern News*, 4 February 1974, 1.
7. Joe Conrad, interviewed by author, 1 April 2016.
8. Martha Moon, 'Dear waka member', undated pānui in a scrapbook owned by Joe Conrad.
9. Joe Conrad, interviewed by author, 1 April 2016.
10. 'War canoe: Peaceful mission', editorial, *New Zealand Herald*, 7 February 1974, 1.
11. *New Zealand Day at Waitangi*, television coverage (excerpts), 1974, NZ On Screen Iwi Whitiāhua: www.nzonscreen.com/title/new-zealand-day-at-waitangi-1974
12. 'First New Zealand Day at Waitangi', editorial, *Te Ao Hou*, March 1974, 32–33.
13. Stanley Conrad, interviewed by author, 10 December 2016.
14. Ibid.

8. Dissent and protest
1. Stanley Conrad, interviewed by author, 10 December 2016.
2. Ned Peita, interviewed by author, 12 April 2021.
3. Stanley Conrad, interviewed by author, 10 December 2016.
4. The first of the invitations occurred soon after approval had been granted for Princess Diana to ride in *Ngātokimatawhaorua* during the coming visit to Waitangi. Incensed that local wāhine were generally not allowed to ride in the waka, a delegation sought and received approval for selected representatives to ride in the waka

in 1982, a year before the royal visit. Included among those to board the waka were: Molly Apiata, Jocelyn Broughton, Desrei Davis, Sharon Edwards, Cherry Marsh, Emily Marsh, Maraea Marsh, Kathleen Mathews, Martha Mathews, Marleen Morunga, Eileen Parore, Maureen Parore, Kiri Potaeand Mayanne Wiki.

5. Aroha Harris, *Hīkoi: Forty years of Māori protest* (Wellington: Huia, 2004), 112.
6. Heke-nuku-mai-ngā-iwi (Hec) Busby, interviewed by author, 31 August 2013.
7. Adams whānau (Anne, Charlene), interviewed by author, 9 July 2021.
8. David Williams, interviewed by author, 9 July 2021.
9. Joanne Hona, interviewed by author, 10 July 2021.
10. Rodger Borman, interviewed by author, 10 July 2021.
11. Harry Te Awa, interviewed by author, 10 July 2021.
12. Greg Barron, Thirty-fifth anniversary reunion, Otangaroa Marae, Kaeo, 4 June 2022.
13. Stanley Conrad, interviewed by author, 10 December 2016.
14. Karen Williams, interviewed by author, 9 July 2021.
15. Charlene Adams, interviewed by author, 9 July 2021.
16. Rauaroha Heta, interviewed by author, 10 July 2021.
17. Karen Williams, interviewed by author, 9 July 2021.
18. Rodger Borman, interviewed by author, 10 July 2021.
19. Rusty Porter, interviewed by author, 10 July 2021.
20. Arena Heta, interviewed by author, 10 July 2021.
21. Stanley Conrad, interviewed by author, 10 December 2016.
21. Ned Peita, interviewed by author, 12 April 2021.
23. Morgan Hemi, interviewed by author, 10 July 2021.
24. Karen Williams, interviewed by author, 9 July 2021.
25. Charlene Adams, interviewed by author, 9 July 2021.
26. 'Emotions run high over historic canoe voyage', *Northern Advocate*, 9 February 1987, 22.
27. Rauaroha Heta, interviewed by author, 10 July 2021.
28. Joanne Hona, interviewed by author, 10 July 2021.

9. The Year of the Waka 1990

1. 'Te Awatea Hou', The Prow: www.theprow.org.nz/maori/te-awatea-hou/#.YorMcu5By5c
2. *Waka: The awakening dream*, NZ On Screen Iwi Whitiāhua: www.nzonscreen.com/title/waka-the-awakening-dream-1990
3. Ned Peita, interviewed by author, 12 April 2021.
4. Karen Williams, interviewed by author, 10 July 2021.
5. Buddy Mikaere, 'Year of the waka', *New Zealand Geographic* 5 (Jan–Mar 1990): 11.
6. Haare Williams, interviewed by author, 8 August 2013.
7. Ibid.
8. Ned Peita, interviewed by author, 12 April 2021.

10. Lessons given, lessons learnt

1. James Robertson, interviewed by author, 12 November 2017.
2. Marty Bercic, interviewed by author, 5 February 2021.
3. Robin Moore, interviewed by author, 10 September 2021.
4. Hoani Tuoro, interviewed by author, 15 March 2021.
5. Ned Peita, interviewed by author, 12 April 2021.
6. Kaupapa Waka — The Safety Report, Ngā Waka Federation in Association with Maritime Safety Authority, 4 October 2011.

11. Tent city

1. The wāhine invited on board in 2020 were Karen Williams, Sarah Williams, Rauaroha Heta, Elsie Rakuraku, Gina Harding, Joanne Hona, Debbie Conrad, Miri Conrad, Reiha Conrad, Waikarere Gregory, Ebony Ranapia, Kayla Pene, Nadia More, Tara Hape and Te Hopuwai Rakuraku.
2. Bess Conrad, interviewed by author, 5 February 2021.
3. Stanley Conrad, interviewed by author, 5 February 2021.
4. Ibid.
5. Joe Conrad, interviewed by author, 4 March 2016.
6. Joe Everitt, interview by author, 5 February 2021.
7. Robin Moore, interviewed by author, 10 September 2021.
8. Brian Wiki, interviewed by author, 5 February 2021.

Further reading

Best, Elsdon. *The Maori Canoe: An account of various types of vessels used by the Maori of New Zealand in former times, with some description of those of the isles of the Pacific, and a brief account of the peopling of New Zealand.* Wellington: Board of Maori Ethnological Research for the Dominion Museum, 1925.

Evans, Jeff. *Heke-nuku-mai-ngā-iwi Busby: Not here by chance.* Wellington: Huia, 2015.

Evans, Jeff. *Waka Taua: The Māori war canoe.* Auckland: Oratia, 2014.

Harris, Aroha. *Hīkoi: Forty years of Māori protest.* Wellington: Huia, 2004.

Nelson, Anne. *Nga Waka Maori.* Auckland: Macmillan, 1991.

Orange, Claudia. *The Treaty of Waitangi.* Wellington: Bridget Williams Books, 2011.

Orwin, Joanna. *Kauri: Witness to a nation's history.* Auckland: New Holland, 2019.

Reed, A. H. *The New Story of the Kauri.* Auckland: A. H. & A. W. Reed, 1964 (3rd edition).

Acknowledgements

Sometimes you get lucky when you start researching a book, and that was the case here. A number of wonderful resources found their way to me during the early days of the hunt. One of the first was a beautifully drawn topographical map that held a surprising and critical clue. Then, soon after, as my search widened, I came across a number of photos of *Ngātokimatawhaorua* taken in 1940, which added depth and welcome descriptive detail to the narrative.

Once I'd committed to writing the book, key introductions were made and doors opened. I met some quite exceptional yet invariably humble people who were willing to share their time and precious memories so I could record their involvement with the waka.

But perhaps the most remarkable discovery was Jim Manley's movie footage. Shot between 1937 and 1940, Manley filmed the felling, preparation and recovery of the kauri trees used to construct *Ngātokimatawhaorua*. He then filmed the waka being finished at Kerikeri, and finally on the water on Waitangi Day itself. Manley's stunning footage, which was eventually turned into the feature film *Mana Waka*, allows us to see for ourselves what it took to bring the waka to life. It is an extraordinary record.

There is, no doubt, much more that could be written about *Ngātokimatawhaorua*; of course there is. Some of it is still hidden away in the memories of the crew and supporters who I didn't have an opportunity to interview, and much of the story is yet to play out, reserved for the coming decades and beyond. That said, I'm confident that what has been included here amounts to the key events from an already rich history.

Ask any author about the challenges faced in researching and writing a book and the list will be long and laughable, so I shan't bore you with mine. Instead, I'll use this space to acknowledge those individuals and organisations who have helped me to complete this tribute to *Ngātokimatawhaorua*.

First I want to thank Chanel Clarke, Mukai Hura, Ralph Johnson, Mori Rāpana, Richard Takimoana, and Caitlin Timmer-Arends from the Waitangi Treaty Grounds; Kahu Kutia and Malcom Duffy from Ngā Taonga Sound & Vision; Katherine Pawley from the Cultural Collections (Special Collections) at the University of Auckland; and Ewen Cameron and Geraldine Warren, both of whom assisted me at the Auckland War Memorial Museum. The knowledge shared by these subject experts was often the difference between me being able to formulate a key part of the narrative and remaining oblivious to its existence.

For assistance during my trip to Kaeo and the surrounding area I'd like to thank Karen Williams, David Williams, Anne Adams, Charlene Adams, Rodger Borman, Morgan Hemi, Arena Heta, Rauaroha Heta, Joanne Hona, Tahua Murray, Rusty Porter, Tony Shepherd and Harry Te Awa, who all took time out of their busy days to share memories of the 1987 voyage to Whangaroa.

And I also need to acknowledge the following individuals who have each contributed to this history of *Ngātokimatawhaorua*: Hotu Barclay-Kerr, Marty Bercic, the late Sir Heke-nuku-mai-ngā-iwi (Hec) Busby, Joe Conrad, Stanley Conrad, Peter de Graaf, Heemi Eruera, Joe Everitt, Mita Harris, Sir Bob Harvey, Robin (Rabbit) Moore, Kipa Munro, Dan O'Halloran, Ned Peita, Amiria Henare (Salmond), Piripi Smith, Hoani Tuoro, Mel Whaanga, Brian Wiki and Ian Wilson.

Special thanks go to Creative New Zealand for enabling me to spend time working on the project at the Michael King Writers Centre; to Whiria Te Mahara New Zealand History Research Trust Fund, Manatū Taonga

Ministry for Culture and Heritage for their financial support; and to Paula Morris and the 2020–21 class of Master of Creative Writing, University of Auckland, for helping usher the manuscript into something worthy of sending to my publisher.

And finally, I'd like to take a moment to recognise the kaihautū, the captains who have served *Ngātokimatawhaorua* and its crew over the years. In chronological order they are Pita Te Hoe Hohepa and Mutu Kapa, Fredrick Augustine (Nicky) Conrad, Alan Karena, Heke-nuku-mai-ngā-iwi (Hec) Busby, Wiremu Wiremu and Joe Conrad. I'd also like to acknowledge the senior kaihoe who have moulded their crews into effective units over the years, as well those who have stepped up and stood in as kaihautū on occasion.

About the author

Jeff Evans is the author of seven works of non-fiction relating to Māori and Polynesian culture. A number of his books are waka related, including *Waka Taua: The Māori war canoe, Ngā Waka o Neherā: The first voyaging canoes* and *Reawakened: Traditional navigators of Te Moana-nui-a-Kiwa*. He also wrote *Not Here By Chance*, the biography of the late Sir Heke-nuku-mai-ngā-iwi (Hec) Busby.

Index

Page numbers in **bold** refer to images.

28 (Māori) Battalion 61, 105, **106**, 107, 110, 126, 135, 140

1990 Commission 188

Acheson, Frank 26, 44–45, 50, 52, 53, 88, 89

Adams, Anne 172–73

Adams, Charlene 173, 179, 186, 238

Adams, Hakopa 172–73

adzes and adzing 28, 36, 64–65, 68, 80
 Matawhao, face of the adze 38
 toki umarua (double-shouldered adze) 82

Alker, Iwa 183

Aotearoa 39, 40–41

archaeology, Moturua Island 200–01

Ardern, Jacinda 214–15

Auckland Niuean group 156

Auckland Samoan group 156

bailers 101, 162, 212, 220

Barclay-Kerr, Hoturoa 93

Bay of Islands Pēwhairangi 8, 9, 29, 92, 94–96, 143, 145, 177, 182, 184, 202

Beachman, John 20

Bercic, Marty 182, 184–85, 201–02, 204–05, 214, 219–20, 221, 223–24, 229

Best, Elsdon, *The Maori Canoe* 67, 82

Biggs, Bruce 86

Bledisloe, Lord Charles and Lady Elaine 109

Bledisloe Domain 213, 216

Blundell, Sir Denis 117

Borman, Rodger 176, 182

Bosch, Ani 176

Boyd 173–74

Britannia 156, **157**

British Museum 84

Brown, Hemowai 152

Brown, Maraea 152

bullock teams 48, 69–70, 71, **72–73**, 74

Busby, Agnes 8, 120

Busby, Heke-nuku-mai-ngā-iwi (Hec) 18–19, 22, 48, 71, 83–86, 98, 114, 139, 149, 155, 160–61, 169, **171**, 181–82, 187, 194

Busby, Hilda 169, **171**, 185

Busby, James 8, 107–09

bushmen and bush camps 48–50, **51**, 61–62, **63**, **66**, 68–69, 89

Calder, Peter 68

Cameron, Ewen 19

canoe house (Te Korowai ō Maikuku; Te Ana o Maikuku Canoe House) 110, 111, 117, 118, 144, 160–61, 229

Canterbury 194

carving 80, 98–99, 137, 189
 contemporary carvings 189
 for *Ngātokimatawhaorua* 83, 84

carving school, Mōtatau 121

carving school, Ngāruawāhia 52, 80

centennial commemoration *see* Te Tiriti o Waitangi (the Treaty of Waitangi), centennial commemoration

Charles, Prince of Wales, visit 1983 169–70, **171**

chips, disposal by burning and burying 67, 80

Clarke, Bella 152

Clendon, Matiu 200

Cloud Pillar 40

Collins, Annie 56–57, 59, 60

Colonial Office, London 128

colonisation impacts 94

Commonwealth Games Arts Festival, 1990 55, 56, 59

Confederated Tribes of Grand Ronde, Tribal Canoe Journey 145

Conrad, Bess 218–19

Conrad, Joe 144–45, 154–55, 163, 214, 225–26
 scrapbook 146, 148–52, 154

INDEX 255

Conrad, Kelli 162
Conrad, Kerewai 145, 218
Conrad, Kiwa 162
Conrad, Margaret 152
Conrad, Nicky 145, 146, 152–53
Conrad, Stanley (Stan) 161, 162–64, 166–67, 169, 178, 180, 184–85, 214, 219–20, 223, 224–25
Conrad, Waimirirangi 146, 215
Cook Islands 195
Cook Islands group, Porirua 156
Cook, James 29
Cooper, Dame Whina 26, 90, 135
Covid-19 pandemic 229
crew *see* kaihoe (crew, paddlers)
Cruise, R. A., *Journal of a Ten Months' Residence in New Zealand* (1820) 94–95
cutty grass (*Carex geminate*) 30

Davis, Felix 223
Davis, May 192
Dawsonia superba (giant moss) 27
Dennis, Jonathan 55, 56, 58
Department of Conservation (DOC), Kerikeri office 19, 20, 21–22
Diana, Princess of Wales, visit 1983 169–70, **171**, 220
Dominion Museum 140
double-hulled voyaging canoes 18
Drummond, Clive 123, 126, 128, 134, 135
du Clesmeur, Ambroise Bernard-Marie Le Jar 29

Edwards, Sharon 192
Elizabeth II, Queen
1974 visit 9, 144–46, **147**, 148–49, 151–56, **157**, 158, **159**, 160–61
1990 visit 195
Eppics Limited 53
Eruera, Heemi 22, 24, 31, 34, 37–38, 39, 40, 41–42, 68–69
Eruera, Jacob 22
Everitt, Joe 176, 177, 226

feathers 76, 86
fibreglass hulls 188
film of the building of the waka taua in 1940 *see Mana Waka*
First World War 104
Fisher, Luke 160
flags
New Zealand flag 158, 166, 183
Union Jack 158
United Tribes of New Zealand flag 108, 117, 158
flooring 85–86, 220
Forest Rangers 35
Forster, George 86
Fraser, Peter 105, 126, 138–39
Freeman, James S. 123, 126, 128
fundraising tour, Te Pou o Mangatāwhiri 78, **79**

Gable, Robert 214
Galway, Lord George and Lady Lucia 126, 135, 139
Gardam, Ani 103
Gate Pā, battle of 53
Gates, Buzzy 185
George VI, King 139
Grant, Lyonel 189–90

Hākiro 133
hāngī 75
Hape, Ani 192
Hape, Mita 176
Harris, Bob 98
Harrison, Billy 22
Haruru Falls 228
Harvey, Sir Bob 54–59
haumi (haumi kokomo) 36
haumi joints 81, 82, 84, 85, 114, 151, 161
effect of heavy seas 164
He Whakamaumaharatanga exhibition 110
He Whakaputanga 108
Heke, Hōne 134
Hemi, Morgan 175

Hēnare, Taurekareka (Tau) 45–46, 121, 140

Heperi, Erana 88, 89

Heperi, Eru 95, 103

Heperi, Hohepa 46, 47, 49, 50, **51**, 61, 74, 78, 89

Heperi, Te Hoe Pita 50, **51**, 52, **63**, 70, 81, 88, 89, 90, 93, 95, 103, 116

Heperi, Waka 103, 141

Hepi, Pita 226

Heremaia, Ngawati 98

Heritage New Zealand Pouhere Taonga 109

Heta, Areta 175, 184, 187

Heta, Rauaroha 176, 192

Heta, Te Uru (Eru) 176

Hine-i-te-apārangi 38–39

Hobson Beach 61, 105, 107, 123, 141, 146, 160, 169, 183, 200, 204, 210, 211, 229, **230**

Hobson, William 61, 107, 108, 120, 126, 128–29, 131, 133, 134, 139

hoe (paddles) 17, 83, 88, 105, 118, 126, 146, 163, 176, 178, 181, 195, 196, 205, 216, 221, 223, 229

Hokianga Harbour 39, 43, 96

Hōkūle'a 162, 180

Hona, Acey 174–75

Hona, Joanne 174–75, 176, 187

Hongi, Hare 81–82

ihiihi 86, 152, 183

Jones, Frank Colwyn 69–70

Kaeo 172–73, 174–75, 179

kaihautū 92, 93, 144–45, 146, 181–82, 207, 219, 220, 221, 223–24, 238
   responsibility to teach crews about connection to *Ngātokimatawhaorua* 225–26

kaihoe (crew, paddlers) 9, **12–13**, 89, **91**, 92–93, 155, 162–64, 166, 167, 177, 198, 228–29
   see also hoe (paddles)
   centennial commemoration, 1974 111, 118, 140, 148, 152–53, 233–35

korowai, belts and headbands 88, **91**, 92

Ngātokimatawhaorua's grounding at Wairoa Bay, New Year's Eve 1999 202, 204, 206–08, 210, 211, 212

paddling technique 93, 219, 220–21, 223–24

safety protocols 211–12

seating 220

sections and specialist roles 220

sesquicentennial celebrations, 1990 192, **193**, 194, 195–96

training 152–53, 163–64, 173, 174, 176, 177–78, 179, 212, 215–16, **217**, 228, 229

Whangaroa County centennial celebrations, 1987 172–82, 183–85, 186–87, 238–39

women 88, 93, 198, 215, 236

kaikaranga 176, 183, 184, 186, 214, 237

Kaikohe 44, 100

kaituki 92, 101, 111, 206, 220, 227–28

kaiurungi (steersman) 174, 205, 220, 227

Kāmira, Himiona 86

kapa haka 153, 179

Kapa, Mutu 46, 93, 96

Kapua, Eramiha 80

karakia 90, 169, 180, 184, 192, 200, 228
   to appease Tāne Mahuta 52, 65, 67, 80

Karena, Alan 145, 153, 163, 167, 177, 178

karu atua 86, 152

Katipa, Rawiri 53

Kauere, Rei (Rē) 46, 95, 96, **97**, 98, 103, 135, 140

kaumātua 9, 15, 19, 26, 57, 104, 105, 141, 155, 166, 167–68, 169, 200, 212, 214, 219, 238
   sesquicentennial celebrations, 1990 192, 194, 195
   Whangaroa County centennial celebrations, 1987 172, 176–77, 178, 180, 181

Kaupapa Waka event, 1990 Commission 188–91, 196, **197**

INDEX 257

kauri 11, 19–20, 21, 30–31, 188
  exports 30
  naval demand 29–30
  suitability for waka building 11, 28–29
kauri dieback 25, 28
kauri for building *Ngātokimatawhaorua*
  celebration of safe delivery of waka
    sections to Kerikeri 75
  felling 20, 48–50, **51**, 52–53, 61–62, **63**,
    64, 65, 67, 68, 70–
  hauling hull sections by bullock
    team 65, 69–70, 71, **72–73**, 74
  initial shaping and trimming of
    logs 64–65, **66**, 68, 71, 74, 80–81
  modern-day search for original
    location in Puketi Forest 20,
    24–32, 34, 48, 68–69, 70–71
  search for suitable trees 14, 25, 26,
    46–47, 48–50
  seasoning of hull sections 48, 70, 76, 81
  size of the crown 31, 34
  transport of hull sections to
    Kerikeri 48, 70, 74–75
kauri grass (*Astelia trinervia*) 30
kauri snail (pūpūrangi) 27
kāwanatanga 132
Kereama, Waka 36, 80
Kerikeri 75, 80, 81
  delivery of kauri logs from Puketi
    Forest 48, 70, 74–75
  seasoning of hull sections in Kerikeri
    Inlet 48, 70, 76
King, Michael 80, 90
  Te Puea: A life 15, 16
King, Stephen 20
Kira, Sid 176
Kirk, Norman 156, 158
Kirk, Ruth 156
Kissling, Werner 98
Korokī Te Rata Mahuta Pōtatau Te
  Wherowhero 104
Kororāreka Russell 122
kōtuku (heron) 84
Kōtukumairangi (Ngāi Tahu waka) 188
kuia 104, 135, 154, 186, 191–92, 195, 219

Kupe 37–41, 189
  instructions for voyaging to
    Aotearoa 40–43
Kuru, Mereana 152

laminated timber hulls 188
Latimer, Emily 152
Leefe, Agnes Jack 152

Mahuhu o Te Rangi (Ngāti Whātua
  waka) 195, 210
Maikuku 107, 165
Maioha, Sam 98
Māmari 39, 43
Mana Waka, film of the building of the
  waka taua in 1940 53–61, 65, 68, 71,
  74, 93, 148
manaia figures 83, 84
Manley, Reginald George Harwood
  (Jim) 50, 53–60, 61, 62, 65, **66**, 68, 90,
  92, 93, 101, **102**, 119, 123, 148
Manley, William 53
Manley family 56
Manuera, Hemi 45
manūka 30, 85–86
Māori
  confiscation of land 138
  land reform 137
  sport and cultural activities 137
Māori (28th) Battalion 61, 105, **106**, 107, 110,
  126, 135, 140
Māori Land Court (previously Native Land
  Court) 19, 26, 45, 82
Māori Women's Welfare League 90
Māoritanga 18
Maritime Safety Authority 212
Mātaatua (built by Hec Busby) 187
Mātaatua (migration waka) 184
Mātaatua (unbuilt northern waka taua) 44
Mataatua-Puhi 155
Matangirau 45
Matarahurahu 134
Matauri Bay 45
Matawhao (Matahourua) 37, 38–39, 41, 43

258 NGĀTOKIMATAWHAORUA

Matiu, Mei 152
mau rākau 21–22
Maupakanga, Rānui 14, 15, **16**, 34, 35–36, 44, 45, 46–50, 62–63, 65, 69, 71, 81, 103
McBride, Senator Philip and wife 126, 139
McCann, Judith 55
Mikaere, Buddy 192
Mikaka, Eruera 98
missionaries 126, 133, 134
Mita, Merata 56–57, 58, 59, 60, 61, 68
Moka 133
Mokaraka, Hokene 98
moon 42
Moon, Mata 152
Moore, Robin 'Rabbit' 205–08, 210, 227–28
Moranga, Marlene 169
More, Peka 192
Morgan, Hemi 185
Motu, Mei 152
Moturua Island 200–01
Mount Hikurangi 25–26
muka 151
Munro, Kipa 21–22, 24, 25, 26, 31, 34, 48, 119
Munu, Tom 71, 84, 151, 160, 161, 226
Muriwhenua 195
Murray, Ellen 152
Murray, Tahua 176, 183
Mutu, Teresa 152

National Library, Katherine Mansfield Reading Room 61
Native Land Court *see* Māori Land Court (previously Native Land Court)
navigation from Polynesia to Aotearoa 40–43
Nene, Tāmati Wāka 134
New Zealand Day 156, 158
New Zealand Film Archive (now Ngā Taonga Sound & Vision) 54, 55, 58, 61
New Zealand Film Commission 55
New Zealand Forest Service 20

New Zealand Māori Arts and Crafts Institute *see* Ngā Kete Tuku Iho New Zealand Māori Arts and Crafts Institute
New Zealand Wars 53, 94, 110
Ngā Kete Tuku Iho New Zealand Māori Arts and Crafts Institute 189
   see also earlier name School of Māori Arts and Crafts, Ohinemutu
Ngā Tamatoa 165, 166–67
Ngā Taonga Sound & Vision (previously New Zealand Film Archive) 54, 55, 58, 61
Ngā Waka Federation 211–12
Ngāhiraka Mai Tawhiti 231
Ngāi Tahu 111, 188
Ngāi Tawake 133
Ngaiotonga Forest 46, 96, 98
Ngāpuhi 14, 26, 44, 45, 46, 88, 96, 103, 104, 107, 152
Ngāruawāhia 36, 46, 59, 78, 177, 196
   see also Tūrangawaewae Marae; Tūrangawaewae regatta
   carving school 52, 80
Ngata, Sir Apirana 90, 104, 105, 135, **136**, 137, 140
   speech at Whare Rūnanga opening 137–38
Ngāti Hao 134
Ngāti Kahu 21, 44, 45, 111, 152
Ngāti Kahungunu 191–92
Ngāti Kawa 133
Ngāti Kuri 145
Ngāti Kuta 200
Ngāti Maniapoto 189
Ngāti Rāhiri 107, 111
Ngāti Rēhia 21, 22
Ngāti Whātua 21, 44, 45, 152, 195, 210
Ngātokimatawhaorua (ancestral migration waka) 39, 43, 225
Ngātokimatawhaorua (waka taua built by Kauere and Pangari) 96, **97**, 98–99, **127**
   at the centennial commemoration 1974 142–43

gifted to Apirana Ngata 140
race with waka taua built by Poutapu
and Heperi 101, **102**, 103
refurbishment, 2009 98
at Te Tii Marae, then Pukerata
Marae 141
Ngātokimatawhaorua (waka taua built by
Poutapu and Heperi)
see also kauri for building
Ngātokimatawhaorua
at the centennial
commemoration **4**,
1974 101-02, 103, 104,
124–25, 126, **127**, 142–43,
146, **147**, 148–49, **150**, 152,
154–55, 233–35
cultural icon 8, 11
grounding at Wairoa Bay, New
Year's Eve 1999 199–200,
201, **202**, 203–08, **209**,
210–12
Joe Everitt's memories 226–28
kaitiaki 160–61, 176–77
launch and maiden voyage 18,
76, 78, 89–90, **91**, 92–93, 95
origin of name 37–43, 44
passengers 11, 89
refurbishment, 2009 22, 155
refurbishment and relaunch for
visit of Queen Elizabeth
II, 1974 9, 85, 144–46, **147**,
148–49, **150**, 151–56, **157**,
158, **159**, 160–61
straightening of the hull,
1975 160–61
at Treaty Grounds 8–9, **10**, 11,
12–13, 17, 19, 109, 110, 111,
112–13, 114, **115**, 116–17,
119–20, 141
in the Whangaroa County
centennial celebrations,
1987 172–87, 238–39
in the sesquicentennial
celebrations, 1990 144, 155, 191,
193, 194–96, **197**
building and painting
attachments for ceremonial
purposes 86

breach of protocol by a 'pakeha
woman' 52
finish for outside of hull 81–82
flooring 85–86, 220
joining the hull and stern sections
to central section 81, 82, 85
lashing 114
mana of designers and builders 11
nīkau structure to shelter the
waka 78
painting 86
photographs 54, 57, 62, 76, 119,
148
rauawa, tauihu, taurapa and
taumanu 76, 83–84, 85, 86,
114, 116
site 76, **77**, 78
Tainui workers 57
tools 64–65
design
dimensions 14, 64, 88–89, 117
mana of designers and builders 11
ratios 64
Nias, Sir Joseph 120, 123, 126, 128
Nias Track 117, 120, 195
Niue 195
Nukutawhiti 39, 40, 42, 43

Ogle, Jim **51**
O'Halloran, Dan 22, 24, 26, 27–28, 30, 31, 34
Ōkaihau East School 75
Okiato Old Russell 122
Omahuta Forest 34, 83, 119
Ōpua 96, 98, 99, 104, 122
Orange, Claudia, *The Treaty of
Waitangi* 132
orographic clouds 40
Oruanui Forest 36, 46, 53, 68, 78

paddlers *see* kaihoe (crew, paddlers)
paewai 82, 83, 85, 220
Paihia 122
Paikea, Paraire 104, 105
Pangari, Toki Kingi 96, **97**, 98

260 NGĀTOKIMATAWHAORUA

Paora, Nellie 183

Patuone 134

Peita, Ned 99, 117–18, 166, 176, 177, 185, 190, 196, 210–11

Penia 172, 173, 186

Perrin, Ross 211

Pēwhairangi Bay of Islands 8, 9, 29, 92, 94–96, 143, 145, 177, 182, 184, 202

Philip, Prince, Duke of Edinburgh 156, 195

pia houhou 85

Piailug, Mau 19

Pinkham, Kate 192

pitau 84

Poata, Joe 173, 176

Poata, Mere 192

Polynesian Voyaging Society, 'Voyage of Rediscovery' 162

Porter, Rusty 175, 183

Poutapu, Piri (Wiremu Te Ranga) 35, 36, 46, 48, 65, 76, 80, 81, 82–86, 88, 95, 96, 149, 151

protocols while working in the forest 52, 80

puhi kai ariki 86

puhi moana ariki 86

puhi-mākū 86

puhi-maroke 86

puhoro design 86

Puke, Jake 177

Pukerata Marae, Ōtaua 141

Puketi Forest 14–15, 19, 20, 21, 22, 24–26, **32–33**, 34–35, 45, 47–49, 53, 62, 68–70, 96

    see also kauri for building Ngātokimatawhaorua

    'Canoe Track' 15, 19, 20, 26–28, 31, 48, 49, 118–19

    map 20–21, **23**, 24

Pupuke 45

Queen Charlotte Sound 86

Rāhiri 46, 107

Rakatau, Rei 56, 59

Rākaunui 35, 36

Rakuraku, Elsie 169

Rapatini, Hoana 152

Rata, Matiu 156, 160

Rātana, Haami (Toko) 104

Rātana, Tahupōtiki 104–05

Rātana Church 104, 105

rauawa 36, 74, 84, 85, **87**, 98, 114, 116, 149, 178, 183

raupō 86, **91**, 148, 220

Rēkohu Chatham Islands 195

Rere Ki Uta, Rere Ki Tai (The Journey) (documentary) 186

Rewa 133

Richards, Hera 183

Rikihana, Nimera 53

Robinson, James 201

Rose, Akamiria 183

Roux, Jean 64–65

Royal Titles Act 156

royal visits *see* Charles, Prince of Wales, visit 1983; Diana, Princess of Wales, visit 1983; Elizabeth II, Queen

Ruānui-o-Tāne 39, 42, 43

Rutene, Rere Moana 152

safety protocols 211–12

Salmond, Amiria 98

Samuels, Dover 226

Savage, Michael Joseph 126, 139

School of Māori Arts and Crafts, Ohinemutu 35, 80, 137

    see also later name Ngā Kete Tuku Iho New Zealand Māori Arts and Crafts Institute

seasoning of adzed timber 36, 48, 70, 76, 81

sesquicentennial celebrations, 1990 *see* Te Tiriti o Waitangi (the Treaty of Waitangi), sesquicentennial celebrations, 1990

Shepherd, Tony 175, 176

Snowden, Simon 176

Social Security Act 1938 104

State Forest Service 47

sun, rising and setting positions 40, 41–42

taha tangata 84

taha wairua 84

Taheretikitiki 17

Taheretikitiki II (Waikato waka) 144, 188

Tai Tokerau Cultural Group 156

Tai Tokerau District Māori Council 144, 145, 160

Taiapa, Hone 80

Taiapa, Pine 80

Tainui 56, 57, 60, 96, 99, 111

Taipā 37–38

Takapu, HMNZS 180

Tākitimu 40

Tāmaki Paenga Hira Auckland War Memorial Museum 19, 116

Tamatea Arikinui o Te Waka Tākitimu (Ngāti Kahungunu waka) 191–92, **193**, 195

Tana, Rae 152

Tāne Mahuta (god of the forest)

    alternative name, Tāne Matawhao 38

    karakia and offerings to appease 52, 65, 67, 80

Tāne Mahuta (kauri) 29

Tāne Matawhao 38

taniko weaving 88

taonga 132

tapu 34, 49, 50, 52, 53, 59, 76, 107, 135, 153, 180, 225

Tarlton, Kelly, sailing ship *Tui* 146, 190

tauihu (figurehead) 36, 83, 84, 85, 86, **87**, 88, 98, 114, **115**, 116, 152, 183, 189, 190, 226–27

    modern interpretations 189

    pitau style 83

    tuere style 83

taumanu 85, 86

tauparapara 90

Taupiri maunga 57

taurapa 36, 76, **77**, 83–84, 85, 86, **87**, 88, 98, 114, **115**, 116, 183, 189

    stylised 189

Tāwhiao Te Wherowhero 15, 35

Te Ana o Maikuku 107, 108

Te Arawa 111

Te Arawa (Te Arawa waka) 189–90

Te Atairangikaahu, Te Arikinui Dame 56, 57, 59–60, 156

Te Ati Awa 195

Te Aupōuri 44, 45, 93, 111, 145, 152

Te Aurere 18, 161–62

Te Awatea Hou (Te Tau Ihu o te Waka a Māui) 189

Te Kēmara 133, 134

Te Kōhunga museum 109

Te Korowai ō Maikuku 10, **112–113**, 117, 118, 121, 166, 173, 229

Te Kotūiti Tuarua (Ngāti Pāoa waka) 190

Te Patukeha 133

Te Pou Kapua te Tonga-mā-uru 40

Te Pou o Mangatāwhiri concert party 78, **79**

Te Puea Hērangi, Te Kirihaehae (Princess Te Puea) 15, 26, 53–54, 56, 78, 80, 90, 93, 170, 191, 215, 232

    four waka taua built 142–43

    plans for fleet of seven waka taua 15, 16, 17, 35, 53, 78, **79**

    restoration of *Te Winika* 35, 36

    sponsorship of *Ngātokimatawhaorua* 8, 14, 36, 44–46, 47, 69, 81, 90, 95, 96

    two waka taua at Waitangi 95–96, 142

    visit to Waitangi to formally gift *Ngātokimatawhaorua* 103–04

Te Rangatahi (Waikato waka) 143, 188

Te Rangimata (Rēkohu Chatham Islands waka) 195

Te Rarawa 44, 45, 111, 145, 152

Te Rau Aroha museum 109–10, 120

Te Rūnanga o Ngāti Rēhia 21

Te Tai Tokerau 38, 43

Te Tau Ihu o te Waka a Māui 189

Te Tii Bay 179, 190, 191–92, **193**, 194–95, **197**

Te Tii Marae 99, 109, 140, 141, 152, 191, 216

Te Tiriti o Waitangi (the Treaty of Waitangi) 8, 108, 128–29, 138, 165

    English-language version 129–31

262 NGĀTOKIMATAWHAORUA

inconsistencies between English and te reo versions 131–33

signing 92–93, 120, 158

Te Tiriti o Waitangi (the Treaty of Waitangi), centennial commemoration, 1974 8–9, 53, 100–01, 103–05, 107–09, 123, 138, 140, 235–37

food 100, 103, 135, 236

Ngātokimatawhaorua (waka taua built by Kauere and Pangari) 142–43

Ngātokimatawhaorua (waka taua built by Poutapu and Heperi) **124–25**, 126, **127**, 142–43, 146, **147**, 148–49, **150**, 152, 154–55, 233–35

re-enactment of signing 61, 100, 126, **127**, 128, 133–34

Te Tiriti o Waitangi (the Treaty of Waitangi), sesquicentennial celebrations, 1990 144, 155, 191, **193**, 194–96, **197**

see also Kaupapa Waka event, 1990 Commission

re-enactment of signing 195

Te Toki-a-Tāpiri 116

Te Whānau Moana 146

Te Wheke-o-Muturangi 189

Te Wīata, Īna 36

Te Winika 35–36, 82

Temara, Tamahou 214

Tent City 200, 201–02, 205, 213–16, 218–21, 223–32

food 216, 218–19

Tepania, Turoa 176

Thierry, Charles de 108

Thoms, Tommy 50, **51**

Tinana (Muriwhenua waka) 195

tino rangatiratanga 132

Tirikātene, Eruera 104, 105

Tirikātene-Sullivan, Whetu 105

Toetoe, Rosie 192

tohunga tārai waka 14, 35, 64, 103, 160, 188, 189, 196

Tokelau 195

Top Town competition, Waitangi week version 216, 218

tōtara 11, 36, 188, 189

training wānanga, 1970s 152–53, 154, 163, 228

Treaty Grounds, Waitangi 8, 9, 11, 17, 34, 61, 107, 109, 110–11, 120–22, 153, 162, 167, 190, 211, 229

see also Whare Rūnanga, Waitangi

canoe house (Te Korowai ō Maikuku; Te Ana o Maikuku Canoe House) 110, 111, 117, 118, 144, 160–61, 229

kauri stump 118–19

original canoe shed 121–22

Treaty House 108–09, 120, 135, 139, 140, 156, 204

Treaty of Waitangi *see* Te Tiriti o Waitangi (the Treaty of Waitangi)

Tuhi Mata Kamokamo (Ngāti Maniapoto waka) 189

Tumanako (Waikato waka) 143, 188

Tūmatauenga 83, 189

Tuoro, Hoani 205, 208, 210

Tūrangawaewae Marae 54, 59

Tūrangawaewae regatta 17

Tuteao Marae, Te Teko 212

Venus 40, 41

Victoria, Queen 128

von Tempsky, Gustavus 35

waiata 60, 185, 186, 192

Waikare Inlet 96

Waikato 44, 45, 46, 47, 93, 103–04, 138, 142

Waikato waka taua 44, 78, 80, 81, 82, 143, 177, 188

Waikato River 17

Waikato War 35

Wainui Marae 175–76, 187

Waipapa Landing 76, **77**, **87**, **91**

Waipoua Forest 28

Waipoua Forest Trust 20

Wairere, Eka 99

Wairoa Bay 199–200, 202, **203**, 204, 207–08, **209**, 210, 211, 212, 216

wairua 225

INDEX 263

Waitaha whare wānanga 82

Waitangi 76, 104, 107, 108, 143, 156, 162, 165, 173, 179, 190, 196, 213, 226
   see also Te Tii Marae; Tent City; Treaty Grounds, Waitangi

Waitangi Day 161, 164, 165, 177, 179, 199, 213–15, 229, **230**, 231
   change to New Zealand Day 156, 158
   dissent and protest, 1980s 165–67, **168**, 169–70
   threats against Ngātokimatawhaorua 166, 167, 169

Waitangi Māori Committee 156

Waitangi Marae 154, 160

Waitangi Museum 50

Waitangi National Trust Board 34, 50, 118, 119, 141, 144, 160

Waitangi Tribunal 60–61

Waitangi: What Really Happened 109

Waitere, Tene 80

waka
   main form of long-distance transport for Māori 35
   waka bringing first people from Polynesia to Aotearoa 37

waka culture in the education syllabus 215

waka taua 17–18, 94–95
   see also Ngātokimatawhaorua (waka taua built by Kauere and Pangari); *Ngātokimatawhaorua* (waka taua built by Poutapu and Heperi); Waikato waka taua; and names of other individual waka taua
   design 9, 11
   Ngātokimatawhaorua (ancestral migration waka) 39, 43
   symbol of tribal identity, pride and power 8, 17, 94, 232
   Taheretikitiki and *Taheretikitiki II* 17, 144
   Te Puea's plans for seven waka taua 15, 16, 35, 78, **79**

Waka: The Awakening Dream (documentary) 189–90

waka-ama 195, 220–21

Walker, Adrian 20

ware houhou 85

Warena, Toto Wiremu 98

Wellington Tokelau Islands group 156

Whaanga, Mel 58, 93

Whaanga, Moana 56, 57–58

Whaanga whānau 57–59, 60–61

Whangaroa County, *Ngātokimatawhaorua* in the centennial celebrations, 1987 172–87, 238–39

Whangaroa Harbour 173, 174, 184–85, 226

Whare Rūnanga, Waitangi 8, 9, 98–99, 120–21, 135, **136**, 137–39, 146

Whirinaki Forest 189

Whiu, Paddy 176

Wihongi, Ripi 44–45

Wiki, Brian 228–29

Williams, David 172, 174

Williams, Edward 131, 132

Williams, Haare 194

Williams, Henry 131, 132, 133

Williams, Karen 172, 173, 174, 175, 179, 182, 185–86, 191, 192, 238

Williams, Kira 176

Willingdon, Lord Freeman and Lady Marie 126

Windsor, Rachael 152

Wiremu, Linda 192

Wiremu, Wiremu 177, 192, 205, 207, 216

Wirihana, Ropata 46–47, 48, 96

women
   on *Ngātokimatawhaorua* **4**, 88, 93, 169, 192
   woman's violation of tapu 52

First published in 2023 by Massey University Press
Private Bag 102904, North Shore Mail Centre
Auckland 0745, New Zealand
www.masseypress.ac.nz

Text copyright © Jeff Evans, 2023
Images copyright © as credited, 2023

Design by Alice Bell
Front and back cover: *Ngātokimatawhaorua* at Waitangi, 2020.
Photographs by Te Rawhitiroa Bosch, Rawhitiroa Photography.
Inside cover: Map of Puketi State Forest, c. 1920. New Zealand Forest Service,
courtesy of the Department of Conservation.
Pages 2–3: *Ngātokimatawhaorua* at Waitangi, 2014. Photograph by Jeff Evans.

The moral rights of the author and illustrator have been asserted

All rights reserved. Except as provided by the Copyright Act 1994, no part of this book
may be reproduced, stored in or introduced into a retrieval system or transmitted in any
form or by any means (electronic, mechanical, photocopying, recording or otherwise)
without the prior written permission of both the copyright owner(s) and the publisher.

A catalogue record for this book is available from the National Library of New Zealand

Printed and bound in China by Everbest Printing Investment

ISBN: 978-1-99-115119-3

The assistance of Creative New Zealand and the New Zealand History Research Trust
Fund, Manatū Taonga Ministry for Culture and Heritage, is gratefully acknowledged by
the publisher.

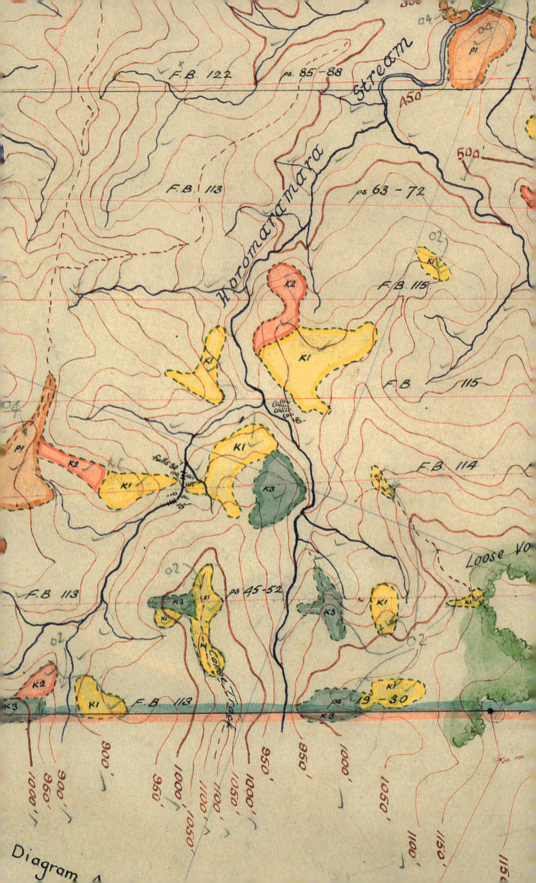